I0824415

The Noma Guide to Building Flavour

The Noma Guide to Building Flavour

René Redzepi
and the Noma Test Kitchen
with Nate French

Photographs
by Evan Sung

Illustrations
by Paula Troxler

Artisan | New York

Introduction by René Redzepi

I still remember the first time I heard Ferran Adrià talk about cooking in terms of language. He said: "Techniques and ingredients are like letters—each one you learn gives you another piece of the alphabet. The more of them you have, the deeper, richer the sentences you can write."

That idea struck me like lightning. It made me think about my own vocabulary, about how limited it was, and how much more there was to learn. Since then I've thought of every new sauce, every strange broth, every oddball fermentation that we've made at Noma as another letter in the pantry. Over two decades we've gathered hundreds of these "letters." Together they've become our words, our grammar, our poetry. This book is that vocabulary written down for the first time.

The Argentine writer Jorge Luis Borges once imagined a library that contained every book that could ever exist, built from only twenty-five characters. If an entire universe can be made from so few letters, imagine what happens when your alphabet runs into the hundreds. That's what we've been doing at Noma: adding letter after letter, building a language of flavour.

A language like this is never built by one person alone. It has taken the work, imagination, and persistence of hundreds of people. And a book like this doesn't, even though my name is on the cover, belong only to me. Believe me when I say this: It's simply the way the world works, a name to lean on. But in reality there could have been dozens of names on that cover.

The Test Kitchen office in the greenhouse.

I guess it all started with Torsten Vildgaard and me, fooling around after hours, one, two, three in the morning, building the next menu. Back then Noma was small, a handful of us in the kitchen, and all the new work had to happen when the doors were shut. Then Søren Westh joined, full of energy. He had a more research-driven approach, where Torsten and I were intuitive, and that balance became the seed of what would grow into the Test Kitchen.

The second big turning point for the Test Kitchen came with Thomas Frebel. His energy, drive, and curiosity gave us a tremendous push. Today he is a partner at Noma, and together with Peter Kreiner and me, we run Noma side by side.

The third phase of the Test Kitchen is led by Mette Søberg; this is the period we are still in. Mette became a central pillar alongside Junichi Takahashi, Riccardo Canella, Mirek Anderson, Rosio Sanchez, and Nate French (an excellent organizational mind who helped make this book a reality).

But there's also Toni Toivanen from Finland, Stu Stalker and Sam Nutter from Newcastle. Malcolm Livingston II (and his daughter Elli!), Álvaro de Juan Sánchez, Gaute Schartau Berrefjord, Mattias Shikatani, and the wizardry of Dhriti Arora. Each of them helped shape this place, and the recipes in this book belong to them, too. This is more than a thank-you . . . it is a deep acknowledgment. Indeed, incredible people have passed through the kitchen doors. Some stayed briefly, others much longer, but each left behind a piece—sometimes a cornerstone, sometimes just a single tile. Together they made the puzzle whole.

When this book is finally in your hands, Noma will have entered its twenty-third year of life. In the beginning we didn't have much. We had ingredients, yes, but not yet the knowledge of how to turn a carrot into a leather, how to coax seaweed into a sauce with the depth of a meat stock, how to transform an ant into a marinade. We didn't know how to find spice in our own region, or even what a spice could be. Out of necessity we began inventing. We needed something that could bring a dish together, something that could bridge one raw ingredient to another.

Slowly, through trial and error, a library of flavours emerged. Hundreds, maybe thousands of items, if you count them all. Some tiny adjustments, others so transformative they became essential. A touch of pine salt can make a dish. A little piece of Noma roasted umami salt on just about anything will make it better than before. Savory fudges, smoked butters, raisin-dark reductions pulled from seaweed, mushrooms, or berries.

These flavours are bridge builders. They are the invisible architecture of deliciousness. And though many of them were born out of scarcity, over time they became our language.

With each year, each season, each journey to somewhere in the world for a pop-up, we've added to that repertoire. We've spent years, even decades, perfecting some of these flavours. They are all in this book: the good ones, the favorites, the ones that truly make a difference.

In the end, this is a book about flavour. But flavour is never just about taste. It's about time and place. It's about the people who shaped it, the failures that led to it, and the stubbornness that kept us searching when nothing worked. It's about how a handful of curious minds, working together over years, can build a language from scratch. This is the Noma pantry.

Mette Søberg and René Redzepi in the Test Kitchen.

What Actually *Is* Flavour?

Inspiration for a new dish at Noma is often sparked by simple curiosity: What happens if we put a pine cone in lye? Can we make something taste like beeswax without the wax? Can we make these sea cucumber gonads into something tasty? (The answer was yes, by the way.) Our creativity is also driven by a desire to surprise and delight our diners, to create something authentic. What if we hid smoke-kissed grilled king crab leg underneath a pile of dried autumn leaves on the plate, so the diner could "forage"?

But no matter what our process is, flavour is our ultimate goal.

But what is flavour? Our good friend, former colleague, and co-creator of the first permanent iteration of our Fermentation Lab (in not-so-permanent shipping containers) Dr. Arielle Johnson explains in her book *Flavorama* that flavour is actually two things, intrinsically linked: taste and aroma.

Taste begins, not surprisingly, in our mouths. Our tongues are full of tiny receptors that accept taste molecules and signal to us that they have found one (or more) of the five tastes: salty, sweet, sour, bitter, and umami. From an evolutionary perspective, each taste held its own key to human survival. Salt is a mineral essential to muscle function and blood flow. Sweet signals something that will give us energy to continue to hunt and/or gather. Sour is a taste that is associated with healthy vitamins. Bitter is a danger signal of something that could poison us. Umami is the taste that signifies the presence of proteins, essential ingredients to repair and build muscle.

Fridges full of flavour.

These five tastes alone, however, don't equal flavour. Flavour needs aroma—what an ingredient smells like. Aroma provides the nuances that, when combined with the basic tastes, are perceived by our brains as flavours—what food actually tastes like. Coupled with aroma, five basic tastes become countless unique flavours.

Aroma receptors (we've got about four hundred of them) are connected to our brains as part of the olfactory bulb. Aroma molecules connect with those receptors when we put food in our mouths and chew; the molecules drift up through our nasal cavity until they encounter the receptors. The olfactory bulb funnels the aromas directly to the part of our brain where they are processed into smells, as many as ten thousand distinct ones. We may think we're tasting flavour with our mouths, but flavour is a team effort of mouth and nose.

The task of the Noma Test Kitchen, and anyone trying to create good food, is to mine the world around them to coax out the flavours. A little bit of science is a valuable tool in that task.

In chemistry, the phrase "like dissolves like" describes a nifty way to figure out the best way to extract flavour from an ingredient, whether you're creating a complex sauce or simply capturing the flavour of rose petals in summer to use later. The "like" here refers to whether a substance is polar or nonpolar.

First, let's take a (quick) moment to talk about electrons. Certain molecules are termed "polar" because their electrons are arranged such that one side is negatively charged and the other is positively charged (and we don't need to understand what "charged" means). Water molecules, for example, are polar, and will easily attract and stick to other polar molecules. Polar molecules are also described as hydrophilic, or "water-loving," meaning they will readily mix with other water-based compounds.

Fat molecules, on the other hand, have a much more rigid structure thanks to their long chains of hydrogen and carbon, which naturally discourage the bunching of electrons. There are no "poles," and therefore fat is classified as "nonpolar." Nonpolar molecules are hydrophobic, meaning "water-fearing," part of the reason water and oil do not mix.

Most aroma compounds are nonpolar, making fat an excellent medium for extracting (dissolving) aromas, leading to delicious substances such as rose oil or smoked butter. The five basic tastes, on the other hand, *are* polar, so you can extract these compounds more efficiently with water or another polar liquid, such as umami-rich dashi.

The "like dissolves like" principle isn't absolute, however; nonpolar compounds can dissolve into polar solutions and vice versa, but the extraction won't be as efficient as when you're combining "likes." And to complicate matters slightly (but to give the chef more options), alcohol and vinegar can dissolve both polar and nonpolar molecules fairly effectively.

The point of knowing about polarity is simply to know that you can enhance some flavours by cooking your ingredient in or mixing it with water and other flavours by doing the same with a fat.

Right: Honeycomb from our beehives. **Following pages:** Chefs at work in the Test Kitchen **(left)**; a dish of wild beach plants **(right)**.

How to Get the Most from the Recipes in This Book

Many of the recipes in this book are straightforward and can be made by anyone in any kitchen. Lemon Thyme Vinegar (page 40) needs only sprigs of fresh lemon thyme and store-bought vinegar. Rose Oil (page 187) uses a neutral oil and whatever fragrant, unsprayed rose petals you can find. And Plum Kernel Cream (page 454), which you can whip to soft peaks and then dollop on any dessert, uses just plums, cream, milk, and sugar. Even something as unusual as Pine Cone Olives (page 73) are simple to make for those who live near forested areas where they can collect tender young pine cones. In many recipes, omitting an ingredient or two is fine; for example, if you can't find dried bergamot skin, arctic thyme, or finger limes, you can still make delicious Pickled Chiles (page 51).

Some of our other recipes are more complex, and you'll need to make additional flavour compounds before you begin the actual recipe. This could be as simple as making a parsley oil, or more time-consuming, like making koji or a fermented product.

A few products used in the recipes, including Wild Rose Vinegar, Mushroom Garum, and Dashi RDX (dashi reduction), are sold by our sister company, Noma Projects (nomaprojects.com).

The best chefs take the most notes.

In the recipe ingredient lists, you'll notice that some ingredients include a cross-reference ("page 000") and others are marked with an asterisk (*). The cross-referenced recipes can be found elsewhere in the chapters; the asterisked recipes are included in our Gastronomique (page 485), which is a deeper library of flavour compounds. The Gastronomique includes, among other things, brief recipes for fermented products. For those who want to dive into our arsenal of ferments, check out *The Noma Guide to Fermentation*.

NOMA TEST KITCHEN VEG 2022
SEAFOOD 2021
2023
JUN
ideas & Recipes
Kyoto
noma
NOMA KYOTO TEST KITCHEN 2023
JUN

Metric Measures

All the amounts in this book are expressed in metric measures, which is how we work at Noma and how most professional kitchens work. Home cooks in most of the world also use metric measures, though Americans still use what's called the US standard system, based on the old British Imperial system. Even if you're not familiar with metric measures, you will soon become a fan; they are easy and intuitive to use, and scaling a recipe up or down is a breeze with metrics.

You do need a digital scale, however, which you can find anywhere. Look for one that can measure at least as low as 1 gram, and pick up an extra battery so you don't have to panic if your scale dies in the middle making of your Nordic Pesto (page 322).

Note also that we express everything in weight (grams/kilograms), rather than using weight for solids and volume (milliliters/liters) for liquids. While the weight and volume equivalencies of most substances are close but not exact, they are close enough for what we're making in this book. And it's a whole lot easier to just plop your container on a scale, tare (zero out) the weight, and add each ingredient than it is to weigh some ingredients and measure others in a measuring cup. We do list temperatures in both Celsius and Fahrenheit.

Recipe Yields

Because our recipes aren't for actual dishes, like a soup, braise, or galette, we can't tell you how many people a recipe "serves." The portion sizes of our recipes depend on what we do with them—we might use one drop (about 1 gram) of Douglas Fir Oil (page 175) to anoint an oyster or 50 grams to make Blueberry Vinaigrette (page 347).

When the Test Kitchen develops a new flavouring, they make a small amount, with all the proportions dialed in. Then when the restaurant kitchen does their mise en place for service, they scale up the recipe and make the amount they'll need for the number of meals they'll serve that day.

You'll be able to discern from the yield line whether a recipe makes a little, such as 15 grams (about 1 tablespoon) for our Danish Curry Powder (page 124), or a lot, such as 2 kilograms for our Black Currant Wood Oil (page 193), our go-to oil, which we use much like an extra-virgin olive oil.

You should make however much you need, though at first, you may not know what that amount is because you're not yet familiar with the recipe's flavour. And that's part of the journey: tinkering, tasting, opening your mind to the possibilities.

In Denmark, wild beach roses are in season in the height of summer.

To Keep Flavours Fresh, Keep Them Cold

You'll notice that some recipes in this book end with an instruction to freeze what you've just made. At the restaurant, for instance, when we produce 200 to 300 liters of elderflower oil in the short window of late spring, we preserve it by freezing. At subzero temperatures, oxidation is greatly slowed, and the oil stays bright.

In most recipes, freezing isn't strictly necessary—cooling is often enough. But the colder you go, the more vivid the flavour will remain later. Cold temperatures slow or halt the changes that dull freshness and color. At very low temperatures, most unwanted molds and yeasts become inactive (though not entirely killed). Chemical reactions like oxidation are also drastically reduced.

Whether you're cooling or freezing, the speed matters: The faster you bring something down in temperature, the less flavour, color, and vitality you lose.

What Is the Flavour of Noma?

As Noma has evolved over the past two decades, our fascination with specific ingredients has ebbed and flowed—we may be obsessed with seaweeds one year, enamored of molds the next. But through the years of Noma's evolution and the creation of hundreds of complex dishes, a cluster of ingredients always seems to be at the center of our menus. These flavours persist because they solve problems and bring joy.

We think of these as the "mother flavours" of Noma, the ingredients that, along with the many ferments woven through our dishes, make us taste like us. These flavours have defined Noma for the past twenty years and will likely continue to define Noma however we evolve in the years to come.

Our affection for these ingredients is not simply because of the way they taste, but because they are so generous—they have so much to give, and they allow us to capture and use their essences in so many flavourful products.

Black Currant

If you've eaten a handful of black currant berries at peak season or even sipped on jammy, deep magenta cassis liqueur, you know the pleasure of ripe black currants. But Noma goes beyond the ripe berry. Every year we pick the unripe berries and salt them to produce bright, tangy capers (page 71) that are delicious; some of us might even say addictively delicious. And the berries themselves almost become an afterthought when compared to all the products we get from the rest of the plant: Young branches of the black currant bush, still green on the inside, are pounded and mashed before being infused into an oil (page 193) with a depth of flavour comparable to that of the finest olive oils. The young shoots are picked at the beginning of spring and used to bring pops of green herbaceousness to dishes (page 45), and the leaves are either pickled or blended into a verdant oil (page 185), redolent with grassy basil flavours and pepper notes.

Elderflower

It's impossible to think of summer in Denmark without the smell of elderflower on the breeze. The clusters of tiny white blooms adorn many dishes during our summer run, but the real work with elderflower lies with stretching this special ingredient to become a year-round celebration. While the flowers are in season, we frantically squirrel away as many of the aromatic blossoms as we can, picking them to add to syrup (page 417), miso (page 488), salt (page 101), oil (page 179), and kombucha, so that even in the darkest winter days, we can offer guests a heightened burst of Danish summer. We even pickle the blossoms (page 44), yielding tiny pickled flowers and elderflower-scented vinegar. After the flowers have given up their petals, the tiny purple elderberries are harvested and processed into fruit leather, and even used to create a facsimile of a balsamic vinegar.

Kelp

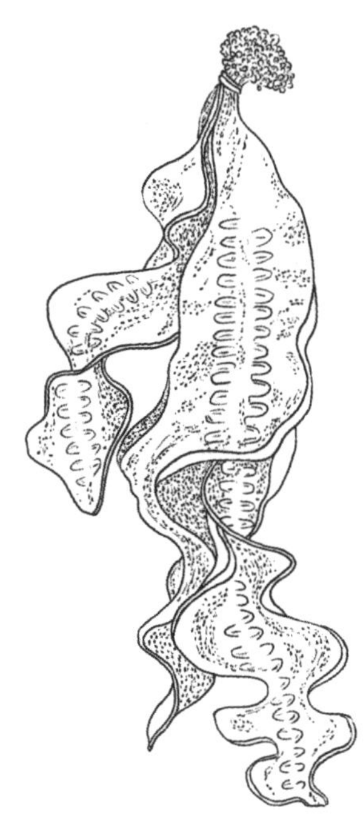

Kelp has become an indispensable ingredient on every Noma menu. A simple cold infusion of kelp and water (page 215) produces a clean, elegant, umami-inflected dashi that serves as a flavourful cooking medium, broth base, or general replacement for water. Reducing this kelp infusion until only the natural salt in the seaweed remains is a daily operation in the Noma kitchen. Noma Umami Salt (page 113) brings a tempered salinity and a tidal wave of sweet-savory richness to any dish in which we use it, whether as a finishing salt, a sauce element, or even ground into spice mixes as a secret flavour booster. Kelp's journey as a dashi flavouring is far from over once it is removed from the infusion: The seaweed can be dried and ground into a powerful thickener and emulsifier that we use to add luxurious body to sauces, or dry-roasted and transformed into an addictive, salty punch of umami (page 115), or simmered with oil (page 170) into a rich, nutty, oceanic condiment. Kelp even finds its way into desserts, simmered in a stock of fruit juice and aromatics and then dried into a chewy, sweet-sour confection (page 436).

Koji

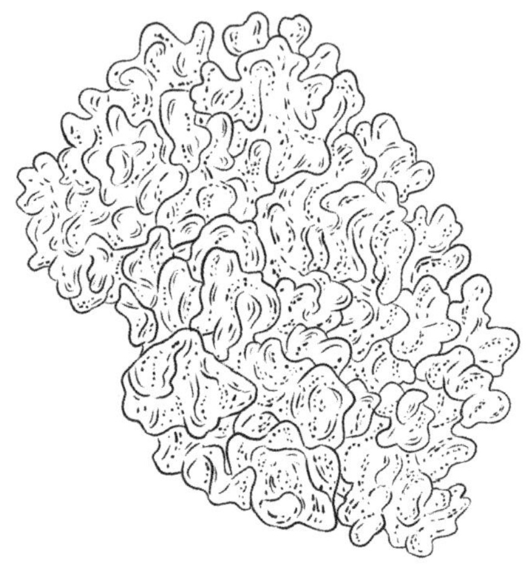

Our use of koji (grains that have been inoculated with the mold *Aspergillus oryzae* and used to create fermented foods) transcends the traditional. Classically, koji is used as a tool, a key to unlock unique flavours in common ingredients. Take soybeans, toasted wheat, salt, and water, add koji, and become awash in the umami-rich tides of a Japanese shoyu. Likewise, miso, sake, and amazake all owe their characteristic flavours to the enzymatic magic of koji. Our koji revelation occurred when we introduced the notion that koji could be its own unique, delicious flavour. We began making koji oil (page 487), confiting koji, flavouring butter with koji (page 203), roasting koji, and fermenting koji, and even went so far as to grill planks of koji, brushing the rapidly caramelizing pieces with a glaze made from still more koji. We adored the fermented fruitiness, the cooked-in-butter nuttiness, the roasted richness, and the barbecued deliciousness that this ingredient offered. It took a simple change of perspective to set us off on a journey to explore the flavour potential of koji, but also to remind us that sometimes the greatest discoveries can hide in the places we least suspect.

Pine

It's hard to remember a time when we weren't aware of the flavour potential of pine. Through years of testing, tasting, and development, we discovered the delicious characters of all the varieties of pine we had growing just beyond our doorstep: Douglas fir, larch, noble fir, Norwegian pine. Their needles were picked to infuse vinegar (page 39) or ground and used to flavour salt (page 100); pine cones were simmered in syrup until fudgy and luscious (page 450), while others were brined until they became "olives" (page 73). Young shoots were used fresh, or pickled for the winter months, and pine bark was used to smoke grilled ingredients, imbuing them with a complex aroma.

Rose

Every summer we scour the Danish countryside, collecting bushels of magenta-hued beach roses, which, along with elderflower, are the harbingers of Scandinavian summer. We'll quickly grill fresh roses over open fire, just until the petals begin to pucker, to uncover a complexity beyond the blossoms' characteristic aromas. At the height of the season, we infuse the delicate petals into vinegar (page 43), grind them into salt (page 105), and blend them into oil (page 187) to preserve the aroma of such a special ingredient and the moment in time in which they bloom. The oil is especially potent, and is used as a finishing oil or as a flavouring agent in emulsions, pastes, and marinades.

1.

Pickling and Preserving

Pickling and Preserving: Revisiting time, unlocking flavour

Seafood Pickles, Ocean, 2024
Top right: Pine cone olives with black currant wood oil, lye-cured pine cone olives, salted noble fir cone. **Bottom right:** Sea cucumber boiled in dashi, frozen, sliced thinly, marinated with elderflower kombucha and unripe sea buckthorn, and served with Japanese quince. **Bottom left:** Brined unripe grapes with pine, pickled wild beach rose petals, preserved ramsons with truffle. **Top left:** Brined Mirabelle plums and gooseberries with ants.

In Scandinavia, winter isn't just a backdrop—it's a force that shapes everything: the culture, the landscape, the way we eat. For as long as people have lived this far north, they've relied on preservation not just to stretch ingredients, but to survive.

By September, the land starts to shut down. The air turns dry and sharp, the days get shorter, and a blanket of cold settles over everything. The land withdraws into itself, locking away its abundance. And for centuries, people here didn't just endure winter—they found ways to keep the warmer seasons alive, one jar at a time.

Understanding preservation means understanding winter. Before electricity, before freezers or fridges, preservation was ingenuity. It was the only way to make it through six months of darkness. A successful harvest in August wasn't a triumph unless you knew how to carry its bounty through to February.

That way of thinking became part of how we cook at Noma. In the early years, when the first frost arrived, it was a moment of real tension. Had we done enough? Had we preserved enough to see us through? But over time, pickled, salted, and preserved ingredients stopped being only about scarcity—they became part of our identity. They started showing up even when ingredients were abundant. That acidity, that tension, that sharpness—the flavour of preservation—became a thread that runs through our food, no matter the season.

What's become clear over the years is that nearly anything can be preserved. We've never met an ingredient we couldn't extend with salt or vinegar. And more than that—preservation doesn't just prolong life, it transforms. Salt, especially: It draws out water, concentrates flavour, and alters texture, sometimes tightening it, sometimes creating

29

30

Sencha-Infused Gingko Nuts, Foamy Smoked Tomato Sauce, and Pine Cone Olives, Kyoto, 2024
Pine cone olives are warmed in sencha butter with fresh gingko nuts and then covered in a foamy sauce of tomato, lacto rice koji water, and smoked butter. The dish is finished with Noma umami salt, larch wood oil, and sudachi zest.

something completely new. Salt unlocks things you can't otherwise access. Likewise with vinegar. I love pickling mushrooms for that reason—the way their structure changes over time is remarkable.

I've thought a lot about preserving food over the years, and I often return to one of my earliest memories. I was a child in what used to be Yugoslavia, spending summers in a small village on the edge of a mountain. We didn't have a fridge. Everything was made from scratch, every day. My aunties would milk cows in the morning, churn the cream into butter by hand, cook all day. One of my strongest memories is of rose cordial, made by boiling rose petals in sugar and diluting the syrup with cold spring water. We'd drink it on the hottest afternoons after running around barefoot. It was sweet and floral and deeply refreshing.

Years later, in my twenties, I was on a beach in Denmark, gathering beach plants: cabbage, coriander, wild beach rose. The scent of those rose petals brought me straight back to that rose cordial. We started pickling the petals, testing every preservation method we knew: salting, smoking, pouring vinegar over them. We packed the jars away and forgot about them. And months later, in the middle of winter, we opened one. The smell of sweet apple vinegar and rose hit us. It was intense. Like the entire memory of summer distilled into a single moment.

Preservation allows us to revisit time. To pull something forward. It's at the core of how we think about flavour at Noma because it creates flavour that's difficult to reach any other way—flavour that holds depth, tension, memory.

Vinegar and Vinegar Pickles

Vinegar is a key player in the Noma larder, its racy acidity providing a bracing freshness as well as the transformational power of acid to change texture and to preserve.

We make some of our vinegars by fermentation, as explained in *The Noma Guide to Fermentation*, and we make others by either whizzing a fresh ingredient into a fairly neutral vinegar base using a high-powered blender or by macerating the flavouring ingredients in the vinegar.

Chiles are preserved with flowers, herbs, and spices.

We may use a splash of flavoured vinegar to give a dish a sparkly contrast, and we also use volumes of vinegar when we make our pickles. These vinegar pickles don't involve fermentation; the ingredients (usually a vegetable or fruit, though we've pickled just about everything from seaweed to sausage) are preserved through acid's ability to inhibit the growth of unwanted organisms.

The most important reason we pickle with vinegar, however, is flavour. Spending time in a vinegar bath infuses any ingredient with bright flavour, creates an appealing texture, and, in many cases, yields a bonus of flavoured vinegar for us to use in other dishes.

When making a flavoured vinegar, you can simply macerate your ingredient in the vinegar, allowing a slow, gentle transfer of flavours. Or you can process the flavourings and vinegar together in a blender, which increases the surface area of the flavouring. This method produces a vibrant vinegar, but you do risk bruising your flavouring ingredient, and the action of blending whips small amounts of air into the vinegar, promoting oxidation. Both of these factors can result in unwanted flavours over time, which is why you should make blended vinegar right before using it, or keep it on ice in the refrigerator if you must make it a day or so in advance.

For our pickles, we typically use two types of commercial vinegar (see page 483), but occasionally we make our own vinegars to create specific flavour combinations: pumpkin vinegar (page 493) for wild chanterelle mushrooms or elderberry vinegar for soft-boiled partridge eggs, for example.

Vinegar pickles are easy to make and quite safe, and they yield not only a delicious pickled item but also liquid gold in the form of flavoured vinegar that can be used as a zesty splash, perhaps to finish a ceviche or salad. The pickling process at its simplest (cold-infused pickling) involves submerging the food to be pickled—flowers or other fragrant, soft-textured items—in vinegar, letting the pickle chill in the refrigerator until the flavours are swapped, and then serving the pickle and/or the now flavour-infused vinegar.

Late-spring vegetables and fruits.

Hot-infused pickling is a slightly more involved but still very straightforward process: Make a flavoured pickling liquid, bring it to a boil, pour it over the ingredients to be pickled, seal, and wait.

At Noma, we make cold-infused pickles with vinegar only, pure and bracing, while for our hot-infused pickles, we use plenty of seasonings (flowers, herbs, spices, dried mushrooms) for a more complex result. The addition of sugar in particular sets our hot pickles apart from our cold ones. The ratio we use for hot-infused pickles is 3:2:1, meaning 3 parts vinegar to 2 parts water (or dashi, in many of our pickles) to 1 part sugar.

37

Pine Vinegar

Makes 500 grams

150 grams Douglas fir needles
500 grams white wine vinegar

Pine vinegar may be the vinegar we make most for the Noma larder because of its versatility, unique freshness, and uncanny ability to tie a dish together.

We call this "pine" vinegar, but we make it with needles from the Douglas fir (*Pseudotsuga menziesii*). You could use other pine varieties in its place, provided they are chemical-free. Douglas fir has a wonderful grapefruit flavour that works especially well in combination with horseradish juice.

Use your Douglas fir needles as soon as you can after harvesting them (or freeze them until ready use) to preserve their full fragrance and flavour. We use white wine vinegar with pine, as it is relatively neutral and balances well with the citrus notes of the Douglas fir.

Blend the fir needles and vinegar together in a Thermomix or other high-powered blender on full speed for 45 seconds, then strain immediately through a fine-mesh nylon sieve into a container set over ice. Reserve in the refrigerator over ice until needed. Use the vinegar the same day you make it; the flavour will deteriorate over the course of a few hours.

Oregano or Lemon Thyme Vinegar

Makes 500 grams

125 grams fresh oregano or lemon thyme sprigs
500 grams apple balsamic vinegar (see page 483), plus more if needed

When oregano and lemon thyme bloom in the warm summer months, they inevitably find their way onto the Noma menu. The tiny blossoms look delicate but pack a powerful punch, one of the things we like most about them. Whether as a seasoning for just-grilled marinated fava beans or arranged on precisely cut crudités of fresh summer berries, these nectar-filled flowers add distinct pops of flavour. But what to do with the flowerless sprigs, which are full of herbaceous leaves? We could only use so much of these for stock or staff meals, so we began pickling them to produce flavoured vinegars.

We love the peppery note of oregano vinegar for seasoning mushroom, roasted onion, or wild game broths. The minty and earthy side of lemon thyme vinegar is an excellent seasoning in a fire-roasted baba ghanoush, or to brighten roasted red peppers. We usually leave the herbs in the bag after aging the vinegar, siphoning off the vinegar as we need it. You can make vinegar with other edible members of the Lamiaceae family, such as mint, basil, or lavender.

Pick through the sprigs and discard any leaves that aren't pristine. Place the herb sprigs in a vacuum bag and add the vinegar (be sure the herbs are covered with the vinegar, adding a bit more if needed). Seal on 100% vacuum. Age in the refrigerator for at least 6 months before using. After you've opened the bag, keep the herbs submerged in the vinegar and reserve in the refrigerator indefinitely.

Fines Herbes Vinegar

Makes 500 grams

70 grams fresh chervil leaves
70 grams fresh flat-leaf parsley leaves
60 grams fresh tarragon leaves
50 grams fresh chives
Liquid nitrogen
500 grams pear vinegar (5% acetic acid)

Freezing delicate herbs with liquid nitrogen before pulverizing and blending them with vinegar allows us to capture their peak flavours without risk of bruising from a knife or blender blade.

Place the chervil, parsley, tarragon, and chives in a bowl. Pour a bit of liquid nitrogen over the herbs to freeze them completely. Transfer the frozen herbs to a Thermomix and blend until powdered, then add the vinegar and blend for 30 seconds to incorporate the flavours. Strain immediately through a fine-mesh nylon sieve into a container set over ice. Reserve in the refrigerator over ice until needed. Use the vinegar the same day you make it; the flavour will deteriorate over the course of a few hours.

Pick through the rose petals and discard wilted petals or debris. Place the petals in a vacuum bag.

Add the vinegar in a ratio of 1 part petals to 4 parts vinegar.

Seal on 100% vacuum and transfer to the refrigerator.

Age in the refrigerator for at least 6 months before use. After opening, reserve in the refrigerator indefinitely.

Pickled Wild Beach Roses

Makes about 125 grams pickled petals and 500 grams vinegar

125 grams wild beach rose petals (or petals from any unsprayed fragrant rose)
500 grams apple balsamic vinegar (see page 483), plus more if needed

Pickled wild beach roses offer us two incredible products for the price of one. The rose petals themselves, infused with fruity aged apple vinegar, are a refreshingly crisp rose-scented accent that we use as we might any other pickle: folded into a rich concoction as an acidic element to cut through fattiness, or served on their own as a bright palate cleanser. The pickled petals are slightly delicate to work with, as they are tender and become a bit floppy in the vinegar, but they can still be manipulated (with some finessing) into their natural heartlike shape. The bonus product is the rose vinegar, the lightly sweet and floral flavour of which is versatile enough to use in dishes from salads to ceviches to grilled vegetables.

Pick through the rose petals and discard any wilted petals or bits of debris. Place the rose petals in a vacuum bag and add the vinegar (be sure the blossoms are covered with the vinegar, adding a bit more if needed). Seal on 100% vacuum. Age in the refrigerator for at least 6 months before using. After you've opened the bag, keep the petals submerged in the vinegar and reserve in the refrigerator indefinitely, retrieving the petals or straining off the vinegar as needed.

Pickled Elderflower

Makes about 125 grams pickled flowers and 500 grams vinegar

- 125 grams elderflower blossoms (a few smaller stems attached is okay)
- 500 grams apple balsamic vinegar (see page 483), plus more if needed

Elderflower is an inextricable part of Noma's flavour palette, and pickling is a great way to preserve its early summer fragrance. As with pickled wild beach roses, this process yields both a delicate pickled flower and a floral-scented vinegar.

Pick through the elderflower blossoms and stems and discard any wilted flowers or debris. Place the blossoms in a vacuum bag and add the vinegar (be sure the blossoms are covered with the vinegar, adding a bit more if needed). Seal on 100% vacuum. Age in the refrigerator for at least 6 months before using. After you've opened the bag, keep the elderflowers submerged in the vinegar and reserve in the refrigerator indefinitely, retrieving the elderflowers or straining off the vinegar as needed.

Pickled Black Currant Shoots

Makes 125 grams

125 grams black currant shoots
500 grams apple balsamic vinegar (see page 483), plus more if needed

In early spring in Scandinavia, black currant buds transform from tiny green sprouts into the shoots of young leaves. These shoots, tender enough to be eaten raw, are delicious when sautéed in butter and lightly salted, and they also can be made into an excellent cold-infused pickle. Dressed with fruity black currant wood oil and served with other pickled items, black currant shoots become part of a palate-cleansing dish. While the vinegar does absorb some black currant flavour, it isn't quite as intriguing as the pickled shoots themselves, so we don't use it as an ingredient.

Pick through the black currant shoots and discard any debris. Place the shoots in a vacuum bag and add the vinegar (be sure the shoots are covered with the vinegar, adding a bit more if needed). Seal on 100% vacuum. Age in the refrigerator for at least 6 months before using. After you've opened the bag, keep the black currant shoots submerged in the vinegar and reserve in the refrigerator indefinitely, retrieving the shoots as needed.

Wild Deer and Autumn Pickles with Horseradish Juice, Forest, 2023
A fallow deer chop is paired with a sauce of deer bones, blueberry reduction, truffle, and fig leaf oil, served with a plate of preserves: Solaris wine leaf, pickled rose petals, brined green gooseberries, brined Mirabelle plum, preserved ramson leaf, black currant caper, preserved Padrón chile with a bowl of horseradish juice and horseradish oil.

Preserved Ramson Around Pickled Quail Egg, Wild Boar Lardo, and Black Currant Caper Paste, Forest, 2022
Black currant capers are transformed into a paste that's spread on lightly pickled quail eggs, which are then wrapped in preserved ramson leaves with wild boar lardo.

Pickled Chanterelles

Makes 500 grams

500 grams button chanterelles
1 kilogram Pumpkin Vinegar*

This recipe first appeared in *The Noma Guide to Fermentation*. Since then, we've adapted the vinegar recipe to work with both butternut squash and pumpkin, and this technique for pickling chanterelles remains a reliable method for preserving peak-season mushrooms. The key is to source high-quality button chanterelles and clean them thoroughly.

Clean and gently rinse the chanterelles and then dry them on clean towels. Place the chanterelles in a clean pickling jar. Heat the vinegar to just below boiling, then pour it into the jar, covering the chanterelles. Let cool completely, then reserve in the refrigerator for up to a couple of months. For unrefrigerated storage, process the mushrooms using the water bath canning method (see page 57), then reserve the unopened jar at room temperature for up to 1 year; after you've opened the jar, reserve in the refrigerator for up to a couple of months.

Pickled Chiles

Makes about 500 grams

About 500 grams mixed fresh chiles

Flowers, Leaves, Citrus

Fennel flowers
Basil flowers
Marigold flowers
1 fig leaf
1 finger lime

Pickling Liquid

600 grams apple balsamic vinegar (see page 483)
400 grams Cold-Infused Dashi (page 215)
200 grams sugar
10 grams dried ancho chile
10 grams dried kelp
3 grams juniper berries
2.5 grams toasted Madagascar pepper
2 grams Dried Bergamot Skin*
1 gram dried rose petals
0.8 gram dried arctic thyme

Twenty years ago, if you wanted to taste chile in Denmark, your best bet was to visit a kebab shop, shake a bit of chile oil on your shawarma, and steal an extra container for later. Even now, you'd be hard-pressed to find the flavour much farther north of Copenhagen. Ever since Noma's Mexico pop-up in 2017, we've been quite chile-crazed, so we were pleased when we discovered Denmark's Gartneri Toftegaard as a source for fantastic chiles. The growers focus on tomatoes, chiles, and other nightshades, having planted and tested over one thousand varieties.

It's hard to go wrong when selecting chiles for pickling, though you might base your choice on your heat tolerance. Keep in mind that chile heat will be tamed a bit by pickling, as capsaicin—the compound responsible for the fire—leaches from the chile into the pickling liquid over time, muting its flavour.

The amount of pickling liquid you'll need for any batch of pickled chiles (or any vegetable) will vary depending on the quantity of chiles, their size and shape, and the volume of your jar. Because it's important to respect the ratio of ingredients in the liquid, you want to be sure you have enough liquid to fill the jar and cover the ingredients; coming up short and adding another big splash of dashi isn't a good option. One way to control this is to do a dry run with your chiles: Pack them into your pickling jar and then fill with plain water to cover. Pour off that water and weigh it; this is the amount of finished pickling liquid you'll need, though you should make a bit more to account for evaporation during boiling. *(Recipe continues)*

We love to chop pickled chiles and fold them with minced salted berries and an aromatic oil to yield a sour-salty-spicy paste. Pickled chiles are also great on their own as a snack or used to dress a rice bowl.

Rinse the fresh chiles. Using a skewer or paring knife, poke a few holes in each one to allow the liquid to penetrate. Place the chiles in a clean pickling jar.

Give the fresh flowers, leaves, and citrus a quick rinse to ensure that there are no critters hitching a ride. Cut the finger lime in half. Add the fennel, basil, and marigold flowers, the fig leaf, and the finger lime to the jar with the chiles.

Make the pickling liquid: Place the vinegar, dashi, and sugar in a medium saucepan and bring to a boil, stirring to dissolve the sugar. Stir in the ancho chile, kelp, juniper berries, Madagascar pepper, bergamot skin, rose petals, and arctic thyme and simmer for a few seconds to rehydrate and activate their flavours.

Carefully pour the pickling liquid and flavourings into the jar, making sure the liquid covers the chiles and other ingredients. Place a weight in the jar to ensure the ingredients stay submerged (we use a sterilized round of food-grade mesh, such as a piece cut from a mesh dehydrator mat, topped with a sterile zip-top bag filled with water). Eventually the chiles will absorb the pickling liquid and sink to the bottom of the jar. Seal the jar and age in the refrigerator for at least 1 week before using.

Store in the refrigerator for up to 3 months; the chiles will develop more flavour and mellow in spiciness the longer they sit. For unrefrigerated storage, process the chiles using the water bath canning method (see page 57), then reserve the pickles in the unopened jar at room temperature for up to 1 year; after you've opened the jar, reserve in the refrigerator for up to 3 months.

Poke holes in the chiles to allow the pickling liquid to penetrate; cut the finger lime in half. Pack the jar with the chiles and aromatics.

Place the vinegar, dashi, and sugar in a saucepan and bring to a boil, stirring to dissolve the sugar. Add the spices and simmer for a few seconds to hydrate the spices and other flavourings.

Pour the hot pickling liquid, along with all the flavourings, into the jar.

Place a weight in the jar to keep the ingredients submerged. Seal the jar and refrigerate for at least 1 week before use. Reserve the finished pickles in the refrigerator for up to 3 months.

Pickled Fennel

Makes about 500 grams

Blanched Fennel
3 kilograms filtered water
30 grams salt
Douglas fir sprigs
Dried kelp
Fennel tops
Fresh lemon thyme (or any aromatic herbs)
Fresh lemon verbena
About 500 grams baby fennel bulbs, halved lengthwise

Fresh Flowers, Berries, and Pine
Fresh fennel flowers
10 to 15 wild beach rose petals
10 to 15 green (unripe) gooseberries
10 grams fresh pine shoots

Fennel can be quite fibrous, so it needs precooking to relax the texture. You want the final pickle to be crunchy, however, so don't cook the fennel until it's fully tender; simply give it a light blanch to soften it to a pleasant level. Alternatively, very thinly slice the fennel and skip the simmering step.

Blanch the fennel: Combine the water and salt in a pot large enough to hold the liquid and the fennel bulbs comfortably. Bring to a boil, stirring once or twice to dissolve the salt. Add the Douglas fir, kelp, fennel tops, lemon thyme, and lemon verbena. Simmer for a few seconds, add the fennel bulbs, and simmer until they are slightly softened; the fennel will only need a few minutes, depending on its size. Transfer the blanched fennel to a rack to cool slightly, then place it in a clean pickling jar.

Give your fresh flowers, berries, and pine a quick rinse to remove any debris or insects, then add them to the jar with the blanched fennel. (If you like, cut the gooseberries in half to expose the flesh before adding them.)

Make the pickling liquid: Place the vinegar, dashi, and sugar in a medium saucepan and bring to a boil, stirring to dissolve the sugar. Stir in the roseroot, chanterelles, horseradish, Konini grains, mustard seeds, rhubarb, and black currant buds and simmer for a few seconds to rehydrate and activate the flavours.

Carefully pour the pickling liquid and flavourings into the jar, making sure the liquid covers the ingredients. Place a weight in the jar to ensure the ingredients are submerged (we use a sterilized round of food-grade mesh, such as a piece from a mesh dehydrator mat, topped with a sterile zip-top bag filled with water). Eventually the fennel will absorb the pickling liquid and sink to the bottom of the jar. Seal the jar and age in the refrigerator for at least 1 week before using.

Store in the refrigerator for up to 3 months; the pickles will develop more flavour the longer they sit. For unrefrigerated storage, process the fennel using the water bath canning method (see page 57), then reserve the pickles in the unopened jar at room temperature for up to 1 year; after you've opened the jar, reserve in the refrigerator for up to 3 months.

Pickling Liquid

600 grams apple balsamic vinegar (see page 483)
400 grams Cold-Infused Dashi (page 215)
200 grams sugar
5 grams dried roseroot
5 grams dried chanterelles
3 grams Dried Horseradish*
3 grams roasted Konini grains or other wheatberry
3 grams toasted yellow mustard seeds
1 gram freeze-dried rhubarb
1 gram black currant buds

Place the water and salt in a large pot. Bring to a boil. Add the Douglas fir, kelp, fennel tops, and herbs. Simmer briefly. Add the fennel bulbs (as Junichi Takahashi does here). Simmer until slightly softened.

Transfer the fennel bulbs to a rack to cool slightly.

Pack the fennel bulbs tightly into a clean pickling jar. Add the fennel flowers, rose petals, gooseberries, and pine.

Pour the hot pickling liquid, along with all the flavourings, into the jar.

Place the vinegar, dashi, and sugar in a saucepan and bring to a boil, stirring to dissolve the sugar. Add the spices to the pickling liquid. Simmer for a few seconds to activate the flavours.

Place a weight in the jar to keep the ingredients submerged. Seal the jar and refrigerate for at least 1 week before use. Reserve the finished pickles in the refrigerator for up to 3 months.

Processing Your Pickles Using the Water Bath Canning Method

At Noma, we have ample refrigerator capacity for our pickles, so we don't often process them for long storage. But if you'd like to store your pickles out of the fridge, you need to can them using a boiling process that kills vegetative bacteria and creates a tight seal that prevents new organisms from sneaking in. Only use this method with high-acid foods (pH 4.6 or lower; the acidity prevents the growth of botulinum spores, which aren't killed by boiling), and only use jars and lids designed for canning.

Here's how to process your pickles:

Sterilize the jars in boiling water and wash the two-piece lids. (Note that the jar pictured on page 59 is not suitable for canning, only for refrigerator pickles.)

Find a pot deep enough for the jars to be submerged by at least 2.5 cm (1 inch) and large enough for water to circulate between the jars. (To keep the jars from clattering against the bottom of the pot, place a wire rack, a silicone mat, or a slim spiral of twisted aluminum foil in the pot.) Fill the pot with water and bring to a boil (100°C/212°F).

Fill the sterilized jars with the pickles and pickling liquid, leaving 1 cm (½ inch) of headspace. Run a sterile knife around the inside of the jar to dislodge any air bubbles. Wipe the rims of the jars with a clean cloth.

Place the flat lid on each jar and screw on the metal rings just tightly enough to keep the lids in place; don't screw the rings on tightly yet, as oxygen needs to escape during boiling.

Using a jar lifter or tongs, place the jars in the pot. When the water returns to a boil, begin timing: Boil 500 ml jars for 10 minutes or 1 L jars for 15 minutes. Add 1 minute for every 300 meters (1,000 feet) above sea level.

Remove the jars from the pot and place them on a wooden surface, a rack, or a kitchen towel (putting hot jars on a cold counter could cause them to crack). Let cool for 24 hours. During that time, the flat lids will be sucked down slightly, forming a tight seal (you should hear a satisfying "ping" when this occurs).

Test the seal by pressing the center of the lid with your finger—it should not pop back up. To double-check, remove the ring and try to lift off the lid; it should remain tightly sealed. Replace the ring and screw it on tightly. If any jars weren't properly sealed, keep the pickles in the refrigerator or reprocess with another round of boiling water. The pickles can be stored in the unopened jars at room temperature for up to 1 year.

59

Salted and Brined Preserves

Salt, like vinegar in the pickles section, does two things for the Noma larder: It preserves, by creating a hostile environment for bacteria and other unwanted organisms, and—most important—it creates flavours in a range of salty condiments that we love.

Ramson buds packed in salt, on their way to becoming capers.

The traditional caper, from the berry of a Mediterranean shrub, has been an inspiration for us. To make capers, you bury the fruit in salt; over time, the salt draws out water from the fruit, which in turn mixes with the salt to create a solution that is then drawn back into the fruit. The process is called osmosis, and it's nature's way of seeking equilibrium—areas of less salty liquid want to equalize with areas of more salty liquid. Once everybody's nicely salty all around, the salt content keeps out the bad stuff and produces a condiment you want to add to your mayonnaise, potato salad, or pan of Dover sole sautéing in foaming butter.

Because we're in Scandinavia rather than Sardinia, we use local caper "equivalents," most often berries from a range of edible shrubs. Smothering the tiny fruits in salt gives the capers a long shelf life and creates flavours beyond just salty to include sweet, tangy, and fruity.

Brined **(left)** and raw **(right)** noble fir cones.

Brine, which at its simplest is salt and water, preserves food in the same way that salt alone does, using the process of osmosis to draw free water from the ingredient to be preserved and replace it with salty water. At Noma, we generally work with an 8% brine (see page 74), which is salty enough to discourage most microbes and still have a nicely balanced flavour.

In the same way that preserving a vegetable or flower in vinegar yields both a pickle and a flavoured vinegar, the liquid left from brining fruit and vegetables (and did we mention pine cones?) is delicious on its own. We even reduce some of our brines to make flavoured salts (see page 107).

63

Ramson Capers

Makes 250 grams

250 grams tender, unripe ramson seeds
Salt
About 500 grams apple balsamic vinegar (see page 483)

Ramson capers sparked an early Noma epiphany: You can use a traditional method from somewhere else in the world and apply it to ingredients in your own backyard. Ramsons (*Allium ursinum*) grow wild in the forests of northern Europe and parts of Asia. They have a cousin called ramps (*Allium tricoccum*) that's native to eastern regions of the US and Canada; the plants can be used interchangeably for cooking. Both plants are an early sign of spring, appearing before deciduous trees leaf out, and as such are cause for celebration for cooks.

Usually, just the ramson leaves are cooked and eaten, but the plants also bear flowers and eventually seedheads after their petals have fallen. We use the seeds while they are still tender to make capers. We never dig up the bulbs of ramsons, because as responsible foragers, we want the perennial plant to return.

When making ramson capers, we salt and then age the unripe seeds in apple vinegar to yield a sweet, oniony, acidic burst of flavour. Need help finishing a sauce? Add some chopped ramson capers, shallots, and parsley. Not sure how to dress your raw, tender squid? Ramson capers or even just their vinegary brine will do the trick.

Wash the seeds and remove any excess stems. Place the seeds in a vacuum bag and add enough salt to cover them completely, then seal on 100% vacuum. Age in the refrigerator for at least 3 weeks before using. The salted seeds can remain in the salt indefinitely, if you wish.

Remove the seeds from the bag and rinse off any excess salt. Gently blot them dry, then weigh them and place in a new vacuum bag. Add two times their weight in vinegar, or enough to cover the seeds completely, then seal on 100% vacuum. Age in the refrigerator for at least 3 months before using. After you've opened the bag, keep the ramson capers submerged in the vinegar and reserve in the refrigerator indefinitely.

Green Gooseberry Capers

Makes 1 kilogram

1 kilogram green gooseberries
80 grams salt

The saltier cousin of the lacto-fermented green gooseberries written about in *The Noma Guide to Fermentation*, salted green gooseberries provide the Noma Test Kitchen with a better-structured but just as preserved green gooseberry to use as a building block for new dishes. Salting the green berries maintains both their structure and their kiwi and star fruit notes, classic gooseberry flavours.

Wash the gooseberries and dry them well. Place the gooseberries and salt in a vacuum bag and mix them around thoroughly. Seal on 100% vacuum. Age in the refrigerator for at least 3 months before using. The gooseberry capers will keep indefinitely in the refrigerator. The salt will eventually dissolve into a brine, which can be used in addition to the capers themselves.

Sloeberry Capers

Makes 1 kilogram

1 kilogram unripe sloeberries
80 grams salt

Sloeberries—large, gorgeous indigo berries, similar to a small damson plum—are the fruit of the blackthorn, or sloe, tree, which is a member of the rose family. On their own, the berries are quite sour and astringent, but when salted, they have an appealing savory tartness. Mature sloeberries have an inedible stone in the center, so forage for the berries when they are small and only a few weeks old; the salt will help tenderize the immature stone to make it edible.

Wash the sloeberries and dry them well. Place the washed berries and salt in a vacuum bag and mix them around thoroughly. Seal on 100% vacuum. Age in the refrigerator for at least 3 months before using. The sloeberry capers will keep indefinitely in the refrigerator. The salt will eventually dissolve into a brine, which can be used in addition to the capers themselves.

Black Currant Capers

Makes 1 kilogram

1 kilogram unripe black currants
80 grams salt

The black currant bush represents the perfect plant for Noma—something can be made from every part of the plant (see page 22). This version of a Noma-style caper is the one we use most commonly in the Test Kitchen.

As with our Ramson Capers (page 64), also an integral member of the Noma larder, the transformation from something not quite edible into a craveable condiment is magical; the result is fruity, tangy, and salty, and just a little bit fleshy. Black currant capers can be used any way you would use store-bought capers and are also delicious enough to snack on by themselves.

Wash the currants and dry them well. Place the currants and salt in a vacuum bag and mix them around thoroughly. Seal on 100% vacuum. Age in the refrigerator for at least 3 months before using. The black currant capers will keep indefinitely in the refrigerator. The salt will eventually dissolve into a brine, which can be used in addition to the capers themselves.

Pine Cone Olives

Makes 1 kilogram

1 kilogram dwarf mountain pine cones (*Pinus mugo*)
Salt
About 1 kilogram Black Currant Wood Oil (page 193)

People have been making olives for thousands of years. Whether lye-curing, brining, salt-curing, sun-curing, or dry-curing, after eight thousand years, the olive-making technique is fairly dialed in. But what would a Scandinavian olive look like? In 2017, the Test Kitchen took on a mission: Create a pine cone olive.

We were comfortable working with pine as a flavouring, but the idea of taking an intensely bitter pine cone from the dwarf mountain pine and turning it into a lemony, salty snack was certainly a novel challenge. And so the work began.

Kevin Jeung, Chef of Research and Production in the Fermentation Lab, tried lye-curing; Test Kitchen head Mette Søberg tried blanching and brining. The lye cure was quicker, but blanching, while more labor-intensive, was easier to control, and the final flavour and texture of the brined fruit was worth the effort. As a result, dwarf mountain pine cone olives that have been blanched, brined, and stored in black currant wood oil are now a charming and delicious staple of our larder.

Set up multiple pots of boiling water (this will make the successive blanching go faster) and an ice bath.
(Recipe continues)

Blanch the pine cones for 20 seconds, then transfer to the ice bath to cool. Using a fresh pot of boiling water each time, repeat the blanching-and-shocking process nine more times. Let the blanched pine cones cool, then drain them.

Weigh the blanched pine cones and make a 10% brine (see below), mixing up enough to cover the pine cones; let the brine cool. Transfer the pine cones to the brine and refrigerate for 10 days.

Drain the pine cones and soak them in fresh water for 30 minutes to remove some of the salt, then drain again. Weigh the pine cones and place them in a vacuum bag with an equal weight of black currant wood oil. Seal on 100% vacuum. Steam in a combi oven set to 90°C (195°F) for 4 hours, then remove the pine cones from the oven. Let cool, leaving the pine cones in the bag, then reserve in the refrigerator for up to 1 year, keeping the pine cone olives covered in the oil after opening the bag.

How to Calculate Your Brine

When calculating brines, it's tempting to start with your target percentage—say, 8%—using the water as your point of reference for your calculation: Add 80 grams of salt to 1 liter of water, dissolve it, and call it a day. But this method doesn't account for the water content of the ingredient being brined. Once you add the ingredient you're brining, whether it's a fruit, vegetable, unripe berry, or protein, its natural water content will dilute the brine, reducing the brine's overall concentration and skewing your original goal of brining at 8%. To brine more accurately, begin by calculating how much water you'll need to fully submerge the ingredient; you can estimate this amount or actually submerge the ingredient and then weigh the water. Combine the weight of the water and the ingredient, and calculate 8% salt based on that total weight. This method compensates for the dilution effect, ensuring that osmosis can do its job properly—and that your results will be far more consistent and effective.

Blanch the pine cones in boiling water for 20 seconds, then transfer them to an ice bath.

Repeat the blanching and shocking, using fresh boiling water each time, nine more times. Drain and weigh the pine cones.

Mix up a 10% brine, transfer the pine cones to the cooled brine, and refrigerate for 10 days. Drain and soak in fresh cold water for 30 minutes, then drain again.

Weigh the pine cones and place in a vacuum bag with an equal weight of black currant wood oil. Seal, then steam at 90°C (195°F) for 4 hours. Let cool, then reserve in the refrigerator for up to 1 year.

Place the noble fir cones in a vacuum bag.

Cover the cones with a cooled 8% brine.

Seal on 100% vacuum and refrigerate for
at least 1 month before use. As the cones rest, the brine
takes on their magenta color.

To use, rinse and peel individual scales from the cones,
discarding their inner seeds. Return the scales to the brine,
vacuum seal, and reserve in the refrigerator for up to 1 year.

Brined Noble Fir Cones

Makes 5 brined cones

5 ripe noble fir cones (*Abies procera*)
5 kilograms 8% brine (see page 74), cooled

When you cut into a ripe noble fir cone, you'll be shocked by the electric pink interior scales, which, when young and with their seeds removed, pack a delightful citrusy, forest-y flavour. But the season for fresh cones is short, so how best to preserve them for later use? Trials were conducted; lacto fermentation and then caper-level salt denatured the cell structure into a slimy mess and was quickly ruled out. Brine became the next logical attempt and, ultimately, the winning technique. As it happens, through the osmotic process, the brine itself develops an incredible flavour and a stunning magenta color, a double reward for our efforts. We use the brine to make Noble Fir Salt (page 108), so make that a triple reward.

Place the noble fir cones in a large vacuum bag, add the brine, and seal on 100% vacuum. Age in the refrigerator for at least 1 month before using. (The cones can remain in the brine indefinitely in the refrigerator.)

When ready to use the cones, remove them from the brine (don't discard it), rinse them lightly, and peel the individual scales from the cones. Remove and discard the inner seed from each scale. Place the peeled scales in a vacuum bag, add the reserved brine, and seal on 100% vacuum. Reserve in the refrigerator for up to 1 year.

Brined Unripe Grapes

Makes 1 kilogram

1 kilogram unripe grapes
8% brine (see page 74), cooled

Denmark isn't known as a wine-making country (not many grapes can thrive in our cold and occasionally gloomy climate), but René was partly raised in Macedonia (part of the former Yugoslavia), a culture that has an ancient wine-making history. A common appetizer in that part of the world is the dolma, usually made with spiced rice and minced meat wrapped in salted grape leaves and steamed. In the early days of Noma 2.0, the Test Kitchen decided to play around with this idea of a "dolma," what it means, and how it can be interpreted. We asked some local vineyards if we could forage a few grape leaves for our research process and ended up with a container full of tender leaves from Solaris grapes, an early ripener with a high sugar content. Some of the leaves still had unripe grapes attached, and they ended up in the Fermentation Lab.

The unripe grapes looked a bit like capers and the lab was awash in brine, so they said "Why not?," brined the grapes, and forgot about them. A few months later, Gaute Schartau Berrefjord, one of the Fermentation Lab chefs, was cleaning out the lab refrigerator and stumbled upon the brined grapes. Like any good mad scientist, he decided to risk a taste. The result? An intensely acidic but addictively briny pop of bright deliciousness. Plus, the brine itself had absorbed wonderful green and aromatic notes from the grapes.

Place the grapes in a large vacuum bag, add enough brine to cover them, and seal on 100% vacuum. Age in the refrigerator for at least 3 months before using. After opening the bag, keep the grapes submerged in the brine and reserve in the refrigerator indefinitely.

Brined Japanese Quince

Makes 1 kilogram

1 kilogram Japanese quince (*Chaenomeles japonica*)
8% brine (see page 74), cooled

In 2018, foraging legend Zenia Samlersen introduced us to Japanese quince (*Chaenomeles japonica*), a wild, thorny deciduous shrub. Similar to traditional quince (*Cydonia oblonga*), Japanese quince is too hard and astringent to eat raw, and benefits from having its cell structure denatured by some means. The two quince species share the same incredible fragrance of citrus, ripe apple, and guava, which was one of the driving factors for wanting to preserve the wild fruit that Zenia brought through our doors. Typically, when we get a crop of traditional quince in the restaurant, it goes straight into our freezer to be juiced and used later. We do the same for Japanese quince, but given its Ping-Pong-ball size, we wanted to try a different method.

We wanted to preserve the flavour and fragrance of the quince without developing new flavours (as lacto fermentation would), so brining was a natural choice. While we couldn't perfectly capture its alluring fragrance, the fruit itself had transformed into a sort of native lemon, a near-perfect embodiment of citrus that we so desperately crave at Noma. Not to mention the added bonus of the quince-infused brine, which has found its way into many dishes over the past six years.

Place the quince in a large vacuum bag, add enough brine to cover them, and seal on 100% vacuum. Age in the refrigerator for at least 1 month before using. After opening the bag, keep the quince submerged in the brine and reserve in the refrigerator indefinitely.

Japanese Quince

Japanese quince (*Chaenomeles japonica*) is a prized fruit at Noma, not only for its amazingly heady perfume but because of its extremely tart, citrus-like flavour, which proved very useful in our earlier days when we chose to limit our ingredients to those found in Scandinavia. Lemons are not one of those ingredients, so we were perpetually in search of sour. Once we realized the potential of Japanese quince, we would ask our forager for as much as could be found that year to freeze for future use. The small fruit, like its larger cultivated cousin, *Cydonia oblonga*, responds well to the mechanical cellular disruption that happens when frozen and thawed. Once frozen, you can slice the quince into wedges, thaw it, and then pick up a wedge and squeeze it like a lemon wedge. We also use the juice, but the fruit is difficult to forage and quantities vary each year based on the weather, so we can't always reserve the juice in large quantities. Cultivated quince, however, can be procured in large quantities and turned into juice by freezing, thawing, and running the fruit through the wine press; the resulting juice is frozen until we're ready to use it.

Suggested Uses

Tangy Chanterelle Relish

Make a warm, chunky relish using Pickled Chanterelles (page 48) as the main player, with chopped Ramson Capers (page 64) for a slightly oniony note and chopped Black Currant Capers (page 71) for fruity overtones. Warm some good olive oil, add chopped garlic, and cook until fragrant and softened, then fold in the chanterelles and the two types of caper. Season with salt as needed. Remove from the heat and let stand for at least an hour to bring the flavours together, then spread the relish on grilled focaccia or spoon it onto a scoop of fresh cheese and serve with crackers.

Green Gooseberry "Mignonette"

Top fresh oysters with a few thin slices of Green Gooseberry Capers (page 67), a small splash of the brine, and a few droplets of Douglas Fir Oil (page 175).

Pickled Fennel Niçoise Sandwich

Split a sandwich roll and moisten the interior with good olive oil and a few drops of the brine from Pickled Fennel (page 54). Layer the bread with sliced tomato, crumbled oil-packed tuna, sliced boiled eggs, and chopped Pickled Fennel. Season with salt, pepper, and more oil and pickle brine as needed.

Shrimp with Black Currant and Rose Tartar Sauce

Sauté shrimp (with their heads on, if possible) in oil with sliced garlic and herbs. Serve slightly warm with a "tartar sauce" made from best-quality mayonnaise mixed with chopped Black Currant Capers (page 71), finely chopped Pickled Wild Beach Roses (page 43), fresh dill, salt, and freshly cracked black pepper. Balance the flavours and loosen the texture a bit with a squeeze of lemon juice.

Fines Herbes Potato Salad

Boil small to medium waxy potatoes in heavily salted water, then drain. While still slightly warm, cut into thick slices or chunks. Dress with Fines Herbes Vinegar (page 41) and toss well so the vinegar is absorbed by the potatoes. Dress with good olive oil, season with salt and pepper, and adjust the acid balance with more vinegar as needed. Finish with a shower of any or all of the fresh herbs used in the vinegar recipe: chervil, parsley, tarragon, and chives.

Pine Cone Martini

Mix up a classic gin martini, using a 5-to-1 ratio of gin to dry vermouth. Stir (please don't shake) with ice until properly chilled, strain into a chilled martini glass, and garnish with a couple of Pine Cone Olives (page 73) on a Douglas fir skewer.

Opposite, top to bottom:
Tangy Chanterelle Relish;
Green Gooseberry "Mignonette";
Shrimp with Black Currant
and Rose Tartar Sauce
Right: Pine Cone Martini

Dried Ingredients, Salts, and Spice Mixes

Dried Ingredients, Salts, and Spice Mixes: Guiding the energy of a dish, shaping how it lands

A handful of dried ingredients. A well-made salt. A good spice mix. These ingredients may not look like much, but together they form the backbone of a kitchen that can move with the seasons and build flavour on its own terms.

We originally leaned into drying as a way to preserve things when they were in season and abundant, but it soon became something more. Drying transforms. It shifts how flavour presents itself. It softens some edges, deepens others, and reveals qualities you don't get when ingredients are fresh.

We've dried flowers for infusions, herbs for seasoning blends, seaweed for powders. One of our best successes is pumpkin bushi (read more about it on page 96), an incredible ingredient that's deep, smoky, elegant. Dried ingredients can act as connective tissue, linking the elements of a dish into something cohesive, something complete.

At Noma, we often talk about salt as both a beginning and an end. It's essential to the cooking process, one of the most important decisions a cook makes. Seasoning too early or too late changes everything. A piece of fish or meat benefits from salting ahead of time, while a broth or sauce might need salt only at the finish. There's no single rule—only feel, repetition, and attention.

In our kitchen, we use salts to shape, not just to season. We mix them with ingredients like rose petals, elderflower, pine, and seaweed. Not simply as a novelty, but because we've found that when you pair a salt with a specific supporting flavour, you can bring more definition to the master ingredient. When the right salt meets the right dish, one plus one makes three—or more.

Abalone Mushroom, Egg Yolk, Kelp, and Gooseberry Pumpkin Spice Mix, Kyoto, 2024
Cured abalone mushrooms are slowly grilled and glazed, then served with egg yolk and cep oil and seasoned with gooseberry pumpkin spice mix.

87

Reindeer Penis Salad with Savory Granola and Spice Mix, Forest, 2021
Slices of brined and pressure-cooked reindeer penis are folded with cooked grains, mustard seeds, and savory granola and mounded on a fig leaf. The dish is seasoned with Douglas fir vinaigrette, showered with herbs, and seasoned with reindeer penis spice mix.

And then there's Noma umami salt, as it's known here. It's become part of our DNA. It's not just a seasoning—it's a finishing element that brings a dish into focus. Kelp is naturally rich in glutamates, the compounds responsible for the flavour of umami, which is why this salt has such complex savory depth. The roasted version gives richness and umami to vegetables or meat. The "sweet" one lifts chocolate and fruit. Ordinary salt enhances—but Noma salt finishes.

In Denmark—and much of Scandinavia—the culinary tradition has been shaped by restraint, including very little use of spices. A Protestant legacy, maybe, where too much pleasure in food was seen as indulgent? Or perhaps it was just because spices were expensive. Either way, for a long time, spices were reserved for special occasions, usually Christmas: the roast pork with clove-scented crackling, the cinnamon rice porridge. But for the rest of the year, food was plain.

Danish cooking is different now, but if we had expanded our imagination back then, we would have realized that spices didn't need to come from faraway places; they were all around us. Because if you go beyond the purist definition—aromatic seeds, roots, and barks—you see that flavour can come from almost anything. Flowers. Fruits. Fermented grains. Dried seaweed. Lichen. The list opens up quickly once you let go of the traditional understanding of what "spice" is supposed to be.

At Noma, we made that shift in mindset and changed how we work when Garima Arora joined our team. She's now a brilliant chef with two Michelin stars and her own restaurants in India and Thailand. Back then, she was the first to show us that our own landscape was full of spices—we just weren't seeing them as such. Our herbs, our dried berries, our wildflowers. She helped us reframe them.

From there, everything opened up. We started building spice mixes. One of the most important was what we called Danish curry powder. Not a curry in the traditional sense, but a layered blend of dried, fermented, and roasted ingredients that brought warmth and depth. We used it in broths and sauces, or to finish a dish. It became a foundation, something that sparked other blends.

Junichi Takahashi, one of our Test Kitchen heads, is behind many of these blends. He has a deep sense of how things work together—how dried seaweed, rose petals, and fermented grains can align into something whole. Many of our most detailed spice recipes are his; some were built over time, while others came together in a single afternoon. But they all start from the same idea: that a spice mix isn't just a seasoning, it's a way of guiding the energy of a dish and shaping how it lands.

Once you start building a pantry of your own—one shaped by what you love, what's available, what you've preserved—you'll find that you have everything you need to create. These are your condiments.

Dried Ingredients

Drying a fresh ingredient at its peak captures the flavour of the season so you can incorporate it into dishes throughout the year. The drying process concentrates flavour and transforms texture. Water leaves, and the tastier parts remain. Soft ingredients turn hard, crisp, and brittle enough to crush, grate, or grind. Combining them with other ingredients becomes as simple as sprinkling a powder. And when you remove enough water from a rose petal or a berry, you deprive the bacteria that cause spoilage of what they need to survive. It's our simplest, and probably oldest, method of preservation.

Air-drying flowers preserves their flavour and color.

Dried Vegetables

Most vegetables are full of water; once dried, they become concentrated sources of flavour, used whole to enhance broths or braises or ground into a powder to be used in spice mixes and other sprinkle-able seasonings.

Fresh vegetables

Peel any vegetable that you would peel if eating raw; otherwise, leave it unpeeled. Cut the vegetables into wedges or slices that will create plenty of surface area. Lay them on a dehydrator tray in a single layer (skin-side down, if applicable) and dry in a dehydrator set to 50°C (120°F) until completely devoid of moisture. Let cool, then transfer to an airtight container (or place in a vacuum bag and seal on 60% vacuum) and reserve at room temperature for up to 1 year.

To transform the dried vegetable into a powder, grind it with a mortar and pestle or in a spice grinder to your desired consistency, keeping in mind that larger pieces will retain their flavour and fragrance longer than smaller ones. Reserve in an airtight container at room temperature until the dried vegetable begins to lose its fragrance.

Dried Flowers and Herbs

Mette Søberg ties up flowers for drying.

Look in the kitchen of an avid gardener and you're likely to see a bouquet of herbs or edible flowers tied with string and hanging at the ready for when the cook wants a pinch of something aromatic. We at Noma are avid gardeners of the highest magnitude (or at least our gardeners are), and dried plants are a welcome member of our flavour larder. You'll see them woven throughout the recipes in this book.

Fresh edible flowers or herbs

Pick over the flowers or herbs and discard any wilted or damaged leaves or blossoms. Lay the flowers or herbs on a dehydrator tray in a single layer and dry in a dehydrator set to 45°C (115°F) until all the moisture has evaporated, then let cool.

Alternatively, keep the flowers or herbs on their stems and gather them into bunches, then tie the stem end and hang the bunches upside down in a cool, dry area, out of direct sunlight, until fully dried.

With either method, transfer the dried flowers or herbs to an airtight container and reserve at room temperature until they lose their aroma. Keep the flowers or herbs as whole as possible in order to preserve their flavour and aroma, crumbling or grinding them only when you're ready to use them.

Semi-Dried Fruit

Drying fruit for grating or grinding is best left to commercial freeze-driers. But to give fruit a luscious, chewy texture and a concentrated flavour, we love semi-drying. We dip or brush the fruit in a flavoured oil, which helps preserve it as well as keep it supple. Koji Oil (page 487) is our standard; it adds just a hint of umami that makes the fruit taste even fruitier. Other fruit-oil pairings we think are fantastic include:

Cherries with lemon thyme oil
Currants with marjoram oil
Japanese quince with Douglas Fir Oil (page 175)
Mulberries with elderflower koji oil
Peeled cherry tomatoes with koji verbena oil
Strawberries with Morita Chile Oil* or Elderflower Oil (page 179)

If the fruit is thin-skinned or looks particularly beautiful when still in a cluster or on a vine, we'll leave them unpeeled in their natural form. For tomatoes and other fruits with firm skins, peeling first gives the semi-dried product a nicer texture.

Each batch of fruit will have its own moisture and sugar content, so you'll need to use your judgment as to drying time. Here are some guidelines to get you started.

Ripe fruit
Oil, for brushing

Arrange the fruit on a dehydrator tray with plenty of space between each piece, then brush the fruit lightly with oil. Dry in a dehydrator set to 60°C (140°F) for 2 to 3 hours for small fruit, such as red currants, or 6 to 8 hours for larger, wetter fruit, such as tomatoes or mulberries. Turn the pieces of fruit every 2 hours as they dry, brushing them with a bit more oil as you do to ensure even drying and a nice final shape. Aim for a final texture that's just slightly less chewy than a good sultana raisin. Let cool, then transfer the fruit to a vacuum bag and seal on 85% vacuum. Freeze for up to a few months.

Bushis: Subtle Smoke, Potent Umami

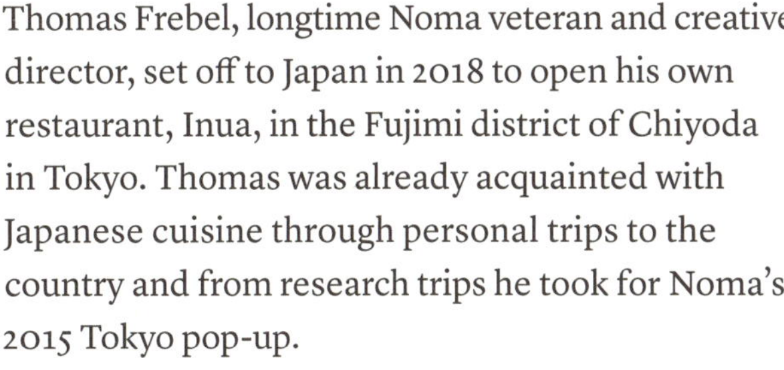

Thomas Frebel, longtime Noma veteran and creative director, set off to Japan in 2018 to open his own restaurant, Inua, in the Fujimi district of Chiyoda in Tokyo. Thomas was already acquainted with Japanese cuisine through personal trips to the country and from research trips he took for Noma's 2015 Tokyo pop-up.

One monumental connection Thomas made while in Japan was with a fourth-generation katsuobushi craftsman named Yusuke Sezaki. Katsuobushi is a time-honored condiment made from bonito that's been fermented, dried, and smoked; the umami-rich fish is shaved paper-thin and used to make the most important base broth in Japan: dashi.

At Inua, Thomas was already using katsuobushi from Sezaki-san because of its incredible quality. One of Thomas's favorite questions is "What else?" And so he began sending every possible fruit or vegetable to Sezaki-san to test in his smokers. The standout was clear: pumpkin bushi.

Sezaki-san takes perfectly ripe pumpkins, splits them in half from stem to base, and dries and smokes them for one to two months. The resulting pumpkin looks more fossilized than edible, but when broken open, its flesh is still bright orange. The flavour is intensely smoky, as you'd expect, but with an umami undertone that rivals aged Parmigiano. It's best grated using a Microplane but can also be sliced into small shavings.

While pumpkin bushi was the standout, Sezaki-san's corn bushi was delicious and is a valued ingredient at Noma. Because corn grows in rows of kernels, it's not as easy to grate, so we grind our corn bushi into a powder or add it whole to broths for additional sweetness and smoky tones.

Blended Salts

Salt on its own will season your dish, but a blended salt will bring it to life. Along with the effects that regular salt has on food—reducing bitterness, enhancing sweetness, boosting umami—blended salt creates a new layer of flavour that's easy to incorporate, whether during cooking or as a final sprinkle of vibrance.

Almost any ingredient is a candidate for blending with salt: flowers, fruits, herbs—even ants. The process is simple: Reduce your flavouring ingredient to a fine consistency (through chopping, grating, and grinding, or by first freezing and then grinding) and then stir it together with salt. The aromatics of the blend can be fleeting, however, so you'll want to capture and preserve them by storing your blended salt in an airtight container in the freezer.

Blended salts are both aromatic and colorful.

Pine Salt

Makes about 100 grams

50 grams Douglas fir needles
Liquid nitrogen
50 grams flaky salt, ground until slightly coarse

Probably our most important flavoured salt, pine salt is made with needles from the Douglas fir, which, confusingly, isn't a fir. Douglas fir is a unique genus in the pine family, and it has the wonderful attribute of tasting like grapefruit. This flavour was especially valuable to us in Noma's early days when we weren't using lemons or other citrus because we were restricting ourselves to Scandinavian ingredients.

To make the salt, we freeze the needles with liquid nitrogen, which allows us to grind them without bruising and potentially muddying the flavours.

The flavour of the salt is ephemeral, so we keep it frozen to prevent the flavour from evaporating. Pine salt can go savory or sweet, another reason it's such an important player in our Noma larder. We've served roasted white asparagus with grilled green asparagus sauce split with Douglas fir oil, horseradish-infused whipped cream, and pine salt sprinkled down the length of the asparagus. On the sweet side, we've fried reindeer moss, dipped it in chocolate, and finished it with a pinch of pine salt. Something as simple as a crisp autumn apple or a pear seasoned with pine salt is amazing.

Place the fir needles in a mortar and freeze with liquid nitrogen. Use the pestle to grind the frozen needles into a fine powder and then combine the powder with the salt. Use right away, or reserve in an airtight container in the freezer.

Elderflower Salt

Makes 40 grams

Dried Elderflower
Fresh elderflowers

Elderflower Salt
30 grams Dried Elderflower
10 grams salt

Elderflower is another elemental Noma ingredient. Blending it with salt gives us an easy-to-use vehicle for adding its floral springtime flavour to dishes. The elderflower can be dried using a dehydrator, or you can simply dry it outdoors if you live in a warm but not humid climate. That describes a Danish summer . . . sometimes.

Dry the elderflower: Break the flower clusters into smaller umbels, but leave them attached to the stem. Place the flowers in a slightly warm, dry, airy space out of direct sunlight and let dry until completely devoid of water. Store the dried flowers in an airtight container or transfer to a vacuum bag and seal on only 50% vacuum to ensure the flowers don't get crushed.

Make the salt: Pick the dried flowers from the umbels and stems and place in a mortar. Grind the dried elderflowers a bit with the pestle, then add the salt to the mortar and grind with the pestle until combined into a coarse mixture. Use right away, keep refrigerated in an airtight container for up to 5 days, or freeze for longer-term storage.

Yuzu Salt

Makes about 10 grams

1 yuzu, fresh or frozen
About 5 grams salt

Yuzu has one of the most iconic and alluring aromas in the citrus world, one that takes over the island of Shikoku in Japan, where most of the world's yuzu is grown, from autumn to early winter. It's a flavour that has become deeply entrenched in the Noma identity throughout our many research trips to Japan and the three pop-ups we have been lucky enough to hold there. Yuzu salt is an excellent way to add the fruit's vibrant citrus aroma and flavour to any number of dishes, from something as simple as steamed spinach to salt-baked turbot.

Grate the zest from the yuzu using a Microplane or a Japanese grater (oroshigane). (Alternatively, using a sharp knife, pare the zest from the yuzu, avoiding the white pith, then finely chop it.) Weigh the zest (you should have about 5 grams) and combine it with an equal weight of salt. Use right away, keep refrigerated in an airtight container for up to 5 days, or freeze for longer-term storage.

Ant Salt

Makes 50 grams

25 grams frozen ants
25 grams salt

We started experimenting with ant salt back in 2010, pairing it with grilled onions, lacto-fermented pears, and Pine Dashi (page 217). The ants brought a bright, citrusy acidity that cut through the dish's wintry richness. While the idea of mixing insects and salt may seem unusual in many Western kitchens, it's a familiar and well-established pairing in other parts of the world. The inspiration for our ant salt came from *sal de chicatana*, a traditional Mexican salt made with toasted flying ants that's often blended with chile and used in mole and salsas, or as a rub. Our Danish wood ants have a naturally lemony tang, and when ground with salt, they create a sharp, aromatic seasoning.

The flavour of ant salt is especially fleeting, as it comes from the formic acid in the insects. As you grind them, they release formic acid aromas, which quickly evaporate, so to capture their unique lemony flavour and perfume, make the salt as close to the time you'll use it as possible.

Grind the ants and salt together with a mortar and pestle until fairly uniformly ground but not completely pulverized. Use right away, keep refrigerated in an airtight container for up to 5 days, or freeze for longer-term storage.

Place the rose petals in a mortar. Add the ants.

Freeze the petals and ants with liquid nitrogen.

Crush and grind the petals and ants with the pestle.
Add the salt.

Continue grinding until the mixture has a slightly coarse but mostly uniform consistency. Use right away, refrigerate in an airtight container for up to 5 days, or freeze.

Rose Petal Salt

Makes 34 grams

20 grams wild beach rose petals (or petals from any unsprayed fragrant rose)
4 grams frozen ants
Liquid nitrogen
10 grams flaky salt

Roses and ants together are not uncommon in nature, so how would roses and ants taste together on a dinner plate? The acidity of the ants naturally balances the aromatic rose wonderfully, and with salt, the combination works well on anything remotely fatty. Use this salt to season a vinaigrette, a fatty grilled fish collar, or a bit of buttery crab.

Place the rose petals and ants in a mortar and freeze with liquid nitrogen, then grind them with the pestle. Add the salt and grind until the mixture is well blended but not too finely ground. Use right away, keep refrigerated in an airtight container for up to 5 days, or freeze for longer-term storage.

Flash-Freezing in a Bowl or Mortar

Liquid nitrogen is a remarkable tool that instantly freezes, bringing ingredients to −196°C (−320°F), which allows us to shatter, blend, grind, or otherwise transform them into a powder. This process increases the surface area of the ingredient, resulting in a hyperpowerful flavour release into the base medium. Maintaining such a cold temperature also prevents the ingredient from oxidizing, so the final flavour remains as pure as possible.

Reduced Salts

We are flavour hunters at Noma, always in pursuit of deliciousness, and our hunt often involves experimenting with common ingredients, including a basic pantry staple: salt. Ordinary salt is evaporated from seawater or mined from deposits left by the vast oceans that once covered the planet, but we've found ways to create other types of salt. While we love a good fleur de sel, we make salt not by evaporating ocean water but by evaporating salty substances that are by-products from other things we make, like the shockingly magenta noble fir salt. Serendipitous salts, if you will.

Brine can be reduced until it crystallizes into salt.

Some of our most important salts are created not from regular salt-based brine, but from the natural glutamates that we coax from kelp when we make our Cold-Infused Dashi (page 215). The flavours in our kelp salts are more umami than salty per se, and this subtle savoriness makes them versatile players in our seasoning lineup.

Noble Fir Salt

Makes about 60 grams

800 grams brine from Brined Noble Fir Cones (page 77)

Seawater isn't the only liquid that can be reduced to produce salt. Former Noma sous chef Riccardo Canella saw the potential in the abundance of brine left over from brining noble fir cones, so he reduced it and created a stunning pine-flavoured magenta salt. The liquid left over from brining other ingredients, such as capers or gooseberries, can be reduced as well, making salts less flamboyantly colored but equally delicious. Through osmosis, which is what brining is all about, salt penetrates the ingredient and in turn, flavour compounds from the ingredient leach into the salty water. We use noble fir salt to season just-steamed vegetables, raw seafood, or autumn fruits such as apples and crisp pears.

Strain the brine through a fine-mesh nylon sieve into a container with a large surface area (to reduce the depth of the liquid) that will fit in your dehydrator. Place the container in the dehydrator set to 60°C (140°F) and dry until completely desiccated. Chip the resulting salt off the bottom of the container in small chunks, then crush the crystals using a mortar and pestle. Reserve in an airtight container at room temperature.

An array of wild Danish seaweeds.

Salt-Baked Black Oyster Mushroom, Warm Mushroom Vinaigrette, Green Rice, and Noma Roasted Umami Salt, Vegetable, 2024
Slices of salt-baked oyster mushrooms are wrapped around green rice seasoned with rose oil and wild beach rose vinegar. The packets are dressed with warm mushroom vinaigrette and topped with shards of Noma roasted umami salt.

Transfer the dashi to shallow containers and dehydrate at 65°C (150°F) until 95% desiccated.

Use a spatula to break up and loosen pieces of the crystallized umami salt (as Thomas Frebel does here).

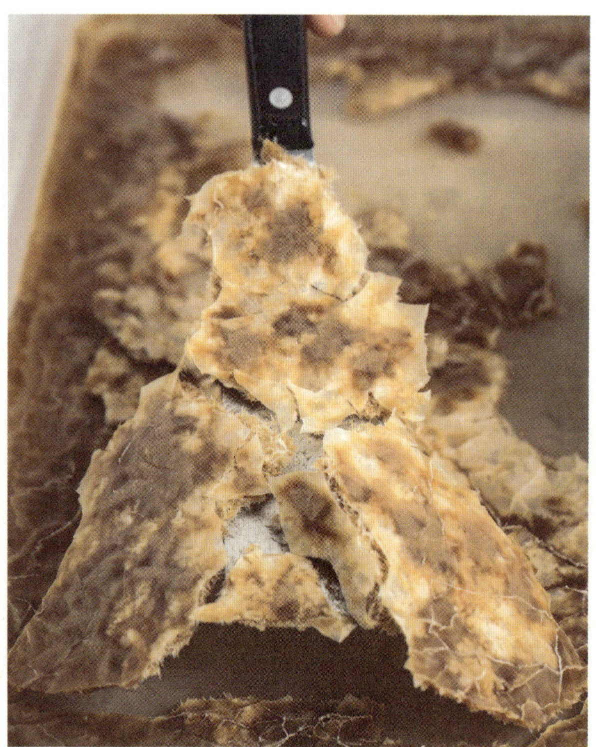

Lift out the salt, keeping it in large pieces.
Use right away or transfer to a vacuum bag, seal on 80% vacuum, and freeze.

To use, break the salt into smaller pieces just before serving.

Noma Umami Salt

Makes about 100 grams

1.5 kilograms Cold-Infused Dashi (page 215)

Noma umami salt goes back to the experimental days of our Nordic Food Lab, a floating think tank situated in a houseboat outside the old Noma. We were attempting to harvest the natural salt and glutamine from kelp. In an effort to mimic the harvesting techniques used in salt flats around the world, we made a hot dashi from the kelp and then slowly dehydrated it in a low oven. The experiment was a success, and umami salt made its way onto the Noma menu, where it remains a hugely important ingredient for us to this day. (We eventually switched our dashi method to a cold infusion for better flavour and consistency.)

We use Noma umami salt not just as a finishing salt, but also as a flavouring agent for a simple butter sauce or as a component of a seasoning paste or fudge. The salt has a crystalline structure, but because it has a fairly high moisture content, it forms a sandy paste when crushed or mashed. Some members of the Test Kitchen refer to this as "sweet kelp salt," but its sugar content is zero. After running some particulate tests to determine the actual composition of our umami salt, we discovered that glycine was the third most concentrated amino acid in the salt. Glycine has a naturally sweet taste, giving the perception of sweetness without any actual sugar. The first and second most concentrated amino acids were glutamic acid and aspartic acid, respectively. Both of these amino acids taste like umami, and rightfully so. Most fermented condiments (fish sauce, soy sauce) have around

0.4% to 2% glutamic acid by weight, and nutritional yeast has around 2.7%. Our umami salt showed a range of 2.76% to 4.2% glutamic acid by weight, meaning it is the most concentrated form of umami next to pure MSG. Literally concentrated deliciousness.

Place the dashi in a saucepan and bring to a boil over high heat. Skim off any scum from the surface and transfer the liquid to two 1-liter containers, filling each about 75% full. Place the containers in a dehydrator set to 65°C (150°F) and dry until 95% devoid of moisture. Use an offset spatula to scrape the resulting salt from the containers. Use right away, keep refrigerated in an airtight container for up to 5 days, or freeze for longer-term storage.

Noma Roasted Umami Salt

Makes about 75 grams

40 grams Roasted Kelp*
1 kilogram filtered water
60 grams fresh kelp

Like our Noma Umami Salt (page 113), the starting point for this salt is cold-infused dashi, but here we transform the kelp in order to develop a richer, deeper flavour. The finished salt has a high amino acid content, so it doesn't crystallize to the point of a sea salt. At room temperature, it can easily be broken or crumbled in your fingers so you can distribute it into your dish.

Place the roasted kelp and water in a vacuum bag and seal on 100% vacuum. Steam in a combi oven set to 60°C (140°F) for 1 hour. Place the fresh raw kelp in an airtight container, strain the roasted kelp liquid through a fine-mesh nylon sieve into the container with the fresh kelp, and let cool. Cover and refrigerate for 12 hours to infuse.

Strain the infused liquid through a fine-mesh nylon sieve, then transfer it to a saucepan and bring to a boil. Pour the hot dashi into a container with a large surface area (to reduce the depth of the liquid) that will fit in your dehydrator. Place in the dehydrator set to 65°C (150°F) and dry until 95% devoid of moisture. Chip the resulting salt off the bottom of the container in small chunks. Use right away, keep refrigerated in an airtight container for up to 5 days, or freeze for longer-term storage.

Place the roasted kelp and water in a vacuum bag.

Seal the bag and steam for 1 hour.

Strain the infused liquid through a fine-mesh nylon sieve, then transfer it to a saucepan.

Bring the kelp infusion to a boil.

Place the fresh raw kelp in a container.

Strain the roasted kelp-infused water through a fine-mesh nylon sieve into the container with the fresh kelp. Refrigerate for 12 hours.

Strain the simmered infusion through a fine-mesh nylon sieve into a shallow container.

Dehydrate at 65°C (150°F) until 95% desiccated. Chip the salt into small chunks or shards. Use right away, refrigerate in an airtight container for up to 5 days, or freeze.

Saffron Kelp Salt

Makes about 75 grams

1 kilogram filtered water
23 grams fresh kelp
1 gram saffron

Rather than change the flavour of the kelp, as we do with Noma Roasted Umami Salt (page 115), this salt is made by changing the flavour of the water used to make the dashi. The addition of a small amount of saffron adds a layer to the already umami-rich salt and produces a vibrantly orange result with a floral overtone.

Place the water, kelp, and saffron in a vacuum bag and seal on 100% vacuum. Cook in a water bath at 60°C (140°F) for 1 hour. Strain through a fine-mesh nylon sieve into a container with a large surface area (to reduce the depth of the liquid) that will fit in your dehydrator. Place the container in a dehydrator set to 90°C (195°F) and dry until completely devoid of moisture. Chip the resulting salt off the bottom of the container. Use right away, keep refrigerated in an airtight container for up to 5 days, or freeze for longer-term storage.

Spice Mixes

Noma began as a restaurant solely focused on ingredients from our own region. We would serve white asparagus, but only if it was grown in Denmark, not Alsace. The paradox was that most of the people who work at Noma are not from Denmark but from other places around the globe—Indonesia, Hungary, and South Korea, to name a few. Over time, the influence of these chefs and the places they came from began to appear on the menu . . . a touch of cumin here, a hint of sumac there . . . non-Scandinavian flavours tiptoeing into our flavour palette.

Spice mixes reflect flavours from around the world.

Once we began producing pop-ups around the world, we embraced ingredients from beyond Scandinavia more fully: seaweeds from Japan, truffles from Australia, dried chiles from Mexico. As our team continued to expand, so did our flavours. Our spice mixes show this clearly; global mash-ups such as woodruff and Japanese quince za'atar are now commonplace for a Noma menu.

Here's a method for making any spice mix:
Toast any seeds or other spices in a dry skillet until fragrant.

Let cool slightly and then transfer to a spice grinder.

Add other ingredients, even those that don't require grinding, such as powdered spice or salt.

Grind to the desired final consistency. If you want some ingredients to retain more texture, add them last and pulse.

Our spice mixes are borderless, and we use them freely across our menus, sometimes as a final seasoning to a dish, other times as a complex undercarriage to a paste or sauce, invisible but powerful. Spice mixes don't go bad, but they do lose their potency rather quickly, so if the aroma of your spice mix isn't making your mouth water, it's time to make a fresh one. We make ours fresh every day.

Danish Curry Powder

Makes about 15 grams

4 grams mustard seeds
4 grams coriander seeds
1 gram fennel seeds
2 grams Dried Ginger Powder*
1 gram saffron
1 gram sumac powder
1 gram vinegar powder
0.5 gram Dried Horseradish*

In 2017—after Noma Mexico, but before moving into our new space for Noma 2.0—we set up a temporary test kitchen behind my house and spent a week working on spice blends. While we had used spices before, this project was about creating concentrated mixes, drawing inspiration from blends like togarashi, furikake, and za'atar. Sweden and Denmark share a tradition of using saffron and cardamom in baking, thanks to the region's historical ties to the spice trade, which got us thinking: Could we use those same spices in savory dishes? That prompted former sous chef Riccardo Canella to develop what we now call Danish curry powder, with saffron as its centerpiece. It's been a quiet pantry mainstay throughout the menus of Noma 2.0.

Toast the mustard, coriander, and fennel seeds together in a dry pan over medium heat until deeply aromatic, then transfer to a spice grinder and let cool. Add the ginger powder, saffron, sumac powder, vinegar powder, and dried horseradish and grind to a fine powder. Reserve in an airtight container at room temperature.

Marigold Spice Mix

Makes about 17 grams

7 grams fennel seeds
0.4 gram dried carrot flower tops
3 grams dried roseroot
4 grams dried marigold flowers
2 grams dried rose buds
1 gram dried arctic thyme

During a research trip to the country of Georgia, we were introduced to an essential Georgian spice blend consisting of equal parts coriander seed, fenugreek, and marigold. We have adapted the idea, preserving the spirit of that bright, slightly bitter trifecta of flavours while tailoring the balance and intensity to fit Noma's dishes.

Toast the fennel seeds in a dry skillet over medium heat until fragrant. Transfer to a spice grinder and let cool. Add the carrot flower tops and roseroot and grind until fine. Add the marigold flowers and rose buds to the spice grinder and pulse, breaking the flowers into smaller bits but not grinding them into a powder; you should be able to clearly see the petals of the marigold. Transfer to an airtight container and stir in the arctic thyme. Reserve at room temperature. Use this spice mix the same day you make it.

Mustard Seed Spice Mix

Makes 31 grams

10 grams yellow mustard seeds
5 grams fennel seeds
4 grams coriander seeds
3 grams black peppercorns
1 gram seeded pasilla chile
5 grams freeze-dried green gooseberries
3 grams juniper berries

This is one of the simplest spice mixes we use at the restaurant. Typically, our spice blends are tailored to specific dishes, adjusted and refined until they strike just the right note. Mustard seed spice mix has taken many forms over the years, with Test Kitchen head Junichi Takahashi often behind those variations; his Jun Spice Mix and other umami-driven blends have appeared on the menu throughout the entirety of Noma 2.0. This version is clean and punchy. If you don't have freeze-dried gooseberries, feel free to substitute sumac powder or dried citrus zest for a similar acidic lift.

Toast the mustard seed, fennel seeds, coriander, peppercorns, and chile in a dry skillet over medium heat until aromatic. Transfer the toasted spices to a spice grinder and let cool. Add the gooseberries and juniper berries and grind to a powder. Reserve in an airtight container at room temperature.

Mushroom Spice Mix

Makes 65 grams

20 grams yellow mustard seeds
10 grams coriander seeds
5 grams fennel seeds
5 grams dried arctic thyme
15 grams dried ceps
10 grams dried morels

Drying mushrooms is one of the oldest preservation techniques, and when fully desiccated and stored in an airtight container, they last indefinitely. While dried mushrooms are often rehydrated for broths or stocks, they can also act as a powerful umami enhancer in spice mixes. Mushrooms are naturally rich in glutamates, and removing their water content concentrates those savory flavour compounds. Mushroom Spice Mix has become a staple during the Forest season, for obvious reasons. The mix is excellent for seasoning mcats or grilled vegetables, or stirring into a mushroom risotto or pasta for added depth.

Toast the mustard, coriander, and fennel seeds in a dry skillet over medium heat until aromatic. Transfer the toasted spices to a spice grinder and let cool. Add the arctic thyme, ceps, and morels and grind to a powder. Reserve in an airtight container at room temperature.

Roseroot Spice Mix

Makes about 50 grams

20 grams coriander seeds
10 grams fenugreek seeds
10 grams dried roseroot
5 grams fennel seeds
5 grams dried arctic thyme
0.65 gram dried carrot flower seeds

On a research trip to Greenland ahead of opening Noma 2.0, the Test Kitchen explored a range of wild herbs, seafood, and traditional techniques. One of the most memorable discoveries was roseroot (*Rhodiola rosea*). The team first encountered it growing near a sunlit stream, where its sharp, floral aroma was immediately striking. Known historically for its medicinal uses, roseroot also carries a distinct and expressive flavour, one that connects deeply to the northern landscape in which it was found. After harvesting a small supply, we began drying and processing the roots back in Denmark, eventually incorporating them into infused oils and spice blends.

Toast the coriander and fenugreek seeds in a dry skillet over medium heat until aromatic. Transfer the toasted spices to a spice grinder and let cool. Add the roseroot, fennel seeds, arctic thyme, and carrot flower seeds and grind to a powder. Reserve in an airtight container at room temperature.

Reindeer Penis Spice Mix

Makes about 30 grams

10 grams juniper berries
6 grams coriander seeds
2 grams black peppercorns
1 green cardamom pod
6 grams dried ceps
2 grams Roasted Yeast*
1.5 grams salt
1 gram Dried Ginger*
0.8 gram fennel seeds

Reindeer penis, as an ingredient, is more about the story than the flavour. We work with members of the Sámi community in Northern Scandinavia, who herd reindeer above the Arctic Circle. During our Forest season, we've served various cuts from the animal—tongue, leg, even brain—all of which are surprisingly delicious. The penis, however, required a long, careful cooking process to render it tender enough to eat. Though it was served with cooked grains, seeds, and herbs, it was this spice mix that tied the dish together. There's no actual penis in the mix, of course (the name was more of an inside joke that stuck), but its ingredients reflect flavours from the reindeer's natural diet: juniper berries, wild mushrooms, and forest herbs.

Toast the juniper berries, coriander, peppercorns, and cardamom in a dry skillet over medium heat until fragrant. Remove the cardamom seeds from the pod and transfer them to a spice grinder along with the other toasted spices, then let cool. Add the ceps, roasted yeast, salt, ginger, and fennel seeds and grind to a powder. Reserve in an airtight container at room temperature.

Cod Jaw with Pumpkin Bushi Spice Mix, Ocean, 2024
Cod jaw is lightly poached in fresh barley koji butter, dressed with a paste of corn bushi powder, semi-dried tomatoes, and black currant wood oil, then finished with a pumpkin bushi paste.

Sweet Preserved Magnolia, Cardamom-Saffron Caramel, and Chocolate, with a Bergamot and Berry Spice Mix, Vegetable, 2024
Fresh magnolia blossoms are preserved in sugar syrup, then spread with cardamom-saffron caramel and brushed with chocolate. The flower is then heavily dusted with dried bergamot skin and berry spice mix.

Berry Spice Mix

Makes 43 grams

5 grams coriander seeds
5 grams fennel seeds
1 gram angelica seeds
15 grams semi-dried strawberries (see page 94)
10 grams Dried Ginger Powder*
5 grams Dried Horseradish*
2 grams dried arctic thyme

In 2019, members of the Noma team traveled to Georgia—one of the most food-centric cultures in the world—for inspiration. We returned with new ingredients and a deep appreciation for the Georgian approach to cooking. A standout dish was *tkemali*, a tart plum sauce that showcases how fruit can be used in savory ways. Inspired by this idea, Test Kitchen head Mette Søberg began playing with dried berries as a seasoning element, landing on strawberries for their bright acidity and floral depth. The resulting spice mix—surprisingly versatile—bridges the line between sweet and savory with ease.

Toast the coriander, fennel, and angelica seeds in a dry skillet over medium heat until aromatic. Transfer the toasted spices to a spice grinder and let cool. Add the strawberries, ginger, horseradish, and arctic thyme and grind until fine. Reserve in an airtight container at room temperature.

Gooseberry Pumpkin Spice Mix

Makes 27 grams

1.5 grams black peppercorns
9 grams Noma Umami Salt (page 113)
6 grams grated pumpkin bushi (see page 96)
6 grams freeze-dried green gooseberries
4.5 grams dried rose buds

We use Noma umami salt in this mix as a flavour booster, but it's the smoky depth of the pumpkin bushi, the perfume of dried roses, the tart punch of freeze-dried green gooseberries, and the warm spice of black pepper that makes this spice mix multidimensional. It delivers acidity, umami, floral lift, and heat, all in one. Originally paired with grilled lobster knuckles and claws, it's equally at home on roasted chicken legs, grilled corn, or anywhere you want to layer brightness and depth.

Toast the peppercorns in a dry skillet over medium heat until fragrant. Transfer to a spice grinder and let cool. Add the umami salt, pumpkin bushi, gooseberries, and rose buds and grind until well blended. Reserve in an airtight container at room temperature.

Woodruff and Japanese Quince Za'atar

Makes 140 grams

Toasted Beechnuts
120 grams beechnuts in their shells

Za'atar Base
23 grams Toasted Beechnuts
4 grams dried arctic thyme
3 grams freeze-dried rhubarb
2 grams freeze-dried lingonberries

Former sous chef Tarek Alameddine, originally from Lebanon, would often return from visits home with za'atar lovingly made by his mother—always to the delight of the kitchen. Inspired by the flavour profile of her blend, we set out to create our own version using ingredients native to our surroundings in Denmark. Test Kitchen head Mette Søberg was developing a dish centered around grilled noble pine, and because za'atar is traditionally used to season grilled vegetables, she tried dusting the pine cone with this woodruff and Japanese quince version of the blend. It clicked immediately, an excellent example of cultural inspiration translated through a hyperlocal lens.

Toast the beechnuts: Remove the beechnuts from their hard shells, spread them on a sheet pan in a single layer, and toast them in the oven at 180°C (355°F) on dry heat for 6 minutes to loosen their skins. Remove from the oven and let cool (keep the oven on). Rub the cooled nuts on a coarse tamis or in a clean cloth to remove the skins. Return the skinned nuts to the sheet pan and toast them again at 180°C (355°F) for 6 to 8 minutes, until lightly browned and fragrant. Let cool.

Make the za'atar base: Combine the toasted beechnuts, arctic thyme, rhubarb, and lingonberries in a spice grinder. Grind until fine.

Make the woodruff za'atar: Transfer the za'atar base to a bowl and add the chopped beechnuts, yarrow powder, woodruff powder, lingonberries, and ground yarrow flowers. Whisk to combine.

Assemble the za'atar: Add the powdered Japanese quince to the bowl with the woodruff za'atar. Season to taste with salt and stir to combine. Reserve in an airtight container at room temperature.

Woodruff Za'atar

32 grams Za'atar Base
24 grams Toasted Beechnuts, finely chopped
6 grams yarrow powder
4 grams woodruff powder
2 grams freeze-dried lingonberries, finely chopped
2 grams ground dried yarrow flowers

Finished Za'atar

70 grams Woodruff Za'atar
70 grams Powdered Dried Japanese Quince*
Salt

Remove the beechnuts from their shells (as Nate French and Mette Søberg do here). Toast at 180°C (355°F) for 8 to 10 minutes to loosen the skins.

Put the toasted beechnuts in a cloth and rub to remove their skins.

Grind the za'atar base ingredients.

Chop the lingonberries.

Toast the skinned beechnuts until light golden.

Let the toasted skinned beechnuts cool, then coarsely chop them.

Combine the za'atar base, chopped beechnuts, yarrow powder, woodruff powder, lingonberries, and ground yarrow flowers.

Add the powdered Japanese quince and stir until blended. Reserve in an airtight container at room temperature.

Suggested Uses

Yuzu-Scented Vegetables

Season steamed greens or other green vegetables with Yuzu Salt (page 102), adding it just before serving so you can enjoy the full hit of fragrant yuzu.

Cacio e Pepe

Make a classic cacio e pepe pasta, with fresh coarsely ground black pepper and freshly grated pecorino. As you add a few ladlefuls of pasta water to the black pepper base, season with some Noma Roasted Umami Salt (page 115), dissolving the salt in the pasta water. Finish the dish with a few small chunks of the roasted umami salt.

Spice-Rubbed Roast Chicken

Coat a chicken leg, bone-in breast, or whole chicken with oil or clarified butter, season generously with Gooseberry Pumpkin Spice Mix (page 133) and salt. Roast in a medium-hot oven until the chicken is fully cooked and the skin is deep golden brown.

Fennel Flower Butter

Crumble dried fennel flowers (see page 93) into melted butter and use to dress a piece of grilled halibut.

Cauliflower Steaks

Sauté a thick slice of cauliflower in foaming butter until beautifully browned, then season generously with Pine Salt (page 100). Peeled white asparagus is also delicious.

Elevated Cocktails

When making a margarita or a paloma, coat the rim of your cocktail glass with salty-sour Ant Salt (page 103).

Tomato-Rose Salad

Sprinkle Rose Petal Salt (page 105) onto cherry tomatoes lightly dressed with a fruity extra-virgin olive oil. Serve the tomatoes as a simple salad or side dish.

Opposite, top to bottom: Yuzu-Scented Vegetables; Spice-Rubbed Roast Chicken
Right: Tomato Rose Salad

Dried Fruit Aperitif

Serve an arrangement of semi-dried fruit (see page 94; tomatoes, cherries, and berries are pictured) as part of a breakfast spread or as a snack to accompany aperitifs.

Saffron Kelp Butter Sauce

Put a generous amount of butter and a big pinch of Saffron Kelp Salt (page 119) in a small saucepan. Melt them together, stirring so the salt dissolves and emulsifies into the butter. Use as a sauce for boiled shellfish, such as lobster or shrimp.

Za'atar Drizzle or Marinade

Mix Woodruff and Japanese Quince Za'atar (page 134) with Black Currant Wood Oil (page 193) or fruity extra-virgin olive oil. Brush onto flatbreads before baking, drizzle onto avocado toast as a seasoning, or use as a marinade for chicken—coat the chicken with the za'atar, marinate for about 2 hours, then roast in a medium-hot oven.

Spiced Mushroom Toast

Grill or sauté some mushrooms, pile them onto a slice of grilled or toasted bread, and season with a generous sprinkle of Reindeer Penis Spice Mix (page 129).

Roseroot Roasted Winter Squash

Mix Roseroot Spice Mix (page 128) with extra-virgin olive oil and rub or brush onto wedges of pumpkin or other winter squash. Roast the squash in a medium-hot oven until it is tender and lightly browned.

Spiced Tempura

Season tempura-fried marigold blossoms with Danish Curry Powder (page 124). Roasted cauliflower florets are also delightful with this spice blend: Toss the florets in oil, salt, and black pepper, then roast until tender with a bit of crispness around the edges. Season with the curry powder and serve.

Opposite, top to bottom:
Dried Fruit Aperitif;
Za'atar Drizzle or Marinade
Right: Spiced Tempura

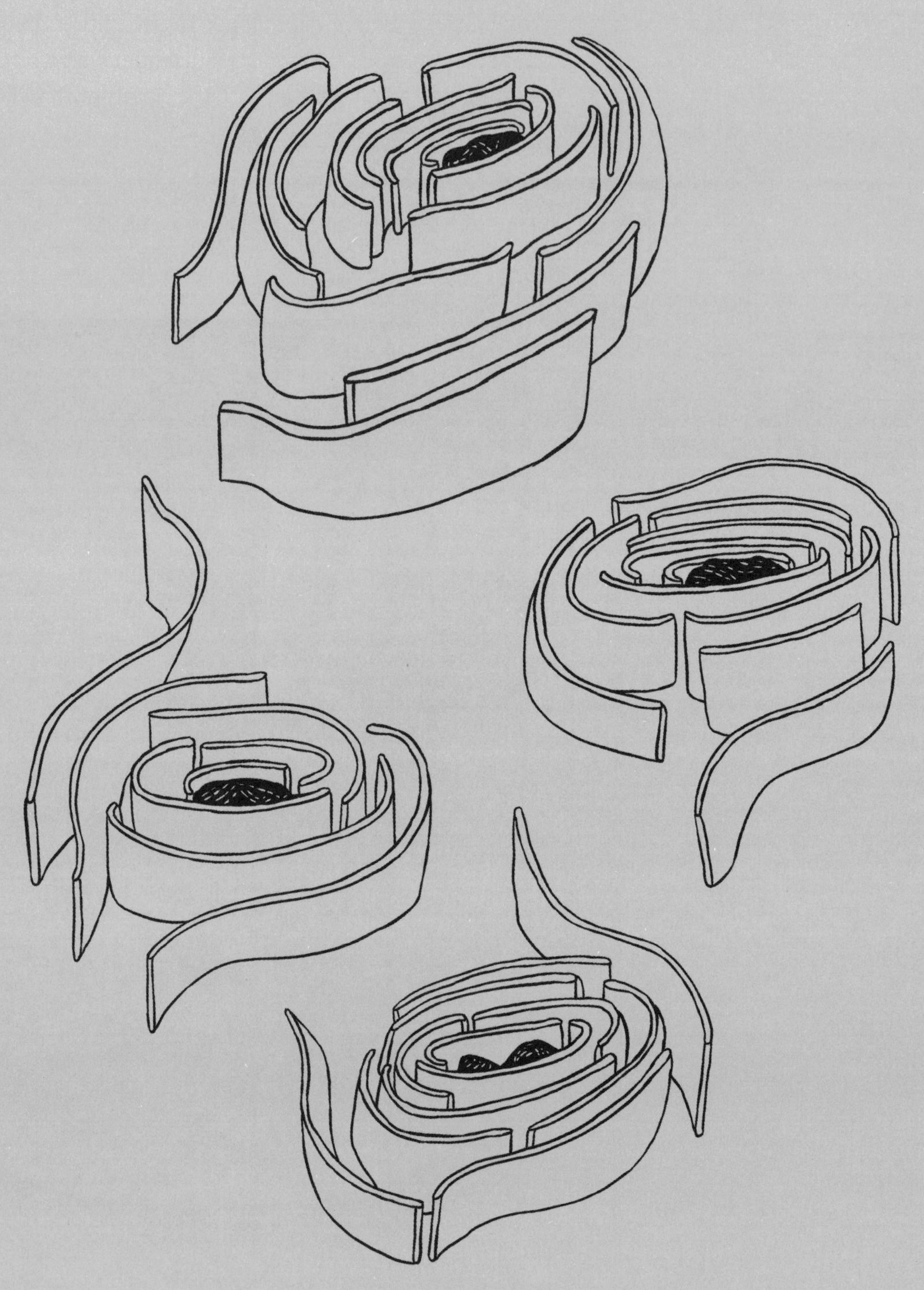

3.

Oils and Butters

Oils and Butters: Carrying aroma, drawing out flavour

The first time I can remember thinking about butter, I must have been five or six years old. My Albanian aunt had just finished milking our cow and was pounding the milk (which I later came to understand was cream) in a big wooden container with a long stick. I didn't quite know what I was watching, but I could feel something was happening. The milk was transforming—changing shape, changing flavour. Later that day, we dipped slices of bread in beaten fresh eggs and fried them in that same butter for a savory Albanian-style French toast. The smell, the crackle, the richness—it's still with me more than forty years later.

Olive oil didn't come into my life until much later, when I started traveling and cooking professionally. After I entered restaurant school in Copenhagen at the age of fifteen, I began to understand fats not just as a way to cook, but as a way to flavour, to build sauces, to carry aroma. To make food delicious.

At Noma, we've gone through many fat phases over the years. For the past five or six years, we've been deep in a phase of using fresh seed and nut oils, pressed right before service: Sunflower seed oil. Linseed oil. Hazelnut oil. Oils that are alive, with flavours that evolve by the hour.

We also infuse neutral oils with seaweed to add umami, or blend them with herbs to extract their green intensity. Fats, for us, are not just a cooking medium—they're part of the structure of cooking, new tools for building flavour.

We've even found ways to taste trees. We capture their flavour by infusing oil with bark, branches, or the tips of black currant and pine, sometimes by blending, even by pounding young tree branches to reveal their aromatic inner flesh. Suddenly, you're eating forest; the flavours are deep, earthy, tannic—

Crudités with Smoked Butter and Fennel, Vegetable, 2024
Thinly sliced carrot, radish, summer squash, turnip, strawberries, along with fresh herb leaves, flowers, seeds, and black pepper are arranged on a sauce made from lacto rice koji water, tomato water, and smoked butter with green fennel tops blended in.

145

Confit King Oyster, Hazelnut Milk, Elderflower Oil, Vegetable, 2023
King oyster mushrooms are confited in koji oil, sliced thin, showered with elderflower blossoms, and served with hazelnut milk dotted with elderflower oil.

subtle, but present. That's only possible because fat knows how to hold on to the scent of wood, drawing it out slowly, gently, in a way that water can't.

Why is fat so good at carrying flavour?

It took me years in the kitchen before I began to understand it properly, but once you see how it works, it changes the way you cook.

The obvious, bold flavours—salt, vinegar, soy, miso—those dissolve easily in water. That's their home turf, so to speak. But the more delicate, fleeting stuff—the smell of toasted hazelnut, of fresh herbs being crushed, of butter just starting to brown—that's a different story. Those molecules are drawn to fat. That's where they open up.

At the core of it is something called polarity (read more about that on page 12). I won't pretend I cared much about polarity when I was starting out, but I feel differently now. Basically, water and fat operate by different rules—they don't mix, and that shapes how flavour behaves. Steep seaweed in water and you get depth, umami. Blend it into oil and you draw out much more of its aroma, the part that hits your nose, not just your tongue.

When most people think of fat or butter in food, they think of dishes that are rich, even heavy. But for us at Noma, fat doesn't just add richness. We use fat because it unlocks things, because it gives access to flavours you can't reach otherwise. Fat holds on to scent; it stretches aroma out in time. It lingers. Fat draws out flavours that would otherwise stay in the dark.

HAZELNUTS OIL
SUNFLOWER BEEF OIL
PUMPKIN SEEDS OIL

Pressed Oils

A freshly pressed oil is somehow more nutty than the nut or seed from which it's pressed, a pure expression of its source—all richness and aroma, no fiber. At Noma, we toast the nuts or seeds before they're pressed, both for deeper flavour and to "activate" the oils and get them flowing more freely. We press the nuts or seeds using a small tabletop appliance that heats as it grinds. When the oil flows from the press, it contains a small amount of sediment, which is typically packed with flavour, so sometimes we'll let the oil macerate with the sediment in the refrigerator and then either pass it through a fine-mesh strainer to clarify the oil or simply wait for the sediment to settle before pouring off the clear oil.

Nuts and seeds are pressed daily to make the freshest oils.

The method is efficient, and though it takes some time, it's mostly hands-off; other than guiding the ingredient into the chamber of the press, the process basically runs itself. Pressing yields oil and also expels the pulp, which is relatively flavourless but can

Toasted hazelnuts, ready to be pressed for oil.

have other uses; we've used it to produce misos and pralines (like Pumpkin Seed Praline, page 458). The pulp also composts well and has been studied as a potential animal feed or biomass energy source.

The enchanting perfume and rich flavour of a freshly pressed oil don't stick around, however; those volatile aroma molecules quickly diffuse and evaporate, so we make pressed oils every day, as close to service as possible. If we find ourselves with extra oil, or if we're pressing an ingredient that has a short window of availability (and so needs to be pressed long before we use it), we'll vacuum seal the oil and stash it in the freezer.

Hazelnut Oil

Makes about 400 grams

1 kilogram raw hazelnuts, skinned, if possible

When hazelnut oil is freshly pressed and still warm from the nut press, it's otherworldly. Seasoned only with a bit of salt, it becomes an elegant and elemental sauce, to drizzle on steamed haricots verts, a green salad with roast chicken, or even a scoop of pure vanilla ice cream. Hazelnuts love to be toasted to a rich brown before pressing, which adds caramel notes to their naturally sweet flavour. Use this same basic method for any nut.

Preheat a nut press for 15 minutes. Spread the hazelnuts over a sheet pan and toast in a 160°C (320°F; 100% fan) oven until they are a rich, even brown, up to about 20 minutes, but start checking early (some nuts are already slightly toasted by the producer). Transfer the warm hazelnuts to the nut press and run them through to extract their oil. Reserve the pulp for another use. Use right away, keep refrigerated in an airtight container for up to 5 days, or freeze for longer-term storage.

Linseed Oil

Makes about 400 grams

1 kilogram linseeds

Depending on where you live, you may call these flaxseeds rather than linseeds, but everyone recognizes the healthful properties of these tiny, oil-rich seeds. (In the US, they're called linseeds when used for nonculinary purposes and flaxseeds when you eat them.) They are packed with fiber and omega-3 fatty acids and are known to help reduce blood pressure. You'll find linseeds in muesli and granola, as well as whole-grain baked goods, and Test Kitchen head Mette Søberg likes to use the pressed oil, which is slightly nutty and earthy, to make Linseed Fudge (page 289). The flavour is subtle, but lightly nutty and buttery.

Preheat a nut press for 15 minutes. Spread the linseeds over a sheet pan and toast in a 160°C (320°F) oven for 30 minutes, stirring them every 10 minutes or so, until fragrant. Transfer the warm linseeds to the nut press and run them through to extract their oil. Reserve the pulp for another use. Use right away, keep refrigerated in an airtight container for up to 5 days, or freeze for longer-term storage.

Fresh Mustard Seed Oil

Makes about 300 grams

1 kilogram yellow mustard seeds

Toasting the seeds just until you begin to smell their fragrance will add complexity to the flavour of the oil, which will be quite spicy. We've used mustard seed oil in a variation of our Lacto Koji Butter Sauce (page 384), a terrific partner for a sautéed piece of mild fish.

Preheat a nut press for 15 minutes. Toast the mustard seeds in a dry skillet over medium heat until toasted and fragrant, about 10 minutes. (Take your time with this process—if you go too quickly, you risk burning the seeds, which will yield a bitter oil.) Transfer the warm mustard seeds to the nut press and run them through to extract their oil. Reserve the pulp for another use. Use right away, keep refrigerated in an airtight container for up to 5 days, or freeze for longer-term storage.

Walnut Oil

Makes about 400 grams

1 kilogram shelled walnuts

Walnut oil, like Hazelnut Oil (page 152), can function as a sauce on its own. Most store-bought versions offer a mild nuttiness but can be bitter and flat in flavour. By blanching the walnuts multiple times to remove tannins, drying them thoroughly, and pressing them warm, the result is a pure expression of walnut flavour. The oil is intensely aromatic, sweet, and free of the astringency of many commercial walnut oils. A pinch of salt in the warm oil and a scoop of ice cream is all you need for a stunning dessert.

Bring 3 large pots of water to a boil and set up an ice bath. Blanch and shock the walnuts three times, each time in a fresh pot of water. Drain them well and transfer them to a parchment-lined tray. Dehydrate in the oven at 80°C (175°F) overnight, or until the nuts are completely dried.

Preheat a nut press for 15 minutes. Meanwhile, use a knife to coarsely chop the walnuts so they'll fit into the auger of the press (do not use a food processor to chop them, which will muddle their flavour). Transfer the chopped nuts to the nut press and run them through to extract their oil, collecting it in an airtight container. Cover and refrigerate overnight to allow the sediment to settle. Strain the oil through a fine-mesh nylon sieve, holding back as much cloudy sediment in the container as possible. Use right away, keep refrigerated in an airtight container for up to 5 days, or freeze for longer-term storage.

Place the sunflower seeds in a bowl, add the beef garum, and stir or toss to coat evenly.

Spread the sunflower seeds in an even layer on a Silpat-lined sheet pan.

Toast the seeds in a 160°C (320°F; 100% fan) oven until they color slightly and the garum bakes in, 8 to 10 minutes.

Run the seeds through the nut press. Taste the oil as it begins to flow; if it's underseasoned, fold more garum into the remaining seeds and continue pressing.

Sunflower Seed and Beef Garum Oil

Makes 400 grams

500 grams raw sunflower seeds
150 grams Beef Garum*,
plus more if needed

With this oil, we go a step beyond a simple pressed nut or seed to exponentially enhance the flavour of the oil by cooking the seeds in garum first, an idea that came from former Noma sous chef Riccardo Canella. Think about a plain toasted pecan. Now think about a pecan toasted with sugar and spices: The pecan flavour is still central, but the seasoned nut has a lot more personality. Other winning flavour combos include lobster garum with hazelnuts and grasshopper garum with walnuts.

Preheat a nut press for 15 minutes. Toss the sunflower seeds with the garum and spread them over a Silpat-lined sheet pan. Toast the seeds in a 160°C (320°F; 100% fan) oven until they color slightly and the garum has been absorbed, 8 to 10 minutes. Transfer the warm seeds to the nut press and run them through to extract their oil. Taste the oil as it begins to come out—it should taste well seasoned and umami rich. If it tastes underseasoned, fold a bit more garum into the unpressed seeds and continue. Use right away, keep refrigerated in an airtight container for up to 5 days, or freeze for longer-term storage.

Macerated and Blended Oils

Letting a potent ingredient—an herb, a flower, the tender tips of an evergreen tree—luxuriate in a neutral oil is an effective way to capture its aromatic power and create a versatile flavouring. We use flavoured oils throughout the Noma kitchen: to brush on fruit as it's drying, to blend into a savory fudge, to finish a sauce or partner with a fresh oyster.

Ceps are confited in oil.

You can encourage the transfer of flavour into oil in a few ways. Blending will massively increase the surface area of your ingredient so its flavours are more accessible. Delicate ingredients that would bruise if chopped, such as rose petals, should be frozen with liquid nitrogen before blending, rendering them brittle without rupturing their cells and releasing the compounds that cause browning and bruising. Even sturdier ingredients like roots need to be grated or ground so they release their flavours more willingly.

When you want to extract flavour and aroma from an ingredient that's a bit more reticent, you need more muscle—in this case, heat. The heat could come from the friction of a blender's furiously whirring blades or from heating in a Thermomix, but most of our hot-infused oils simply get steamed for a short period and then strained and frozen to prevent oxidation. An extreme example is our roasted kelp oil, which undergoes a long process of heating at various temperatures—some Test Kitchen alchemy.

Heat is only the first step, however, as the ingredients still need a period of cold maceration before the solids are strained out and the pure flavourful oil is retrieved.

Ingredient-to-Oil Ratio: Hot Blended Oils

Each oil uses a specific ratio of ingredient to oil. For example, when making floral oils, we typically stay as close to equal parts as possible; however, we sometimes need to add a bit of extra oil so that the blender actually spins and mixes the oil and flowers together.

Recipe	Ingredient	Oil
Ancho Chile Oil	20%	100%
Black Currant Leaf Oil	100%	100%
Chamomile Oil	50%	100%
Elderflower Oil	100%	100%
Lovage Oil	50%	100%
Morita Chile Oil	10%	100%
Parsley Oil	50%	100%
Rose Geranium Oil	50%	100%
Rose Oil	100%	100%
Sea Lettuce Oil	10%	100%

Horseradish Oil

Makes about 1.8 kilograms

2 kilograms neutral oil
1 kilogram fresh horseradish

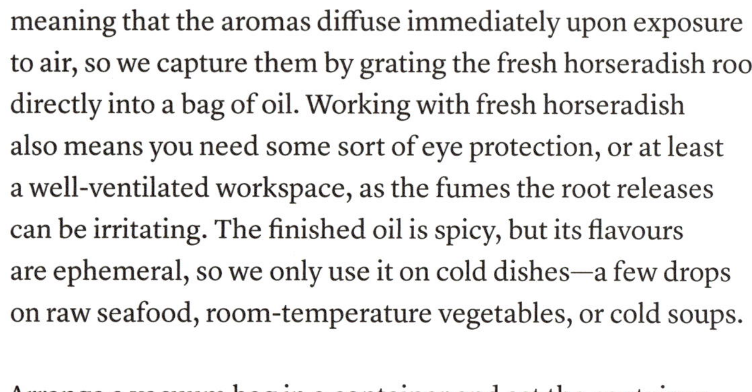

The flavour compounds in horseradish are quite volatile, meaning that the aromas diffuse immediately upon exposure to air, so we capture them by grating the fresh horseradish root directly into a bag of oil. Working with fresh horseradish also means you need some sort of eye protection, or at least a well-ventilated workspace, as the fumes the root releases can be irritating. The finished oil is spicy, but its flavours are ephemeral, so we only use it on cold dishes—a few drops on raw seafood, room-temperature vegetables, or cold soups.

Arrange a vacuum bag in a container and set the container over an ice bath. Pour the oil into the bag and, using a fine grater, grate the horseradish directly into the oil. Seal on 100% vacuum and refrigerate over ice overnight.

Strain the oil through a fine-mesh nylon sieve, pressing on the pulp for maximum extraction. Use right away, keep refrigerated in an airtight container for up to 5 days, or freeze for longer-term storage.

Rhubarb Root Oil

Makes about 3 kilograms

1 kilogram rhubarb roots
3 kilograms neutral oil, plus more as needed

We use rhubarb root for its earthy yet fruity-tangy flavour. The root contains oxalic acid, the same compound that makes the leaves of the rhubarb plant toxic (if you eat five kilos at a time), but when consumed in small quantities, it is completely harmless.

Wash the rhubarb roots, then transfer them to a large bucket of water and use a paring knife to peel them; drain and rinse well. Slice the peeled roots into 3 mm (⅛-inch) thick slices and lay them on a dehydrator tray in a single layer. Dry in a dehydrator set to 45°C (115°F) until completely devoid of water.

Weigh the dried roots (you should have about 500 grams, 50% of the original weight), transfer to a vacuum bag, and add three times their weight in oil. Seal on 100% vacuum and refrigerate for 8 to 12 hours to infuse. Strain the infused oil through a fine-mesh nylon sieve into an airtight container; cover and reserve in the refrigerator. Transfer the roots to a clean vacuum bag, add twice their weight in oil, and seal. Refrigerate for 8 to 12 hours to infuse. Strain and reserve the infused oil as you did for the first batch. Transfer the roots to a clean vacuum bag, add an equal weight of oil, and seal. Refrigerate for 8 to 12 hours to infuse.

Stir together the three batches of infused oil. Use right away, keep refrigerated in an airtight container for up to 5 days, or freeze for longer-term storage.

Cep Oil

Makes 1.8 kilograms

1 kilogram frozen ceps
2 kilograms neutral oil

Make this oil with the trimmings from fresh ceps (also known as porcini or boletes, or as Karl Johan mushrooms in Scandinavia) or with less-than-perfect specimens rather than just-foraged beauties that you'll want to showcase fresh. Cep oil is extremely versatile, suitable as a seasoning and as a component of cold sauces such as mayonnaise, and because the oil is essentially "cooked" already, you can use it as a cooking medium if you keep the heat moderate.

We use ceps from Sweden, a country that harvests millions of kilograms of this mushroom per year. They are typically dried or frozen; freezing forms ice crystals inside the mushrooms, disrupting their structure. This makes them quite soft and spongy when they defrost, and consequently ready to absorb the oil and give up their mushroomy flavour.

Place the ceps and oil in a vacuum bag and seal on 100% vacuum. Steam in a combi oven set to 80°C (175°F; 100% fan, 100% steam) for 8 hours. Let cool, then transfer the bag to the refrigerator overnight to infuse.

Strain the oil through a fine-mesh nylon sieve into an airtight container. Use right away, keep refrigerated for up to 5 days, or freeze for longer-term storage. Vacuum seal the ceps separately and freeze for another use.

Mirabelle Blossom Oil

Makes 500 grams

10 grams dried Mirabelle plum blossoms
500 grams oil

Mirabelle plum trees are often the first tree to bloom in the spring in Denmark. They grow around a small lake near the restaurant, and from far away, the profusion of delicate white blossoms looks like snow. It's magical. We dry the flowers for tisanes, but we realized we could capture their flavour in oil as well. The result is elegant, almondy, with a slight bitterness. One beautiful application from a Noma menu was a frozen shrimp and rose oil mousse served on top of this Mirabelle blossom oil like a cloud, with a dusting of lacto plum powder and toasted beechnuts.

Place the blossoms and oil in a vacuum bag and seal on 100% vacuum. Steam in a combi oven set to 85°C (185°F) for 3 hours. Remove from the oven and refrigerate overnight to infuse.

Strain the oil through a fine-mesh nylon sieve into an airtight container. Use right away, keep refrigerated for up to 5 days, or freeze for longer-term storage.

Blue Mussel Lips with Fresh Cheese, Blue Mussel Sauce, and Rose Oil, Ocean, 2025
Cooked and sliced blue mussel lips are draped across fresh cheese, piped with rose fudge, and dressed with blue mussel sauce and dots of rose oil.

Young Bamboo with Squid Broth and Koji Oil, Kyoto, 2023
Tender young bamboo shoots are lightly poached and nixtamalized, then thinly sliced and brushed with a corn bushi and umami salt paste. The bamboo shoots are served with a squid broth infused with jasmine and split with koji oil.

Pheasant Spice Oil

Makes about 3 kilograms

Unsalted butter
2 pheasants (1.6 kilograms total), broken down into 8 pieces each
6 bay leaves
20 grams juniper berries
20 grams black peppercorns
4 pasilla chiles, seeded
3 kilograms neutral oil

Making an oil from roast pheasant may seem surprising, but not when you think about how well oil unlocks aromas that water can't (see page 12 for more on this). We use a neutral oil as a base, and the result is deeply flavoured, rich with dark spices and a hint of the game bird from the oils that the pheasant renders during cooking. One memorable use on a Noma menu was grilled wild greens dressed with Lacto Koji Butter Sauce (page 384) made with pheasant spice oil.

Smear a bit of butter on each piece of pheasant. Place the pheasant pieces on a wire rack set over a parchment-lined gastro pan and roast in the oven at 200°C (390°F; 100% fan) for 12 minutes. Reduce the oven temperature to 170°C (340°F; 70% fan) and roast for 20 minutes more, until golden brown and crisp. Remove from the oven and let cool.

Transfer the cooled pheasant pieces to a large rondeau and add the bay leaves, juniper berries, peppercorns, chiles, and oil. Heat over medium heat until the mixture reaches 100° to 110°C (212° to 230°F), then cook at this temperature for 4 hours (start the timer as soon as the oil comes to temperature). Remove from the heat and let cool, then transfer the oil and the pheasant pieces to a container. Refrigerate overnight to infuse. Strain the infused oil through a conical strainer, then strain through a fine-mesh nylon sieve into an airtight container. Use right away, keep refrigerated for up to 5 days, or freeze for longer-term storage.

Fresh Barley Koji Oil

Makes 1.6 kilograms

1 kilogram fresh Barley Koji*
2 kilograms neutral oil

Koji provides so much to Noma's flavour arsenal that we think of it as one of our "mother flavours" (see page 22). Slow cooking and eventual caramelization of the koji infuses this oil with a subtle undertone of umami depth that, when finished, is an ideal medium to use for cooking.

A surprising discovery about our koji oil is that it seems to be gluten-free, despite barley being a grain that contains gluten. We suspect that the gluten content dissipates in barley koji due to the fermentation processes that occur thanks to *Aspergillus oryzae*. We are still running tests on this matter, but we recently conducted a lab analysis of the gluten content in barley koji oil that yielded a result of less than 3 mg/kg of gluten in the oil. For comparison, the threshold for a gluten-free product is less than 20 mg/kg.

Using gloved hands, crumble the koji into individual grains. Place the koji and oil in a saucepan and heat over medium heat until the koji begins to bubble. Reduce the heat to maintain a low simmer and cook for 8 hours.

Let cool to room temperature, then strain the oil through a fine-mesh nylon sieve into an airtight container, pressing on the sediment to maximize yield and flavour (reserve the barley koji sediment for other uses). Use right away, keep refrigerated for up to 5 days, or freeze for longer-term storage.

Roasted Kelp Oil

Makes 400 grams

250 grams fresh kelp
500 grams neutral oil

This oil embodies the idea of liquid umami. We use a few droplets to add richness to a dish or a few spoonfuls as a sauce. We pulverize the kelp to create the most surface area possible, which allows for maximum flavour extraction, and then we heat the kelp with oil over many hours and many temperature changes—not an oil to be made à la minute!

We've used roasted kelp oil throughout our many menus: paired with fish roe on potatoes cooked in roasted koji mole, as well as on citrus segments dressed with Pine Salt (page 100), pickled long peppers, and salted sansho leaves, all finished with roasted kelp oil. We reserve the sediment, too, and use it to cure raw seafood, as its salt content is high, even after so much cooking.

Lay the kelp in a single layer on a dehydrator tray and dry in a dehydrator set to 60°C (140°F) overnight.

Transfer the dried kelp to a Thermomix and blend on high speed for 30 seconds, until powdery with a few larger pieces. Weigh the powder, then add twice its weight in oil and blend for an additional minute. Transfer the mixture to a rondeau and heat to 160°C (320°F), then cook, stirring continuously, for 15 minutes (start the timer only after the oil has come to temperature). Adjust the heat to lower the oil temperature to 150°C (300°F) and cook for 1 hour, stirring every 5 minutes. Lower the oil temperature to 140°C (285°F) and cook for 1 hour, stirring every 5 minutes. Continue this process, lowering the oil temperature by 10°C (15° to 20°F) every hour until you reach 80°C (175°F), then leave the oil to cook at 80°C (175°F) overnight.

Bring the oil temperature back up to 130°C (265°F) and cook for 15 minutes, then lower the oil temperature to 120°C (250°F) and cook for 1 hour. Remove from the heat and let cool a bit. Transfer the mixture to a Thermomix and blend on full speed for 5 minutes. Strain the oil through a fine-mesh nylon sieve into an airtight container. Use right away, keep refrigerated for up to 5 days, or freeze for longer-term storage. Store the sediment separately.

Place the dried kelp in a Thermomix.
Blend the kelp until it's powdery with a few larger granules.

Weigh the kelp powder and measure out twice that weight in oil.

Heat the mixture to 160°C (320°F), then cook, stirring continuously, for 15 minutes. Lower the oil temperature to 150°C (300°F) and cook for 1 hour, stirring every 5 minutes.

Continue cooking, lowering the oil temperature by 10°C (15° to 20°F) every hour until you reach 80°C (175°F), then cook at 80°C (175°F) overnight.

Add the oil and the kelp powder to the Thermomix and blend again for 1 minute.

Transfer the kelp-oil mixture to a rondeau.

Bring the oil temperature back to 130°C (265°F) and cook for 15 minutes, then lower the oil temperature to 120°C (250°F) and cook for 1 hour. Let cool a bit. Blend the kelp oil on high speed for 5 minutes.

Strain the oil through a fine-mesh nylon sieve.
Use right away, refrigerate in an airtight container for up to 5 days, or freeze. Store the sediment separately.

Rose Geranium Oil

Makes about 400 grams

300 grams fresh rose geranium leaves
Liquid nitrogen
600 grams neutral oil

Rose geranium leaves produce a deep green oil with a flavour that is floral, slightly sweet, and herbaceous. Your well-trained nose will detect notes of rose, lemongrass, and mint, with a bit of bitterness as well. Rose geranium oil is a bit more perfumy compared to other oils we make, so it should be used sparingly. Similar to Lemon Verbena Oil (page 177), we process the raw leaves with liquid nitrogen to pulverize them without damaging the cells. The oil is then blended for a longer period of time than the lemon verbena because the rose geranium can take the heat. To extract as much oil as possible from the geranium leaves, we spin the oil using a centrifuge, but you can make this oil without one.

Place the rose geranium leaves in a stainless-steel bowl and freeze with liquid nitrogen, then transfer them to a Thermomix and blend on high speed for 10 seconds to create a fine powder. Add the oil and blend on high speed for 5 minutes. Transfer the blended oil to a container set over an ice bath to cool it down as quickly as possible. Cover and refrigerate over ice overnight to infuse.

Strain the oil through a fine-mesh nylon sieve and set aside. If you have a centrifuge, distribute the pulp evenly among centrifuge bags, vacuum seal the bags, and spin the pulp to maximize yield. Strain off the resulting oil, add it to the rest of the flavoured oil, and stir to combine. Use right away, keep refrigerated in an airtight container for up to 5 days, or freeze for longer-term storage.

Douglas Fir Oil

Makes about 900 grams

450 grams Douglas fir needles
100 grams fresh flat-leaf parsley leaves
Liquid nitrogen
1 kilogram neutral oil

You'll see Douglas fir used throughout this book, along with references to its grapefruity flavour, an aspect we cherish. But as with grapefruit, Douglas fir can be bitter. Freezing the needles with liquid nitrogen before blending allows us to capture their aroma without the bitterness, and parsley provides an additional green-mineral flavour to balance the resinous pine citrus notes.

To extract as much flavour as possible from the Douglas fir needles, we spin the oil using a centrifuge, but you can make this oil without one.

Place the Douglas fir needles and parsley leaves in a stainless-steel bowl and freeze with liquid nitrogen, then transfer to a Thermomix. Add the oil and blend on high speed for 1 minute. Strain the oil through a fine-mesh nylon sieve and set aside. If you have a centrifuge, distribute the pulp evenly among centrifuge bags, vacuum seal the bags, and spin the pulp to maximize yield. Strain off the resulting oil, add it to the rest of the flavoured oil, and stir to combine. Use right away, keep refrigerated in an airtight container for up to 5 days, or freeze for longer-term storage.

Place the lemon verbena leaves in a container and freeze with liquid nitrogen. Transfer the frozen leaves to a Thermomix.

Blend into a very fine powder. Add the oil and blend again until smooth, up to 1 minute (but no longer, to ensure the oil doesn't become warm).

Transfer the lemon verbena mixture to a vacuum bag and seal. Refrigerate overnight to infuse.

Strain the lemon verbena oil through a fine-mesh nylon sieve set in a container over ice. Use right away, refrigerate in an airtight container for up to 5 days, or freeze.

Lemon Verbena Oil

Makes about 600 grams

500 grams fresh lemon verbena leaves
Liquid nitrogen
500 grams neutral oil

Fresh lemon verbena is brilliantly aromatic, but once you apply heat or bruise the delicate herb, the aroma disappears, so cold infusion is the way to capture and preserve its lemony perfume. We spin the lemon verbena in a centrifuge to extract as much flavour as possible from the leaves, but you can make this oil without one.

Place the lemon verbena leaves in a container and freeze with liquid nitrogen, then transfer to a Thermomix and blend on high speed for 45 to 60 seconds to create a fine powder. Add the oil and blend for 1 minute to thoroughly saturate the lemon verbena with the oil and ensure that the herb will not oxidize. Transfer the mixture to a vacuum bag and seal on 100% vacuum. Refrigerate overnight to infuse.

Strain the oil through a fine-mesh nylon sieve and set aside. If you have a centrifuge, distribute the pulp evenly among centrifuge bags, vacuum seal the bags, and spin the pulp to maximize yield. Strain off the resulting oil, add it to the rest of the flavoured oil, and stir to combine. Use right away, keep refrigerated in an airtight container for up to 5 days, or freeze for longer-term storage.

Parsley Oil

Makes about 300 grams

250 grams fresh
flat-leaf parsley leaves
500 grams neutral oil

Parsley may not be sexy, but it provides a versatile herbal flavour that works well with a vast number of ingredients. Like black currant leaves (see page 185), parsley reacts well to heated blending, and produces a vibrantly colored oil with an excellent aroma. Because of the herb's year-round availability, parsley oil has become a workhorse in our flavour larder.

Blend the parsley and the oil together in a Thermomix on high speed for 7 minutes. Transfer the blended oil to a container set over an ice bath to cool it down rapidly, then cover and refrigerate (still over ice) overnight to infuse.

Strain the oil through a fine-mesh nylon sieve and set aside. If you have a centrifuge, distribute the pulp evenly among centrifuge bags, vacuum seal the bags, and spin the pulp to maximize yield. Strain off the resulting oil, add it to the rest of the flavoured oil, and stir to combine. Use right away, keep refrigerated in an airtight container for up to 5 days, or freeze for longer-term storage.

Elderflower Oil

Makes about 500 grams

750 grams picked elderflower blossoms
750 grams neutral oil

Following pages: When it's time to pick elderflower, the whole team comes together, including the front of house, kitchen, and office staffs. Hundreds of kilos of elderflower are processed to produce oil, vinegar, and more.

Elderflower is an extremely special ingredient for us, and one that is available fresh for only a few weeks each year. When the bushes begin to bloom, we get deliveries literally by the truckload. We rally all hands that are available (which usually means everyone from the dishwashers to the head chef), crank up the German techno music, and have an elderflower-picking party.

We have experimented with using liquid nitrogen to remove the blossoms from the branches, which works, but when the blossoms defrost, they start to oxidize immediately, so you have to be even faster with the oil-making process—not a worthwhile trade-off.

Blend the elderflowers and the oil together in a Thermomix for 7 minutes. Transfer the blended oil to a container set over an ice bath and place in the refrigerator overnight to infuse.

Transfer the infused oil to a fine-mesh nylon sieve hung over a container, cover, and refrigerate for 24 hours to strain. Use right away, keep refrigerated in an airtight container for up to 5 days, or freeze for longer-term storage.

Place the black currant leaves and oil in a Thermomix.

Blend on maximum speed for 7 minutes, then transfer to a container set over ice to cool rapidly.

Transfer to a vacuum bag and seal. Refrigerate over ice overnight to infuse.

Strain through a fine-mesh nylon sieve, pushing on the solids to extract as much oil as possible. Use right away, refrigerate in an airtight container for up to 5 days, or freeze.

Black Currant Leaf Oil

Makes about 300 grams

500 grams young black currant leaves
500 grams neutral oil

Black currant is one of Noma's "mother flavours" (see page 22). We use it to flavour oil and more, even sautéing its tender young leaves the way we would any leafy green. Black currant leaf is a good example of a sturdy herb whose flavour—green and herbaceous, with berry, floral, and woody notes—is best extracted through heat. We consume lots of this versatile oil, so we use a centrifuge to extract as much oil as possible from the blended pulp. It is excellent in vinaigrettes or when used to provide a fruity-herbal note to sauces made with game.

Blend the black currant leaves and the oil together in a Thermomix on maximum speed for 7 minutes. Transfer the mixture to a container set over an ice bath to cool it rapidly, then cover and refrigerate (still over ice) overnight.

Strain the oil through a fine-mesh nylon sieve and set aside. If you have a centrifuge, distribute the pulp evenly among centrifuge bags, vacuum seal the bags, and spin the pulp to maximize yield. Strain off the resulting oil, add it to the rest of the flavoured oil, and stir to combine. Use right away, keep refrigerated in an airtight container for up to 5 days, or freeze for longer-term storage.

Place the rose petals and oil in a Thermomix.

Blend on high speed for 7 minutes. The color will change from deep pink to a darker mauve due to the heat generated by the blender.

Transfer the blended rose petals to a vacuum bag, seal, and refrigerate overnight to infuse.

Strain the rose mixture through a fine-mesh nylon sieve into a container over ice. Use right away, refrigerate in an airtight container for up to 5 days, or freeze.

Rose Oil

Makes about 500 grams

750 grams wild beach rose petals (or petals from any unsprayed fragrant rose)
750 grams neutral oil

Rose oil was born when Thomas Frebel, Lars Williams, and Rosio Sanchez were heading up the Test Kitchen. They were working on a dish featuring a technique for cooking beets that required roasting the beets at an extremely high temperature (250°C/480°F) until they literally burned, then peeling the burnt bits off, butterflying the beets, and cooking them further at a lower temperature until they took on a meatlike chewiness. At the same time, the team had been working on ways to preserve the extremely fleeting Danish rose season. They captured the flavour by blending rose petals with oil. The pairing of deeply earthy, sweet, and textural beets with floral rose oil was a match made in heaven.

Blend the rose petals and the oil together in a Thermomix on high speed for 7 minutes. Transfer the mixture to a container set over an ice bath to cool it rapidly. Place the oil in a vacuum bag, seal on 100% vacuum, and refrigerate overnight to infuse.

Strain the oil through a fine-mesh nylon sieve. If you have a centrifuge, distribute the pulp evenly among centrifuge bags, vacuum seal the bags, and spin the pulp to maximize yield. Strain off the resulting oil, add it to the rest of the flavoured oil, and stir to combine. (The spun pulp can be reserved and used as a starter for rose kombucha.) Use right away, keep refrigerated in an airtight container for up to 5 days, or freeze for longer-term storage.

Pounded Oils

The pounded-oil process began with a delivery from our forager: black currant buds, the tiny swellings along the branches that become leaves and berries as the season progresses. Noma creative director Thomas Frebel fell in love with their flavour, and used the tiny buds in various spice mixes and pastes, chopped them up and added them to a seasoned yogurt, or cooked them with vegetables.

A hammer is a useful tool for making our wood oils.

Picking the buds on a large scale was too labor-intensive for our forager, so his next delivery was of whole black currant branches. Thomas loved the aroma of the branches, which inspired him to use them to make an oil.

Nowadays, if you walk through the Noma courtyard, you're likely to see a couple of chefs de partie with hammers in hand, working through piles of branches, pounding away to split them open and reveal their tender aromatic interiors, soon to be submerged in oil.

Larch Wood Oil

Makes about 250 grams

100 grams thin young larch branches, with needles attached
300 grams neutral oil

Larch wood has a more resinous flavour than black currant, with a slight bitterness that is reminiscent of extra-virgin olive oil. Pick larch wood in late spring when green shoots are growing on the branches.

Pound the larch branches with a hammer or mallet to split open the wood, revealing the aromatic flesh inside. Immediately place the wood in a vacuum bag, pour in the oil, and seal on 100% vacuum, then seal the bag in a second bag to prevent any loss if the inner bag is punctured by a twig. Steam in a combi oven set to 60°C (140°F; 100% fan) for at least 4 hours or up to overnight. Let cool, then refrigerate overnight to infuse.

Strain the oil through a fine-mesh nylon sieve into an airtight container and compost the wood. Use right away, keep refrigerated for up to 5 days, or freeze for longer-term storage.

Cherry Wood Oil

Makes about 150 grams

100 grams tender wild cherry wood branches
200 grams neutral oil

We used cherry wood oil for the first time in 2015 during our Tokyo pop-up. At the time, we had just begun to explore the potential of infusing oils with young black currant wood, and cherry wood felt like a natural evolution of that technique, given the cherry tree's cultural resonance in Japan. We used it on a dish of Nagano squash confit served with Lacto Koji Butter Sauce (page 384), roasted kelp, and salted cherry blossoms. The cherry wood oil added a final aromatic layer: soft, woody, and ephemeral.

Using a hammer (on a hard surface), a mortar and pestle, or a wood chipper, break the cherry wood into small pieces to expose the aromatic inner flesh of the branches. Immediately place the exposed wood in a vacuum bag with the oil and seal on 100% vacuum. Seal the bag in a second bag to prevent any loss if the inner bag is punctured by a twig. Steam in a combi oven set to 60°C (140°F; 100% fan) for at least 4 hours or up to overnight. Let cool, then refrigerate overnight to infuse.

Strain the oil through a fine-mesh nylon sieve into an airtight container and compost the wood. Use right away, keep refrigerated for up to 5 days, or freeze for longer-term storage.

Break the black currant branches into small pieces.

Immediately place the wood into a vacuum bag. Add the oil and seal on 100% vacuum. Seal in a second bag for security.

Steam in a combi oven set to 60°C (140°F; 100% fan) for at least 4 hours or up to overnight. Let cool, then refrigerate overnight to infuse.

Set a container over ice and strain the oil through a fine-mesh nylon sieve into the container. Use right away, refrigerate in an airtight container for up to 5 days, or freeze.

Black Currant Wood Oil

Makes about 1.8 kilograms

1 kilogram young black currant wood branches
2 kilograms neutral oil

Black currant wood oil is Noma's olive oil. It's mild enough to be versatile but has a distinctive flavour that can be described as green and herbaceous with a fruity back note, a slight pine resin characteristic, and a slight floral undertone. The perfume industry values black currant buds, which have a similar flavour profile, for the same reason we do: their seemingly foreign yet familiar and entirely enticing aroma.

Using a hammer (on a hard surface), a mortar and pestle, or a wood chipper, break the black currant wood into small pieces. Immediately place the wood in a vacuum bag, pour in the oil, and seal on 100% vacuum; seal the bag in a second bag to prevent any loss if the inner bag is punctured by a twig. Steam in a combi oven set to 60°C (140°F; 100% fan) for at least 4 hours or up to overnight. Let cool, then refrigerate overnight to infuse.

Strain the oil through a fine-mesh nylon sieve into an airtight container over ice and compost the wood. Use right away, keep refrigerated for up to 5 days, or freeze for longer-term storage.

Butters

At Noma, we love butter, but we don't think of it as an all-purpose cooking medium the way another fine-dining kitchen might. Our use of butter is more specific to the context of a dish. We use butter in our butter sauces (pages 381–403), sure, and we do cook with whole fresh butter (Danish, of course) when we seek its nutty, creamy flavours. Pan-roasted turbot in fragrant foaming butter is hard to beat.

Fresh barley koji simmers with butter.

But we like to take our butter to the less-explored corners of the flavour world. We smoke it, split it to use the whey, brighten it with fruit, or infuse it with koji for some savory funk. We take our brown butter way past "nutty," all the way to where the risk is burning but the reward is deeply aromatic and potent, and worth taking a chance on.

Smoked Butter

Makes 1 kilogram

1 kilogram cold unsalted butter, cut into 2 cm (¾-inch) cubes

Whenever we get excited about a new technique or ingredient, we tend to use it in every way we can think of. Smoking is a traditional preservation method in Scandinavia, so when Noma was finding its Nordic identity, we smoked everything we could get our hands on. Because fat is extremely good at absorbing flavours (see page 12), including smoke, smoked butter was a clear winner in all those tests. It's remarkable, in a way, that you can do something so simple to an ordinary ingredient and transform it into a vehicle with so much flavour.

We usually use hay to produce the smoke, which yields a light result, but we've also used birch and pine (in a limited capacity, as aerosolizing pine resin can create harmful fumes). We have used a variety of smoking devices to smoke butter, including an offset hot smoker, a smoking gun, and a cold smoker. All the devices work, it just depends on what equipment you have. Whichever method you use, cut the butter into cubes to create a lot of surface area on which to capture the smoke flavour, and keep the butter cold and solid as it smokes.

Set up an offset cold smoker. Fill a smoking coil with wood dust and light the dust with a bit of white-hot charcoal. Place the butter in a container and set it on one of the top racks of the smoker. Smoke the butter until it smells rich and smoky, about 30 minutes. Use right away or transfer to a clean airtight container and reserve in the refrigerator for up to 3 days, or use to make Smoked Butter Whey (opposite).

Smoked Butter Whey

Makes about 300 grams

1 kilogram Smoked Butter (opposite)

Butter whey is a flavourful by-product of clarified butter—lightly tangy, subtly lactic, nutty, and just a touch sweet. Smoked butter whey carries all those qualities, but with an added layer of depth from the smoke, making it even more compelling. When clarifying smoked butter, the whey that separates from the butterfat is small in quantity but powerful in flavour. We first used it in our cured egg yolk sauce; originally, we intended to season the sauce with the smoked butterfat, but the brightness and complexity of the whey quickly took center stage. Since then, we've leaned into using just the whey to bring a smoky, lactic depth to sauces. It's a surprisingly versatile seasoning agent.

Heat the smoked butter in a pot over low heat until it splits to yield clarified smoked butter and smoked butter whey. Carefully pour off the clarified butter from the whey. Use right away or reserve the two in separate airtight containers in the refrigerator for up to 3 days.

Brown Butter

Makes about 5 kilograms

5 kilograms unsalted butter, cubed

At Noma, we take our brown butter to the edge. While most instructions for brown butter caution the cook to pull the butter from the heat as soon as the milk solids turn deep golden brown in order to avoid burning, we push those limits further, cooking the butter until it looks almost black.

The trick is to take your time. You want to arrive at the point where the clarified liquid butterfat itself tastes nutty; if you stop when the milk solids are lightly caramelized, the resulting clarified butter will taste like any other clarified butter, with just a hint of caramelization.

Butter melts at between 90° and 95°C (195° and 205°F), water evaporates from the butter at 100°C (212°F), and milk solids brown between 120° and 150°C (250° and 300°F). We aim for 165°C (330°F), monitoring the level of heat carefully when we reach 150°C (300°F) and pulling the pan off the stove 5 to 10 degrees before that target, since the butter temperature will continue to rise, especially if you're making a large quantity (in the same way a piece of meat will continue to cook off the heat due to "carryover cooking"). As the butter reaches the target temperature, stir it to distribute any pockets of hotter or cooler butter, then immediately strain the butter into a container set over an ice bath to cool. The butter will resolidify as it cools. The French would call this *beurre noir*, and we find it to be the deepest, most round-flavoured brown butter possible. It also has an extremely fragrant aroma that will quite literally take over your entire cooking space.

Heat the butter in a large saucepan over medium-low heat until it splits, bubbles, and caramelizes to a very deep, rich brown, whisking often to reincorporate the milk solids to yield an evenly browned final product and taking care not to let it scorch. Remove the pan from the heat when the butter reaches around 155°C (310°F) and allow carryover cooking to bring it to a final temperature of 165°C (330°F). Strain the brown butter through a fine-mesh metal sieve (not a nylon sieve, as the butter is too hot) into a container set over an ice bath and let cool to room temperature. Use right away or transfer to an airtight container and reserve in the refrigerator for up to 1 week or freeze for up to 3 months.

Place the butter in a large saucepan. Cook over medium-low heat until the butter melts and separates, the water cooks off, and the butter begins to brown.

Whisk frequently as the butter cooks to keep the milk solids from settling to the bottom of the pan and to brown the butter evenly.

The butterfat will be deep amber.

Set a bowl in an ice bath and strain the butter through a fine-mesh metal strainer into the chilled bowl to stop the cooking.

Continue cooking, monitoring the butter so it doesn't burn, until it reaches about 155°C (310°F), then remove from the heat; you'll reach the target temperature of 165°C (330°F) through carryover cooking.

The milk solids will be a dark brown.

Whisk the butter to speed the cooling.

The strainer will capture most of the milk solids.
Use right away, refrigerate in an airtight container for up to 1 week, or freeze.

Crumble the fresh koji into individual grains or small clumps. Melt the butter in a large saucepan and add the crumbled koji.

Simmer the koji for 8 hours, until it has caramelized slightly and the butter is a rich, nutty brown.

Strain the oil through a fine-mesh nylon sieve into a clean container.

Press on the koji solids to extract as much butter as possible. Use right away, refrigerate in an airtight container, or freeze.

Fresh Barley Koji Butter

Makes about 1.6 kilograms

1 kilogram fresh Barley Koji*
2 kilograms unsalted butter

Noma has a massive love affair with koji, but we don't always want to include the actual grain in a dish; usually, we just want the flavour. Longtime Noma veteran Thomas Frebel solved that problem by creating koji butter, an umami-rich butter that can be brushed onto other ingredients or used as part of a sauce. The barley koji for this recipe cannot be frozen—it must be freshly made, as the flavour of frozen koji will be muted in comparison to fresh.

Making fresh barley koji butter also yields a bonus: butter-soaked koji solids, which we have turned into a paste and used when salt-baking a guinea hen. We spread a layer of koji-butter paste (which you peel off but don't eat) between the meat and the salt dough, which adds a light umami flavour and prevents the meat from becoming too salty.

Crumble the fresh koji into individual grains. Melt the butter in a large saucepan over medium heat, then add the crumbled koji. Reduce the heat to maintain a low simmer and cook for 8 hours, until the koji has caramelized slightly and the butter is a rich, nutty brown. Let cool slightly, then strain the butter through a fine-mesh nylon sieve, squeezing the sediment to maximize yield and flavour. Use right away, reserve an airtight container in the refrigerator until needed, or freeze.

Simmer the quince and dried carrot flower with the butter until the quince is soft, about 1 hour. Let cool.

Transfer the butter and fruit to a mortar and pound with the pestle to break down the quince and create a chunky puree.

Transfer the mixture to a tamis lined with a fine-mesh nylon sieve and push it through the sieve with a scraper. Scrape the smooth butter from the underside of the tamis and transfer it to a bowl.

Whisk the butter until smooth, then set the bowl over ice and continue whisking until the butter is thick and somewhat lightened in color. Use right away or refrigerate in an airtight container for up to 3 days.

Japanese Quince Butter

Makes about 2.5 kilograms

1.6 kilograms unsalted butter
2.2 kilograms Japanese quince
30 grams dried carrot flowers

Test Kitchen head Mette Søberg started with the notion that citrus works well with butter, so perhaps Japanese quince would as well. After giving the quince a long bath in warm butter, in which it softened and released its flavour, she decided that rather than straining out the flavouring fruit, she would mash it into the butter, which yielded a silky emulsion with the richness of butter and the acidity and floral notes of the quince. Quince butter is now a staple ingredient in our pantry; it's excellent brushed on top of raw seafood, cooked into sweet late-summer pumpkin or corn, or brushed onto smoked fish.

Melt the butter in a medium rondeau over medium heat, then add the quince and carrot flowers. Simmer until the fruit becomes tender, about 1 hour. Let cool, then transfer the mixture to a mortar and pound with the pestle until the fruit is pulverized into a chunky puree (do this in batches, if necessary). Pass the butter through a tamis lined with a fine-mesh nylon sieve, pressing it through with a scraper, then transfer it to a bowl.

Whisk the butter until smooth to give it a lighter texture and more volume, then set the bowl over an ice bath and whisk until the butter has the consistency of a thick buttercream. Use right away or transfer to an airtight container and reserve in the refrigerator for up to 3 days; bring it to room temperature before use.

Suggested Uses

Rose-Scented Brown Rice

Give a simple grain a fragrant dimension: Cook brown rice in Roasted Kelp Dashi (page 216) and then finish with a small drizzle of Rose Oil (page 187).

Spring Vegetable Salad with Lemon Verbena

Toss together a few spears of raw asparagus, thinly sliced on an angle, a handful of fava beans, lightly steamed English peas, and a few julienned radishes. Dress with lemon juice and Lemon Verbena Oil (page 177). Season with salt and black pepper, and serve on a bed of fresh sheep's-milk cheese or whipped ricotta.

White Asparagus with Cep Mayonnaise

Make a mayonnaise with egg yolks, whisky vinegar (apple cider vinegar also works nicely), a few drops of lemon juice, and Cep Oil (page 164). Taste and season with salt and black pepper. Peel some white asparagus and poach in salted water just until crisp-tender. Spoon the cep oil mayonnaise over the warm asparagus and finish with more pepper.

Sautéed Corn with Japanese Quince Butter

Cut the kernels from a few ears of corn and flash-sauté them with just a bit of clarified butter until warmed through and tender, then toss with a spoonful of Japanese Quince Butter (page 205). Season with salt.

Smoked Butter–Basted Steak

Season a steak generously with salt and black pepper, then sear it in a cast-iron pan with a bit of neutral oil. Toss in a few garlic cloves and thyme sprigs and a big spoonful of Smoked Butter (page 196). Cook the steak to your desired doneness while basting with the foaming smoked butter.

Charred Onions with Hazelnut Oil

Grill a few spring onions over a hot fire until they're fully charred, then move them to a cooler part of the grill and cook until the interiors steam to tenderness. Peel off the charred layer, slice open the interior flesh, and season with freshly pressed Hazelnut Oil (page 152) and flaky salt. You could substitute thick slabs of sweet onion for the spring onions.

Opposite, top to bottom:
Rose-Scented Brown Rice;
White Asparagus with Cep Mayonnaise;
Smoked Butter-Basted Steak
Right: Charred Onions with Hazelnut Oil

4.

Broths and Other Flavourful Liquids

Broths and Other Flavourful Liquids: Clarifying flavour and intention

About fifteen years ago, I was in Japan, speaking with one of the great master chefs. We talked about the core differences between Western and Japanese cooking. It was a generous conversation. At one point, he said something that has stuck with me ever since:

"In our cooking, we take things away. In the West, you add."

I'm still not sure I fully understand what he meant, but I keep going back to that phrase, especially when we're working through a new idea at the restaurant. Are we adding? Or are we taking away? Not in a negative sense, of course—it's more about whether we're getting to the essence of a thing. Are we clarifying? Or are we just layering on more than we need?

On that same trip, I found myself in a kitchen where nearly everything was built around broths. No heavy reductions. No dense meat stocks that had been cooked for twelve hours. Just light broths that were somehow still rich, savory, and mouth-filling. That became a kind of quiet inspiration. I started asking myself: Could we, in our part of the world, with our ingredients, our mindset, our culture—could we get there, too? Could we create that kind of clarity and depth without relying on meat?

So over the years, we began working on broths of our own. Not the traditional kind where you simmer bones and skim fat for hours—more like infusions. Most of them vegetarian, many even fully vegan. We started to find new ways to bring out flavour—using plants, kelp, toasted grains, dried seaweed. We kept stripping things back. And often, what we were left with was better than what we started with.

Forest Broth, Kyoto, 2024
A broth of wild Japanese mushrooms, seaweeds, and pine is split with pine, cep, and wasabi oils and served in a bowl of autumn leaves.

211

Kuzu and Fresh Cheese with Sorrel and Verbena Kombucha Broth, Vegetable, 2024
Kuzu noodles made with lacto-fermented honey are served with fresh cheese floating in a broth of sorrel juice and lemon verbena kombucha.

A great example is mushroom kelp broth, a broth that, when done right, guests often assume must be meat-based. But it actually came from a place of practicality. We'd been making dashi in large volumes, using thick sheets of kelp, and every time we strained them out, we were left with this beautiful spent seaweed. In an effort to upcycle, Noma creative director Thomas Frebel had the idea of simmering the kelp again, this time in a mushroom broth, seasoned with condiments. He brought the broth to a simmer . . . and then forgot about it for two days (timing we now use intentionally). What emerged was a fresh broth, rich and savory, and a piece of seaweed, transformed. We began drying it, slicing it, and using it across the menu: in desserts, in ceviches, in all corners of the kitchen.

We also use juices not simply as beverages, but as ingredients—to finish a dish, to season it just before it hits the table. One of the best, and most dangerous, is horseradish juice. If you ever juice fresh horseradish root, wear goggles. Clear the room. The vapor hits the air like a weapon. People cry. But that juice, just a few drops on a raw oyster or in a dressing—it's incredible.

The first time we made that horseradish juice, walking home at the end of the night, I asked myself: What else can we do here? That one question led us into a long phase of technical exploration, after which came this: Clarity had become its own craft.

Broths and juices offer clarity: in flavour, in structure, in intention. They can be rich, deep, bright, but always clean. That's their strength.

Cold-Infused Dashi

Makes 1 kilogram

60 grams fresh kelp
1 kilogram cold filtered water

Our original method of making dashi was pretty classic: Add 23 grams of kelp to 1 kilogram of water, cook it at 60°C (140°F) for one hour, shock it in an ice bath, strain it, and away you go. All that changed after a trip to Hokkaido. The seaweed producer prepared a dashi for Thomas Frebel, Rosio Sanchez, and Lars Williams, then the heads of the Test Kitchen, so they could sample the seaweed, but he used a cold-infused method, simply leaving the seaweed to infuse in water overnight. The result was an umami broth unlike any they had tasted before, exceedingly clear and potent. Not using heat allowed the more delicate flavour compounds to come to the fore, in the same way that a cold-brewed coffee can express flavours you won't get in a hot coffee. Heat changes everything. Even the texture of the liquid was different than the dashi from our old method, slightly more viscous because the naturally occurring carrageenan in the seaweed remained intact. Needless to say, cold-infused dashi has become our new standard. We make it almost daily, and it's on the menu in many forms, including our Noma Umami Salt (page 113).

Place the kelp in the water and refrigerate overnight (or for at least 8 hours) to infuse.

Remove the kelp and strain the dashi through a fine-mesh nylon sieve. The sooner you use the dashi, the better, but it can be reserved in an airtight container in the refrigerator for up to 3 days.

Roasted Kelp Dashi

Makes 1 kilogram

23 grams Roasted Kelp*
1 kilogram filtered water

We make this dashi as the first step in our Noma Roasted Umami Salt (page 115), an incredibly flavourful seasoning that makes pretty much anything taste amazing. We also use the roasted kelp dashi as a base for sauces, or as a seasoning tool—to balance the flavour and consistency of a butter sauce, for example.

Place the kelp and water in a vacuum bag and seal on 100% vacuum. Steam in a combi oven set to 60°C (140°F) for 1 hour, then transfer the bag to an ice bath to cool. Strain the dashi through a fine-mesh nylon sieve into an airtight container. The dashi is best used the day it's made, but it can be reserved in the refrigerator for up to 3 days.

Pine Dashi

Makes 1 kilogram

- 60 grams Dried Norwegian Spruce*
- 1 kilogram Cold-Infused Dashi (page 215)

This is a very Noma interpretation of dashi, created by Thomas Frebel, who has an affinity for evergreens. Instead of seasoning the final kelp-infused broth with katsuobushi (dried and smoked bonito, used in traditional Japanese dashi), we season it with Norwegian spruce needles. This very Scandinavian ingredient doesn't have the smokiness or savoriness of smoked fish, but it does add a bit of acidity and a refreshing aroma. This dashi is excellent on its own, as the base for a larger, more complex broth, or as a cooking medium for various ingredients. We've used pine dashi in a seaweed hot pot and cooked pears and onions in it as well.

Place the spruce and dashi in a vacuum bag and seal on 100% vacuum. Steam in a combi oven set to 60°C (140°F) for 1 hour. Strain the dashi through a fine-mesh nylon sieve into an airtight container. The dashi is best used the day it's made but can be reserved in the refrigerator for up to 3 days.

Yeast Broth

Makes about 150 grams

400 grams filtered water
60 grams Peaso*
20 grams Roasted Yeast*
12 grams freeze-dried gooseberries

The search for umami is a through line in Noma's creative process; we're always exploring ways to enhance savoriness, especially beyond the sources you might find in traditional European cuisine, such as cured meat or aged cheese. Noma chef Thomas Frebel was inspired by Vegemite when he wanted to create an umami-rich broth. The Australian spread gets its savory flavour from brewer's yeast. Here we roast fresh yeast to achieve the same effect. We often reduce yeast broth (page 260), but we also serve it as a broth unto itself, as in a dish of shrimp enclosed in nasturtium leaves, ravioli-style, seasoned with cured radish, Pine Vinegar (page 39), horseradish juice (see page 237), and rhubarb and surrounded by yeast broth.

Place the water, peaso, yeast, and gooseberries in a Thermomix and blend until thoroughly homogenized. Transfer to an airtight container and freeze.

Remove the frozen brick of yeast broth from the container and place it on a tamis lined with a fine-mesh nylon sieve set over a clean container or hang it in a cheesecloth-lined perforated gastro pan set over a deep gastro pan to catch the liquid as it thaws. Let stand in the refrigerator for 2 to 3 days, until completely thawed and devoid of any further easily extractable liquid. Do not press on the residual solids. (For more about ice-clarifying, see page 240.) Strain the broth through a fine-mesh nylon sieve. Use as soon as possible, or reserve in an airtight container in the refrigerator for up to 3 days.

Maitake Broth

Makes 3 kilograms

1 kilogram maitake mushrooms
Fresh Barley Koji Oil (page 169)
2 kilograms Pine Dashi (page 217)
1 kilogram Peaso Water*
Reduced White Wine*
Salt

This broth is an adaptation of one from Thomas Frebel's former restaurant in Tokyo, Inua. At Noma, we use pine dashi as the base. The key lies in gently smoking the maitakes over an open grill to infuse them with a delicate smokiness and evaporate some of their moisture, concentrating their flavour. The resulting broth is clean, layered, and evocative of forest and flame. Once the broth is complete, the mushrooms are typically strained out and used for staff meals.

Place the maitakes in a vacuum bag and add enough koji oil to cover them. Seal and cycle through the vacuum sealer to compress the mushrooms. Remove the mushrooms, and reserve the oil to use in the future. (If you don't have a vacuum sealer, just press the bag of oil-covered mushrooms with a moderate weight for a few hours.)

Transfer the maitakes to wire racks and position them above a grill, high enough for them to absorb the latent smoke from grilling other food but not close enough to get any heat. We smoke our maitakes for 2 days.

Preheat the oven to 250°C (480°F). Transfer the mushrooms to a clay pot or Dutch oven and add the dashi and peaso water. Place the pot in the oven and cook for 30 minutes. Strain the broth and season with reduced white wine and salt. Use the broth as soon as possible, or reserve in an airtight container in the refrigerator for up to 3 days.

Place all the ingredients in a stockpot and bring to a simmer. Simmer overnight.

Strain the broth through a conical strainer and then again through a superbag.

Transfer the strained broth to a clean stockpot and bring to a simmer, skimming off any residue that rises to the surface.

Simmer for 36 hours, until the broth is rich and reduced. Use right away, refrigerate in an airtight container for up to 2 days, or freeze.

Mushroom Kelp Broth

Makes about 2 kilograms

10 kilograms filtered water
1 kilogram Lacto Cep Water*
500 grams thin outer pieces of kelp
250 grams muscovado sugar
250 grams dried ceps
130 grams dried morels
70 grams dried trumpet mushrooms
50 grams freeze-dried lingonberries

This is a two-in-one recipe: It produces intensely flavoured braised kelp and a super-tasty broth that can be reduced to a syrupy glaze. Braised Kelp (recipe follows) was the original incarnation; we would braise the thick center-cut of a blade of kelp until fully tender and plump, then slice it to use in various ways. But the cooking liquid is incredibly delicious, so now we make the broth even when we're not creating braised kelp. The reduced broth goes into one of our most important sauces, Kelp Mushroom Truffle Sauce (page 395). You could also use this rich broth in simpler ways, perhaps as a glaze for sautéed mushrooms.

Place the filtered water, lacto cep water, kelp, sugar, ceps, morels, trumpet mushrooms, and lingonberries in a large stockpot or rondeau and bring to a boil. Reduce the heat to low, cover, and simmer overnight.

Strain the stock through a conical strainer and transfer it to a superbag; squeeze it through the superbag into a clean pot to extract as much liquid as possible. Cook over low heat, keeping the liquid just below a simmer so that only the occasional bubble breaks the surface and skimming off any residue that rises to the surface, for 36 hours. The broth will become rich and syrupy, but not as thick as a glaze. Strain through a fine-mesh nylon sieve. Use right away, refrigerate in an airtight container for up to 2 days, or freeze for longer-term storage. Use the broth as is or reduce it further, depending on its final use.

222

How to Braise Kelp

To braise thick kelp, divide the ingredients in the Mushroom Kelp Broth recipe (page 221)—except the kelp—evenly between two stockpots. Add 250 grams thick center-cut pieces of kelp to one pot and 250 grams thin outer pieces of kelp to the other pot. Simmer both pots overnight as directed.

Carefully remove the thick center-cut pieces of kelp from their pot and reserve them. Strain both pots of stock through a conical sieve, combine them, and then squeeze the stock through a fine-mesh sieve such as a superbag.

Transfer the liquid to a clean stockpot and add the reserved thick kelp pieces. Cook very slowly for 36 hours, or until the kelp just begins to lose its "al dente-ness." Remove from the heat and allow the kelp to cool in the liquid. Transfer the cooked thick kelp pieces and the broth to an airtight container and reserve in the refrigerator for up to 5 days. Make sure to use clean utensils when retrieving the kelp from the broth so you don't introduce pathogens.

Grilled Koji, Squid Broth, Kyoto, 2024
Sea snails are confited, then thinly sliced and laid across pieces of just-grilled barley koji. The dish is finished with a broth made of clarified squid stock, squid reduction, and Noma umami salt, and autumnal flowers and herbs.

Mussel Broth, Ocean, 2024
A warm broth of mussel stock seasoned with sencha cream and bergamot is sipped through an arrangement of fresh seaweeds.

Place the raw shrimp in a Thermomix and add an equal weight of water or dashi. Blend until smooth, about 2½ minutes.

Pour the shrimp slurry into a vacuum bag and seal well, then seal the first bag in a second one.

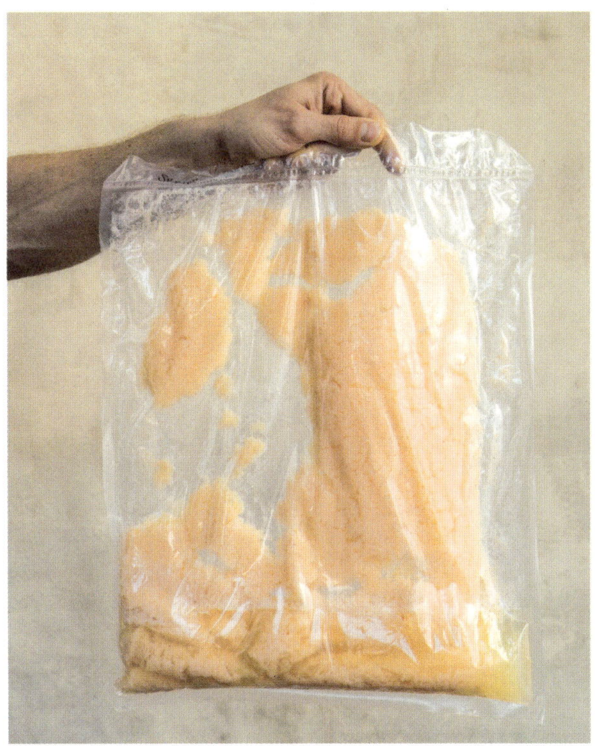

Steam at 100°C (212°F) until the shrimp solids coagulate and separate from the broth.

Pour the clarified shrimp stock and the cooked shrimp protein through a fine-mesh nylon sieve into a container over ice. Use right away, refrigerate for up to 2 days, or freeze.

Shrimp Stock

Makes about 750 grams

500 grams peeled and deveined raw shrimp
500 grams Cold-Infused Dashi (page 215) or filtered water

This type of seafood stock can be served unreduced as a broth, but we usually reduce these stocks to a glaze, to be brushed onto the same seafood—shrimp glaze on shrimp, lobster glaze on lobster tail—to intensify the essential flavour, in the same way that a French chef might serve a veal demi-glace with a veal chop.

Place the shrimp and dashi in a Thermomix and blend until smooth, about 2½ minutes. Transfer the mixture to a vacuum bag and seal on 100% vacuum, then seal the bag in a second bag (a shrimp slurry leak can make an unfortunate mess). Steam in a combi oven set to 100°C (212°F; 100% fan) for 45 minutes, until the proteins coagulate and the clarified broth separates from the solids. Strain the clarified broth through a fine-mesh nylon sieve into a container set over an ice bath. Use right away, reserve in an airtight container in the refrigerator for up to 2 days, or freeze for longer-term storage.

Self-Clarifying

"Self-clarifying" is a clever technique that we often use to make seafood broths, transforming raw shrimp, lobster, or squid protein into intensely flavoured clear broth. (We've used this method with other proteins as well, but shellfish suits our needs best.) The process uses the same principle that's in play when making a French consommé, in which raw proteins coagulate when heated and capture the solid particles in the stock. For consommé, you whisk egg whites (and sometimes chopped aromatic vegetables and raw ground lean meat for more flavour) into cold stock and then slowly simmer everything. As the egg whites coagulate, they grab the tiny solid bits in the stock, eventually floating to the top of the stockpot and forming a solid mass referred to as a raft. After an hour or so of gentle simmering and ladling the broth through the raft, you're left with a crystal-clear consommé; the raft is lifted off and discarded. Winemakers sometimes use a similar technique (minus the meat and vegetables) to clarify wine.

At Noma, we use the same principle of protein coagulation in our method, but rather than introduce egg whites, lean meat, or other outside flavours, we let the proteins in the main ingredient do all the work, hence "self-clarifying." We blend the raw shellfish with water or other liquid to make a slurry and then steam it in a vacuum bag, which causes the liquid to separate out from the coagulated proteins and other solids. We're left with a pure liquid essence of our main ingredient, which is quite versatile and is also beautiful on its own, as when we served lobster broth seasoned with Rose Oil (page 187), a few drops of vinegar, salt, and nasturtium flower petals.

Smoked Fish Broth

Makes 3.5 kilograms

3 kilograms turbot bones or cod bones
2 kilograms cod heads
Neutral oil
5 large shallots, coarsely chopped
1 kilogram white wine
10 kilograms Cold-Infused Dashi (page 215)

This preparation leans more toward a fumet than a traditional broth, with a few key twists. The smoked fish bones add a deep, savory bass note, while the use of cold-infused dashi instead of water contributes an additional layer of umami. It's particularly well suited for use as the base for a rich butter sauce. Once reduced, the broth can be clarified using the ice filtration method (see page 240) or, for a more classical approach, with an egg white raft (see opposite).

Rinse the fish bones, remove the gills and the blood line behind the neck, and cold-smoke the bones and heads for 2 hours. Remove from the smoker. Brush the smoked bones with oil, place them on wire racks, and roast in the oven at 220°C (430°F) on dry heat until well caramelized, 12 to 15 minutes.

Heat some oil in a large pot (large enough to hold all the fish and the dashi) over medium heat. Add the shallots and cook until lightly caramelized. Deglaze with the wine, then cook until the wine reduces to form a glaze. Add the roasted bones to the pot and pour in the dashi. Bring to a boil, skimming continuously for clarity, then reduce the heat to maintain a simmer and cook for 40 minutes. Turn off the heat and let stand for 1 hour to allow the flavours to meld. Carefully strain the stock through a fine-mesh nylon sieve into a clean pot. Simmer until the stock has reduced to about 3.5 kilograms. Let cool, then use right away, keep refrigerated in an airtight container for up to 2 days, or freeze for longer-term storage.

Crab Stock

Makes about 600 grams

2 kilograms crabs (brown crabs or Dungeness crabs work well)
Filtered water

Like Shrimp Stock (page 227), this recipe self-clarifies (see page 228), but unlike the shrimp, the crab must be steamed first so the meat can be removed from the shell before blending. That means the crab is cooked twice before the final clarification step. The result is a pure, sweet crab flavour that can be reduced to a caramel or served on its own. One memorable presentation involved pouring it from a crab "flask"—the shells of two brown crabs (*Cancer pagurus*) fused together with beeswax. We typically use brown crab for its flavour and meat yield, but the method works with any crab variety, especially those with a generous meat content.

Place the crabs in a steamer and steam at 80°C (175°F) for 20 minutes. Let the crabs cool, then pick the meat and weigh it; you should have about 500 grams. Transfer the picked meat to a Thermomix with an equal weight of filtered water. Blend on high speed for 1 minute, then at speed 6 for 29 minutes more.

Meanwhile, bring a pot of water to a boil. While the crab mixture is still hot, transfer it to a vacuum bag and seal on 100% vacuum, then seal the bag in a second bag. Place the bag in the boiling water and cook for 1 hour, until the proteins coagulate and the clarified broth separates from the solids. Strain the clarified broth through a fine-mesh nylon sieve into a container set over an ice bath. Use the broth the same day you make it.

Mussel Broth

Makes about 1 kilogram

5 kilograms mussels
2 shallots, sliced
1.5 kilograms white wine

Briny, tart, and deeply savory, mussel broth is one of our go-to utility broths. Emulsify it with butter for a quick sauce to pair with fish. Reduce it to a caramel for a hit of salty-sweet depth. Or use it as a base for steaming a second round of mussels.

Rinse any grit from the mussels, scrubbing them as necessary, and remove any visible beards. Heat a large rondeau over high heat. Add the mussels, shallots, and wine to flash boil and steam the mussels, covering the pot with a lid and agitating it to stir the mussels around. Reduce the heat to maintain a simmer and cook until the mussels open, releasing their juices. Remove from the heat, still covered, and let cool.

Strain the broth through a fine-mesh nylon sieve, weigh it, and transfer it to a clean pot. Bring to a simmer and cook until it has reduced to about 66% of its starting weight, tasting it as it reduces (if reduced too far, it can become bitter). Let cool, then transfer to an airtight container and freeze.

Remove the frozen broth from the container and place it on a tamis lined with a fine-mesh nylon sieve set over a container or hang it in a cheesecloth-lined perforated gastro pan set over a deep gastro pan to catch the liquid. Refrigerate for 2 to 3 days, until completely drained and thawed. Do not press on the solids. (For more about ice-clarifying, see page 240.) Strain through a fine-mesh nylon sieve into an airtight container. Use right away, refrigerate for up to 2 days, or freeze for longer-term storage.

Juicing Through a Superbag

The simplest juicing method involves pressing the ingredient to force out the juice. You can easily coax the juice from a soft, moist ingredient such as a berry or currant by squeezing it through a strainer of some kind simply using your hands; the strong, fine mesh of a superbag is ideal.

Squeeze and twist the bag to extract as much juice as possible; keep the juice over ice as you work.

Good for superbag juicing:
Soft fruit such as white currants, red currants, raspberries, and wild blueberries.

Juicing with a Wine Press

For greater quantities, or for tougher ingredients, we enlist the help of a time-honored mechanical force: a wine press.

Line the wine press with cheesecloth and collect the juice in a container set over ice, to keep flavours as fresh as possible. If using ingredients that have been frozen and thawed, be sure to incorporate any juices that accumulated in the vacuum bag during thawing.

Good for wine press juicing:
Large quantities of relatively soft ingredients, such as currants or berries, and for ingredients that have been frozen and thawed, such as potatoes or Japanese quince.

Freezing Before Juicing

Another way to extract juice efficiently is to freeze and then thaw the ingredient before you juice it. The freeze-thaw step ruptures the cell walls of the food, allowing the juices (containing water, sugars, acid, and other soluble compounds) to flow more easily. As the water within each cell freezes, it expands slightly, forming sharp ice crystals that pierce the cell membrane and disrupt the pectin networks. In fact, pectinase and cellulase enzymes become active during the defrosting process, which helps further break down cell walls. The result is a flavourful juice that is slightly more viscous due to the dissolved pectin. After the ingredient is completely frozen, let it thaw at room temperature in the sealed bag in order to collect any free-running juice before you press it further.

Good for freeze-thawing: Rhubarb, quince, potato.

Fast Machine Juicing (Centrifugal Juicer)

Ideal for firm or fibrous ingredients, a centrifugal juicer slices and grinds the ingredient with a super-fast rotating blade and then spins the resulting pulp, forcing out the juice. The trade-off for that power and speed is the risk of oxidation. The forces at work in a centrifugal juicer introduce air into the ingredient, creating a bit of froth. Most of the froth subsides, leaving you with clear juice, but any introduction of air contributes to quicker oxidization, changing the flavour and color of your juice ever so slightly and potentially hastening spoilage.

As you feed your ingredient into the juicer, check occasionally to see whether fibrous matter is accumulating on the blades and remove it as needed.

Good for fast-juicing:
Fibrous vegetables such as peapod husks, or tough roots such as horseradish, ginger, and turmeric.

Horseradish Juice

Not the most common juice, but critically important to us, sweet-spicy horseradish juice is one that we have used on almost every menu since the beginning of Noma. In our early days, we avoided ingredients that did not come from our region, including black pepper and hot chiles. Horseradish was a common Scandinavian ingredient that could provide the pleasurable shock of pepper heat for us, so for years it was indispensable.

Horseradish root is quite fibrous, so a centrifugal juicer is required; you'll need to scrape off the fibers that collect during the juicing process so they don't clog up the machine. A note of caution: Allyl isothiocyanate, the spicy compound in horseradish (also found in mustards and wasabi), will fill the air as you juice the root, so wear goggles or take other precautions so you don't suffer a culinary teargas attack. We collect the horseradish pulp to use as a "cure" for radishes, horseradish's milder cousin in the brassica family.

Slow Machine Juicing (Masticating)

A masticating juicer (also called a cold-press juicer) works by slowly turning a screwlike auger that crushes the ingredients and presses the pulp through a filter. Slow juicers produce a slightly thicker juice than centrifugal juicers.

Slow juicers don't overheat the ingredients; this cooler process retains more nutrients, keeps colors truer, and avoids oxidation.

Good for slow-juicing: Sorrel; tender herbs such as lovage, parsley, and cilantro; nuts such as walnuts, hazelnuts, and almonds (when first blended with water into a slurry).

Clarifying by Boiling

Boiling is a simple method for clarifying fruit and vegetable juices. The high temperature will denature the proteins in the juice, which causes them to coagulate and clump together, allowing them to be easily skimmed off.

Skim the juice as it boils until mostly clear, then strain it through a fine-mesh nylon sieve.

Good for clarifying by boiling:
Rhubarb, celery, cucumber, and quince juices.

Ice-Clarifying

Ice-clarifying is an ingenious method for rendering liquids crystal clear, best used when you don't want to alter the flavour of the liquid by heating and skimming it. We use the technique to produce an expressive, pure liquid extraction from an otherwise cloudy medium, whether that's a juice, broth, lacto ferment, or other flavourful liquid. Open a refrigerator at Noma and you'll see multiple setups of frozen liquids suspended over containers to collect every drop of clarified broth or juice as it slowly melts out.

To ice-clarify, the liquid (juice or broth) is frozen into a block and then allowed to slowly thaw in a fine-mesh nylon sieve or cheesecloth suspended over a container to capture the clarified juice.

Pure water freezes at 0°C (32°F), but when the water contains other particles, the freezing point is lowered. Salt or sugar, for example, dissolved in water lowers the water's freezing point because the salt or sugar interferes with the formation of ice crystals. In the process of freezing a juice or broth, pure water freezes first and starts the formation of a lattice of ice, separating from the other particles, which concentrate and centralize in the ice. Freezing a liquid slowly (vs. in a blast chiller) produces larger, purer ice crystals, giving the solutes more time to separate and centralize. Conversely, freezing a liquid quickly may result in less efficient separation and potentially

Place the frozen block on a fine-mesh tamis set over a container or wrap the frozen block in cheesecloth and place it in a perforated gastro pan set over a deep gastro pan to catch the liquid as it thaws.

Refrigerate until fully thawed, capturing the juice in the lower container. Take care not to disturb the solids remaining in the tamis or cheesecloth after thawing.

a less clear broth. Whether you freeze your liquid slowly or quickly, it's critically important that the liquid is frozen solid or the process will be ineffective.

When the frozen liquid is thawed, the melting point of the mass is at its lowest, causing the concentrated sugars and flavour compounds to melt and drain first. As the sugars leave the mass, the freezing point of the mass increases, meaning that the last drippings of meltwater are mostly that: water. That being said, in order to maintain consistency in our recipes, we always allow the mass to completely thaw to ensure that the level of sugars in the finished solution is as congruent as possible across subsequent batches. It's also important to thaw your juice or broth in the refrigerator, or you run the risk of a cloudy liquid caused by thawing the mass too quickly, or wild yeast affecting the thawed liquid and potentially leading to spontaneous fermentation and off-flavours.

A side effect of this method is that pectin (if present in the original liquid) is clarified out as well, resulting in a liquid that won't become tacky when reduced to a glaze.

Good for ice-clarifying: Vegetables such as red pepper; fruits such as tomato and green gooseberries (blended with water); broths such as dashi.

PEASO
GREEN GOOSEBERRY

STRAWBERRY AND CHERRY
RED PEPPER

Suggested Uses

Fresh Fruit Juice Spritzer

Fill a tall glass with ice, pour in about 100 grams of your chosen juice (red gooseberry is pictured here), then top off the glass with sparkling water or sparkling wine.

Umami-Rich Farro with Peas and Prosciutto

Sauté chopped shallots in butter, add farro, and cook to toast the farro slightly. Ladle in some Yeast Broth (page 218) and cook until the farro is tender, adding more broth as needed. Fold in fresh English peas and diced prosciutto. Finish with some Parmigiano-Reggiano for even more umami.

Mussels Steamed in Broth, Tomato Water, and Pine Dashi

Pour some Mussel Broth (page 231), ice-clarified Tomato Water (page 488), and Pine Dashi (page 217) into a large pot (use mostly mussel broth, with the other two liquids as accents). Add a handful of chopped semi-dried tomatoes (see page 94) and bring to a boil. Add cleaned mussels, cover the pot, and steam until the mussels have opened. Finish with a handful of chopped fresh herbs and serve with grilled bread on the side.

Smoked Fish Potato Gratin

Thinly slice 2 or 3 leeks and sauté until tender; season lightly with salt and pepper. Slice a few potatoes about 5 mm (a scant ¼ inch) thick and arrange them in rows in a small baking dish and season lightly with salt. Tuck the sautéed leeks in between the rows of potato. Distribute a few sprigs of thyme over everything and pour over enough Smoked Fish Broth (page 229) to just barely cover the potatoes. Top with a few bits of butter, then cover the baking dish and bake in a moderate oven until the potatoes are very tender and have absorbed most of the broth.

Summer Crab Soup

Simmer fresh corn kernels, chopped onion, and finely chopped fresh green chiles in Crab Stock (page 230) until the vegetables are tender. Finish by adding a few spoonfuls of chopped fresh tomato and a sprinkling of chopped fresh cilantro.

Mushroom Noodle Broth

Make a pot of Maitake Broth (page 219), but don't strain out the mushrooms. Cook ramen noodles (or any type of noodle) in water until tender, then drain well and transfer to the broth. Serve hot.

Pages 242–243:
Ice-clarified waters and juices.
Opposite, top to bottom:
Fresh Fruit Juice Spritzer; Mussels Steamed in Broth, Tomato Water, and Pine Dashi
Right: Mushroom Noodle Broth

5.

Reductions, Skins, Caramels, and Fudges

Reductions, Skins, Caramels, and Fudges: Concentrating flavour for a new kind of seasoning

Before there was Noma, I worked in a small French restaurant in Copenhagen called Pierre André. It was an intimate space with just thirty seats, the kind of kitchen where you lived elbow to elbow with the other cooks. I was young, still learning, and for four years, I watched everything the chef, Philippe Houdet, did. Together, we ran the restaurant like a machine.

What stuck with me most was how Philippe built flavour. Every night when we left, the stoves would be lined with pots of stock: chicken, veal, oxtail, fish fumet. In the morning, we'd strain and reduce them, layer by layer, until they were as rich and deep as anything you'd find in the great kitchens of France. That was the foundation.

That method of layering flavour—slowly, carefully—is the backbone of most Western cooking. And it followed me for a long time. But at Noma, our path shifted, and we started wondering: What if we reduced things nobody else was reducing?

One of our first breakthroughs was reduced potato water. Lars Williams and Thomas Frebel were working on a dish in our Test Kitchen and discovered that if you clarified the liquid from juiced potatoes and reduced it slowly, it turned into a kind of syrup: sweet, savory, umami-rich. It was the first time we had tasted that kind of intensity from something so ordinary.

These reductions quickly became game changers, unlocking flavour, adding depth and complexity in ways that traditional stocks couldn't achieve. Something as simple as cucumber can slip in like a secret ingredient, adding richness without the cloying stickiness that meat-based sauces often leave behind.

Fresh Milk Skin, Grilled Rose Ice Cream, Berries, Vegetable, 2024
A tender fresh milk skin (Nordic yuba) is draped over grilled rose ice cream and served with wild strawberries, raspberries, tayberries, dewberries, lavender, and fresh rose petals.

Around the same time, Junichi Takahashi from the Test Kitchen brought in a dish during one of our Saturday-night project sessions. It was winter. Everyone was working late, presenting dishes to each other. I remember it was cold and quiet in the kitchen when Jun stepped up with a dish of cooked red peppers.

Barbecued King Crab with Rose Fudge, Ocean, 2025
King crab leg is first cured in koji and rose peaso, then poached in pine dashi, and finally grilled with rose oil and a mix of reductions. The crab is served with lemony Japanese quince and a silky rose fudge to be brushed onto the crabmeat.

A decade or so ago, red peppers in Denmark weren't exactly promising. In winter, they were usually bland and watery, so I wasn't expecting much. But when I tasted Jun's offering, I was shocked. I thought the peppers were spread with a thin layer of butter, but instead, he'd seasoned them with something entirely new—a kind of savory fudge. Velvety, deeply sweet, umami-rich. As powerful in flavour as a meat stock.

Jun had grown up in Japan with seasonings like miso and soy sauce, concentrated flavours used to finish dishes. And now here he was in Denmark, looking for something that could do the same. He mixed soft butter, a Nordic staple, with one of the new vegetable syrups we'd been experimenting with—and boy, did it work. It came together in a way that felt completely new on that late Saturday night.

More than a decade later, those savory fudges are everywhere in the kitchen. They're as important to us as soy sauce is to a sushi chef.

As with so many of the epiphanies that have shaped Noma into what it is today, one of the biggest began with an accident. We had just gotten a set of dehydrators, and I asked, "What happens if we dry stock instead of reducing it on the stove?"

So we tried it with chicken stock. The next morning, I found a thin, glassy layer at the bottom of the dehydrator tray. It cracked like sugar. Crispy chicken stock. The flavour was intense, but sticky. Too much. Too heavy.

We tried it with game stock next and learned that if you stop the drying at just the right moment, before the stock fully crisps, the result is like a caramel. Pipeable, spreadable, and deeply savory.

Over the years, we've made caramel with just about any broth or protein liquid you can imagine—rabbit, mussel, oyster.

The result of all this experimentation—reductions, skins, fudges, caramels—is a new kind of seasoning, the Nordic way of doing what the French do through a demi-glace, or what most of Asia does with soy sauce or the many versions of miso.

Every culture has its own way of concentrating time into flavour, whether through aging, fermenting, or boiling down to a single drop. And at Noma, these techniques offer a glimpse into the future of flavour that's both modern and rooted in tradition. Flavours built on the legacies of great kitchens like those of France and Japan. But it's also about challenging ourselves to see beyond the obvious, to push beyond what's known, opening doors to flavours that aren't just new, but necessary.

Reductions

For a cooking technique that takes the least amount of effort for the biggest reward, look no further than reductions. This (mostly) hands-off technique takes the flavour of the original ingredient, whether stock, juice, vinegar, or any other flavourful liquid, and dials it up to the max. We use reductions as secret weapons, slipping them into savory fudges and pastes, using them to glaze grilled foods or deliver a shot of umami to a dish that needs some punch.

Cucumber juice is reduced to a savory syrup.

Reducing is simply evaporating much or all of the water in a liquid, leaving you with more of the liquid's flavourful compounds, which could include sugars, amino acids (aka umami), and, in the case of animal-protein-based stocks, collagen. You can use a pan on the stovetop or a dehydrator to accomplish the goal; a dehydrator usually takes longer, but it avoids flavour changes that can occur with higher heat. Make sure your liquids are well skimmed and finely strained before reducing them.

Cucumber Reduction

Makes about 300 grams

4 kilograms cucumbers

Cucumber reduction evolved from our longtime practice of drying vegetables to add to vegetable stocks. We used dried cucumber frequently, so cucumber was a logical candidate for the Test Kitchen's experiments with reduced vegetable juices. When raw, cucumber has a nice combination of sweet and earthy flavours, but because the vegetable contains so much water, the flavours are very delicate, almost bland. When reduced, however, that combination becomes more intense yet stays nicely balanced, making it a versatile reduction for layering flavours in pastes, providing a vegetal backbone for fudges (see page 285), adding intense flavour to a sauce, or incorporating into a glaze for grilling.

Juice the cucumbers (skin on) with a centrifugal juicer and strain the juice through a fine-mesh nylon sieve into a large saucepan. Bring it to a simmer, skimming off the chlorophyll and other compounds that rise to the surface, then remove from the heat and let cool slightly. Strain the juice again through a fine-mesh nylon sieve. Pour the strained juice into shallow containers and place them in a dehydrator set to 60°C (140°F). Reduce the cucumber juice slowly until syrupy (about 60°Bx as measured by a refractometer); if you run a spatula through the reduction, it should leave a trail. Your actual yield will depend on how juicy and how sweet your cucumbers are. Use right away, keep refrigerated in an airtight container for up to 5 days, or freeze for longer-term storage.

Pass the skin-on cucumbers through a centrifugal juicer.

Strain the juice through a fine-mesh nylon sieve. Transfer to a large saucepan and bring to a simmer.

Strain the cucumber juice again, pour it into shallow containers (as Mette Søberg does here), and place the containers in a dehydrator set to 60°C (140°F).

Reduce the cucumber juice until syrupy (about 60°Bx as measured by a refractometer); if you run a spatula through it, it should leave a trail.

Simmer until a layer of chlorophyll develops on the surface, then skim off the chlorophyll.

Use the finished cucumber reduction right away, refrigerate in an airtight container for up to 5 days, or freeze.

Peaso Water Reduction

Makes about 300 grams

4 kilograms filtered water
600 grams Peaso*

The idea of a peaso reduction sprang from our process of making peaso. Barley koji and split peas are packed together in a container and compressed with a weight. As the mixture ferments, a liquid seeps up to the surface—it's essentially a tamari, a soy sauce–like liquid that's a by-product of miso making.

Our peaso tamari is delicious and full of umami, but the quantities are minimal . . . and we wanted more. So we devised a process to extract the flavour in liquid form, then reduced the liquid to intensify it. Peaso water reduction has many uses in the Noma kitchens: A simple gloss brushed onto steamed vegetables elevates them to another level. And a splash enhances almost any sauce with indescribable sweet-savoriness.

Blend the water and peaso together, transfer to an airtight container, and freeze. Remove the frozen brick from the container and place it on a tamis lined with a fine-mesh nylon sieve set over a clean container or hang it in a cheesecloth-lined perforated gastro pan set over a deep gastro pan to catch the liquid. Refrigerate for 2 to 3 days, until completely thawed.

Weigh the liquid, then transfer it to shallow containers and place them in a dehydrator set to 60°C (140°F). Reduce the peaso water to 8% of the liquid's initial weight (about 63°Bx as measured by a refractometer). Use right away, keep refrigerated in an airtight container for up to 5 days, or freeze for longer-term storage.

Dashi Reduction

Makes about 100 grams

Dashi Base
1 kilogram filtered water
15 grams fresh kelp
40 grams katsuobushi

Reduction
800 grams Dashi Base
100 grams Mushroom Garum*
100 grams sake
10 grams muscovado sugar

Noma creative director Thomas Frebel developed this reduction during his time in Japan, a culture in which dashi is fundamental. Reduced dashi is one more versatile and convenient source of umami in liquid form; it's a halfway point between liquid dashi and our Noma Umami Salt (page 113).

Dashi reduction is brilliant when added to pastes or used as an intense seasoning for sauces and other dishes. You can slip it in pretty much anywhere you want a subtle savory note. It's perfect with other seafood because of the katsuobushi in the reduction, but it also works well with vegetables and meat.

Make the dashi base: Combine the water and kelp in a pot and bring to a boil. Add the katsuobushi, turn off the heat, and let stand for 10 minutes to infuse. Strain the liquid through a fine-mesh nylon sieve.

Make the reduction: Combine the dashi base, garum, sake, and sugar in a saucepan and heat over low heat, swirling the pan until the sugar has dissolved. Transfer to a shallow container and place in a dehydrator set to 65°C (150°F). Reduce until the liquid reaches 67°Bx as measured by a refractometer. Use right away, keep refrigerated in an airtight container for up to 5 days, or freeze for longer-term storage.

Yeast Broth Reduction

Makes about 75 grams

800 grams filtered water
120 grams Peaso*
40 grams Roasted Yeast*
24 grams freeze-dried gooseberries

This is the reduction of the Yeast Broth (page 218) also developed by Thomas Frebel when he went in search of umami.

Place the water, peaso, yeast, and gooseberries in a Thermomix and blend until thoroughly homogenized. Transfer to an airtight container and freeze.

Remove the frozen brick of yeast broth from the container and place it on a tamis lined with a fine-mesh nylon sieve set over a clean container or hang it in a cheesecloth-lined perforated gastro pan set over a deep gastro pan to catch the liquid as it thaws. Let stand in the refrigerator for about 24 hours, until completely thawed.

Weigh the liquid, transfer it to a shallow container, and place in a dehydrator set to 60°C (140°F). Reduce to 8% of the liquid's initial weight (63°Bx as measured by a refractometer). Use right away, keep refrigerated in an airtight container for up to 5 days, or freeze for longer-term storage.

Beet Reduction

Makes 300 grams

1.5 kilograms beets
15 grams fresh kelp
3 grams freeze-dried black currants
10 grams green gooseberry juice
0.5 grams powdered pectin

Beets are a very Danish vegetable. They grow well here, and they last throughout the long winter in traditional root cellars. Here we have transformed them by roasting and then juicing them, reducing the beet juice, and combining the reduction with other ingredients that complement their sweet, deeply earthy flavour.

Peel the beets, wrap them in aluminum foil, and roast them in the oven at 200°C (390°F) until fully tender, about 1 hour. Let cool, then juice the beets with a centrifugal juicer and strain the juice through a conical sieve; you should have about 600 grams.

Combine the beet juice and the kelp in a small saucepan and bring it to a boil. Skim the juice, reduce the heat to maintain a low simmer, and cook until the liquid has reduced by half. Transfer the reduced beet juice to a Thermomix and add the black currants, gooseberry juice, and pectin. Blend until completely incorporated, then transfer the mixture to a saucepan. Bring it to a boil, reduce the heat to maintain a simmer, and cook until syrupy, about 10 minutes. Strain through a fine-mesh nylon sieve and let cool. Use right away, keep refrigerated in an airtight container for up to 5 days, or freeze for longer-term storage.

Blueberry (Bilberry) Reduction

Makes about 150 grams

2 kilograms wild blueberries (bilberries)

At Noma, fruit juice is used in both sweet and savory dishes. We use wild blueberries from Sweden (which aren't actually blueberries but a cousin called bilberries—the name "blueberry" just stuck). North Americans may forage a fruit called huckleberries, which have similar traits to Swedish bilberries.

The berries are ripe in late summer, well timed for dishes on our Forest menus, such as the grilled wild sika deer chops that we glazed with blueberry reduction and Smoked Butter (page 196) and served with Kelp Mushroom Truffle Sauce (page 395). Wild blueberries (and bilberries!) are very delicate when raw, which is why freezing and reducing them works well.

Blend the blueberries in a Thermomix until well pureed. Transfer the blueberry puree to 1-liter airtight containers, leaving room for expansion, and freeze. Remove the frozen blueberry puree from the container and place it on a tamis lined with a fine-mesh nylon sieve set over a clean container or hang it in a cheesecloth-lined perforated gastro pan set over a deep gastro pan to catch the liquid. Refrigerate for 1 to 2 days, until completely thawed. Wring out the thawed solids to extract all the remaining juice. Transfer the juice to shallow containers and dry in a dehydrator set to 60°C (140°F) until it reaches 80°Bx as measured by a refractometer. Your yield will depend on how juicy and sweet your blueberries are. Use right away, keep refrigerated in an airtight container for up to 5 days, or freeze for longer-term storage.

Shrimp Reduction

Makes about 100 grams

500 grams Shrimp Stock (page 227)

Years ago, we served a dish of sweet shrimp wrapped in steamed nasturtium leaves to resemble ravioli and paired with cured radish, Pine Vinegar (page 39), and Yeast Broth (page 218). Just before service, the chopped shrimp were seasoned with pine vinegar, salt, and a small spoonful of shrimp reduction to deepen their flavour. Seasoning an ingredient with a concentrated version of itself is a common technique in the Test Kitchen, and one that consistently yields dishes with remarkable depth and clarity.

Strain the stock through a fine-mesh nylon sieve into a nonstick saucepan. Cook over medium heat, stirring continuously with a silicone spatula, until the reduction coats the back of a spoon. Transfer the reduction to a small airtight container and refrigerate until it sets into a gel (like chicken stock). Use right away, keep refrigerated for up to 5 days, or freeze for longer-term storage.

As with many dishes at Noma, our skins began with inspiration from Japan. In Japanese cuisine, *yuba* (soy milk skins or tofu skins) are made by gently heating pans of soy milk until a skin forms on the surface. The skins are lifted off and dried, to be used as wrappers or fried until crispy, among many other delicious uses.

Milk is cooked to form a delicate caramelized skin.

We interpreted that Japanese tradition using an iconic Danish ingredient: cow's milk. We use these simple milk skins in dishes such as an assortment of grilled vegetables with a "crepe" of Nordic yuba draped over the top. We also make skins with a hotter method that results in a caramelizing of the milk sugars and proteins.

Our duck skins are an example of how we follow a concept down the rabbit hole. Noma chef Thomas Frebel was in pursuit of the savory flavours of reduced chicken stock and wound up creating these ethereal discs with intense meaty flavour.

Fresh Milk Skin (Nordic Milk Yuba)

Yield varies

800 grams organic whole milk
200 grams organic soy milk
30 grams milk protein powder

We have brought equipment back from our many trips to Japan, including a yuba machine, an electric double boiler that holds a consistent temperature. Before we had this machine, we would use saucepans on our induction stovetops to hold milk at a low temperature when making milk skins; you can do the same if you don't have a yuba machine.

When we make our milk skins, we add milk protein powder and a touch of soy milk to get the right balance of protein and liquid. The first few skins are quite fragile, but as the water content in the milk evaporates, the skins become sturdier. The delicate wrappers—Nordic yuba—impart their sweet, milky flavour to whatever is within.

Set a yuba machine to 85°C (185°F). Combine the milk, soy milk, and milk protein powder in a container and blend with an immersion blender. Strain the mixture through a fine-mesh nylon sieve, then transfer it to the yuba machine. If you don't have a yuba machine, heat the mixture in a large saucepan over low heat to 85°C (185°F). Cook the liquid at this temperature for 10 minutes, then skim off the first skin and any bubbles that rise to the surface.

Adjust the heat to lower the temperature of the milk mixture to 75°C (165°F) and cook, fanning the surface of the liquid, for 10 to 12 minutes more, until a second skin forms on the surface. Using your fingers, lift the skin and lay it on a sheet of oiled parchment paper, with the top side of the skin facing down. Repeat, making as many skins as you can (and using more oiled parchment as needed) until you can no longer produce skins with the consistency that you want due to changes in the protein content of the evaporating milk.

Let the skins dry for about 20 minutes and then cut them into portions according to your desired use. The skins should be used the same day you make them, but will keep in the refrigerator for up to a few hours.

Caramelized Milk Skin

Makes 4 skins

Rice Slurry
50 grams sushi rice
50 grams water

Milk Skin
20 grams Rice Slurry
1 kilogram whole milk (3.5% fat, if possible)

A natural progression from our Nordic yuba (page 266), these caramelized milk skins are made using higher heat, which reduces the milk more quickly and caramelizes the milk sugars, creating a golden brown color and a caramel flavour. Because no sugar is added, caramelized milk skins are useful for both savory and sweet applications. Make sure you're using a pristine nonstick pan—no chips or scratches. A light spritz of water is useful when removing the skin from the pan, but try not to use it while the milk is reducing and caramelizing or you run the risk of the skin sticking. The finished skin should be sprayed with water to make it more pliable and easier to store.

In an early dish featuring caramelized milk skins, we shaped the skins into cups (the way you might shape a tuile to fill with fruit and cream), dried them in a dehydrator until crisp, and then filled them with delicate ribbons of frozen smoked cod liver, all seasoned with a tiny bit of Noma Umami Salt (page 113). The delight came from the textural contrast between the smooth shaved cod liver and the crisp, sweet milk skins. We've also used caramelized milk skins as a sort of dumpling wrapper, draped around soft cheese and herbs, and topped with preserved truffle, or to encase seared reindeer brains as a delicate handheld pie.

Make the rice slurry: Blend the rice and water in a Thermomix until thoroughly homogenized. Strain the mixture through a fine-mesh nylon sieve.

Make the milk skin: Mix the rice slurry very well, as it may have settled. Combine the milk and slurry and mix well, without incorporating too much air.

Heat a 28 cm (11-inch) nonstick pan over high heat until just before the pan begins to smoke. Pour in 230 grams of the milk mixture; the liquid will begin to flash boil. Reduce the heat to very low. When steam begins to waft from the milk mixture, set the burner to 100°C (212°F) and cook until the mixture forms a lightly caramelized skin, about 30 minutes. Spray the skin with water to moisten it and render it pliable, then carefully loosen it from the sides of the pan with a stiff rubber spatula. After loosening it, you can pull it back from the pan with your fingers and transfer it to a sheet of parchment paper. Top with another sheet of parchment, wipe out the pan, and repeat, using 230 grams of the milk mixture for each skin.

Duck Skin

Makes 3 to 5 kilograms stock, up to 200 skins (yield is highly variable)

5 whole chickens
5 whole ducks
5 kilograms chicken wings

At Noma, a duck skin isn't *really* a duck skin (no surprise) but it has the same addictive, savory flavour as actual crispy roasted duck skin or the caramelized drippings at the bottom of the pan after you've roasted a plump chicken. The difference is the delicate texture of a Noma duck skin, which at first bite is crisp like a thin sheet of ice and then disappears as soon as it hits your tongue.

You can create this intense poultry flavour by reducing stock until it becomes a demi-glace, as you would in a French kitchen. The collagen in meat means the texture of a meat-based demi-glace is quite tacky and sticks to your mouth, so we attempted to replicate that addictive flavour but with a light, crisp, glasslike texture. The result was our duck skin (which we make with duck and chicken).

The process is elaborate and involves making a stock the "wrong" way—wrong in the eyes of a classically trained French chef, anyway. Rather than simmering your vegetables and poultry bones gently, skimming off the foam and fat that rise to the surface, and aiming for a clear broth, here we boil the stock hard, which incorporates more fat and proteins into the liquid, making it cloudy. It's a bit like making a good tonkatsu pork broth for Japanese ramen. In our duck skin method, we skim the fat, reduce the broth, and then add back the fat. In addition to all this boiling, skimming, reducing, and enriching, we throw in some whirlpool-making . . . and probably a bit of magic. The process certainly seems alchemical, and to be honest, not every Noma cook is able to create a duck skin, so if you try these, don't be discouraged if you don't succeed at first. You'll still have a pot of tasty and protein-rich stock.

Put the whole chickens, ducks, and chicken wings in a couple of large stockpots, add cold water to cover, and bring to a boil. Skim the stock lightly to remove any foamy scum, then boil the stock vigorously for 1 hour. Reduce the heat to maintain a gentle simmer and cook the stock overnight (or for at least 12 hours). Strain the stock through a fine conical strainer into a clean container; discard the solids. Let the stock rest, undisturbed, until it has settled.

Skim off the fat from the surface and reserve it. Transfer the skimmed stock to a medium stockpot and return it to a simmer. Simmer until the stock has reduced to a light glaze the color of caramel. Remove from the heat and strain the glaze.

Transfer about 800 grams of the glaze to a medium saucepan and add a heaping spoonful of the reserved fat. Bring the mixture to a boil, stirring with a metal spoon as its temperature rises. When the mixture is close to boiling, swirl it with the spoon to create a whirlpool. When it reaches a boil, turn off the heat and let stand, completely undisturbed, until a skin has formed on the surface, about 15 minutes. Using a palette knife, carefully cut the skin away from the sides of the pot, then use the palette knife to lift it free and carefully transfer it to a parchment paper square. Top with another parchment paper square and set aside. Repeat the boiling-swirling-resting process to produce more skins. Note that the first few skins you produce will be quite brittle. They will become thicker naturally as the amount of fat in the pan and the glaze itself reduce. This balance can be adjusted by adding spoonfuls of fresh glaze or additional fat. At this stage, the skins can be reserved in the refrigerator for up to a few hours before crisping. *(Recipe continues)*

To crisp a duck skin, heat a nonstick skillet over the lowest possible heat. Peel off one piece of parchment from a duck skin, then place the skin in the pan parchment-side down (yes, you're cooking the parchment along with the skin). Cook until the skin bubbles gently and begins to crisp. Use a palette knife to carefully pick up the parchment square with the duck skin attached. Invert the crispy skin onto a new parchment square and remove the "cooked" parchment square. Place the skin (on its new parchment square) on a dehydrator tray; repeat the process until you have filled the tray. Dry the skins in a dehydrator set to 60°C (140°F) until completely crisp. (Alternatively, skip crisping the skins in a pan and just lay them on a parchment-lined dehydrator tray. Dry in the dehydrator until completely crisp; this will take a few hours.)

Once crisp, use the skins as needed; they can be held at 60°C (140°F) until you're ready to use them, but humidity will cause them to become soggy. The skins can be easily cut into different shapes using a small paring knife or the edge of a palette knife, depending on how you plan to use them.

Place the reduced duck-chicken glaze in a medium saucepan.

Add a heaping spoonful of the reserved fat and bring the mixture to a boil, stirring with a metal spoon.

When the glaze is almost boiling, swirl it with the spoon to create a whirlpool. Turn off the heat and let stand, undisturbed, until a skin forms on the surface.

Carefully cut the skin from the sides of the pot using a palette knife and gently transfer the skin to a square of parchment. Repeat the process to make additional skins.

Caramels

What if you could make a reduction of a reduction? At Noma, our savory caramels are just that: flavourful liquids reduced beyond a simple glaze, to the point where the sugars and proteins are transformed by heat into something much deeper and darker—a malleable, pipeable, savory toffee.

Mussel caramel in its final stage.

Making a caramel takes careful management, because too much reducing results in bitterness.
We finish the reduction in hot oil to prevent it from sticking to the pan, allowing us to push the reduction to the absolute edge, where all water content is gone and all that remains are the savory proteins, amino acids, and sugars.

Caramels add a punch of flavour to a dish with just a small potent droplet. Our first savory caramels were most often used during the Forest season, but they also found their way into the Ocean season, where we made them using oysters, mussels, and shrimp.

Rabbit Caramel

Makes about 100 grams

1 whole rabbit, butchered into small pieces
Butter
1 kilogram Cold-Infused Dashi (page 215)
15 grams dried ceps
10 grams fresh lemon thyme
2 grams juniper wood
1 apple, coarsely chopped
20 grams Cep Oil (page 164)

One of our early savory caramels was made from rabbit. Former Noma sous chef Riccardo Canella reduced a beautiful rabbit stock until it was insanely intense with rabbity flavour and then combined it with a spiced oil. We served the rabbit caramel in a deceptively simple dish of semi-dried tomatoes and strawberries (see page 94) into which the caramel was piped. The dried fruit was arranged in a ramekin; its appearance was unassuming, but its flavour was otherworldly.

Arrange the rabbit pieces on a wire rack in a roasting pan, top each piece with butter, and roast in a combi oven at 190°C (375°F; 100% fan) on dry heat until well browned. Remove the rabbit from the oven and let cool. Transfer the rabbit to a rondeau and add the dashi, dried ceps, lemon thyme, juniper wood, and apple. Bring to a boil, then reduce the heat to low and simmer the stock for 1 hour. Strain the stock through a tamis lined with a fine-mesh nylon sieve and measure its volume. Pour the strained stock into a clean pot and simmer over medium heat until reduced by about 80%. Strain the reduced stock.

Heat the cep oil in a nonstick skillet over medium heat. Slowly add the reduced stock and cook, stirring continuously with a silicone spatula to prevent the stock from spattering, until all the water has evaporated and the reduction has become thick and fudgy. Be careful not to overreduce the stock or it can become bitter. Transfer to an airtight container and let cool. Use right away or refrigerate for up to 2 days.

Arrange the rabbit pieces on a rack in a roasting pan and top each piece with butter. Roast the rabbit at 190°C (375°F) until well browned.

Transfer the rabbit to a rondeau and add the dashi, dried ceps, lemon thyme, juniper wood, and apple; bring to a boil, then reduce the heat and simmer for 1 hour.

Cook over medium heat until the stock has reduced in volume by about 80 percent.

Strain the reduced rabbit stock.

Strain the rabbit stock through a tamis lined with a fine-mesh nylon sieve (as Nate French does here).

Measure the volume of the strained stock and pour the stock into a clean pot.

Heat the cep oil in a nonstick skillet over medium heat. Slowly add the reduced rabbit stock to the oil.

Cook, stirring continuously, until the reduction is thick and fudgy. Let cool, then use right away or refrigerate in an airtight container for up to 2 days.

Bearamel

Makes about 100 grams

400 grams bear meat (ideally with a high meat-to-fat ratio), cut into 4 cm (1½-inch) cubes
2 kilograms Cold-Infused Dashi (page 215)
30 grams dried ceps
20 grams fresh lemon thyme
4 grams juniper wood
2 apples
40 grams Cep Oil (page 164)

After a research trip to Japan during which we dined on bear hot pot at a hunters lodge, we were eager to explore the notion of serving bear in Scandinavia. This bear caramel is part of a rather distinct dish, the Bear and Duck Skin Baba. It's essentially an aebleskiver—a round Danish pancake—moistened with bear consommé and served with a spoonful of bearamel on the side.

Place the bear meat on a wire rack set over a parchment-lined sheet pan and roast in the oven at 190°C (375°F; 100% fan) for about 30 minutes, until well caramelized. Transfer to a rondeau and add the dashi, dried ceps, lemon thyme, juniper wood, and apples. Bring to a boil, then reduce the heat to maintain a simmer and cook for 1 hour. Strain the stock through a fine-mesh nylon sieve and measure its volume. Pour the stock into a clean pot and simmer over medium heat until reduced by 80%. Transfer the reduced stock to a container.

Heat the cep oil in a nonstick skillet over medium heat until the oil shimmers lightly. Slowly add the reduced bear stock and cook, stirring continuously with a silicone spatula to prevent the stock from spattering, until all the water has evaporated and the reduction has become thick and fudgy. Be careful not to overreduce the stock or it can become bitter. Transfer the reduction to an airtight container and let cool, then cover. Use right away or refrigerate for up to 2 days.

Place the mussels, wine, and kelp in a rondeau, cover, and bring to a boil. Reduce the heat and simmer until the mussels are cooked; strain the cooking liquid into a container.

Pour the mussel stock into a large skillet. Add the peaso reduction and umami salt.

Bring the mussel stock to a simmer, stirring frequently and skimming any foam from the surface.

Simmer the mussel stock until thick, glossy, and reduced to the consistency of soft caramel. Let cool, then use right away or refrigerate in an airtight container for up to 2 days.

Mussel Caramel

Makes 100 grams

Mussel Stock
2.5 kilograms mussels
750 grams white wine
2 grams fresh kelp

Mussel Caramel
500 grams Mussel Stock
6 grams Peaso Water Reduction (page 258)
2 grams Noma Umami Salt (page 113)

Mussel caramel is made with just a few ingredients: mussels steamed in white wine with a bit of kelp for extra umami. The resulting liquid is delicious and can be ice-clarified (see page 240) and used as a broth, but for mussel caramel, we often just filter the broth and then cook it down with peaso water reduction and Noma umami salt.

Make the mussel stock: Rinse any grit from the mussels, scrubbing them as necessary, and remove any visible beards. Heat a large rondeau over high heat. Add the mussels, wine, and kelp. Cover and agitate the pot to stir the mussels around. Reduce the heat to medium and cook until the mussels open and release their juices, 3 to 4 minutes. Reduce the heat to low and simmer for 10 minutes more. Remove from the heat and let cool, still covered, for 10 minutes. Strain the liquid through a conical strainer, then strain again through a tamis lined with a fine-mesh nylon sieve into a container set over an ice bath to rapidly cool the stock. (The stock can be reserved in the refrigerator for up to 2 days.)

Make the mussel caramel: Combine the mussel stock, peaso water reduction, and umami salt in a large nonstick skillet. Bring to a simmer over medium heat, stirring frequently and skimming off any foam, then cook, stirring continuously, until it becomes thick and glossy and has the consistency of soft caramel. Transfer the reduction to an airtight container and let cool. Use right away or refrigerate for up to 2 days.

Fudges

A savory fudge at Noma is a vessel for flavour, one that doesn't seem to have an analog in other parts of the culinary world. Test Kitchen head Junichi Takahashi invented the first Noma fudge during a Test Kitchen session, where the chefs let their imaginations roam. That fudge became a template for many other fudges, all (or most) based on a quartet of ingredients: a vegetable reduction, oil, Peaso Water Reduction (page 258), and butter. The other chefs took this formula and riffed on it like mad. Cucumbers gave way to other vegetables; neutral oil expanded to include flavourful oils such as chili oil, mushroom oil, and rose oil; and simple unsalted butter was replaced with more potently flavoured brown butter and even beeswax.

Savory fudge has a silky sheen and is creamy and pipable.

Top to bottom:
Black currant wood fudge, morita chile fudge, vegetable fudge.

The key for the cook is to hold fudge at the proper texture and temperature—silky and emulsified, pipeable like buttercream frosting. It's a surprising roller coaster of creamy, savory, acidic, sweet, and umami all wrapped into one bite. The cook also needs to pay attention to the temperature of the ingredient or dish on which the fudge will be served. Black currant wood fudge would be delicious on raw fish, but if the fish is too cold, the butter in the fudge will solidify and the texture won't be right. Conversely, if the main ingredient is too hot, the fudge's emulsion will break and the flavours lose their balance. Room-temperature to slightly warm ingredients are ideal, though there are exceptions to this rule. A pat of cold elderflower fudge is the perfect complement to a freshly cooked Danish new potato.

Vegetable Fudge

Makes 80 grams

35 grams unsalted butter, at room temperature
20 grams Peaso Water Reduction (page 258)
15 grams neutral oil
10 grams Cucumber Reduction (page 255)

Think of this as the "master recipe" for fudge. The formula was developed by Junichi Takahashi, head of Noma's Test Kitchen, and once Jun had worked out the winning proportions, it was easy for the other chefs to create variations.

Bring a saucepan of water to a simmer and set up an ice bath. Combine the butter, peaso water reduction, oil, and cucumber reduction in a heatproof bowl that will fit over the saucepan. Begin off the heat, whisking thoroughly but gently, without aerating the mixture. If the butter isn't blending well, set the bowl over the simmering water for a few seconds and whisk to soften it; conversely, if the mixture looks too loose and at risk of separating, whisk it over the ice bath. Continue gently whisking until the fudge is thick and creamy but not stiff. Use right away or transfer to an airtight container and reserve in the refrigerator for up to 5 days.

Linseed Fudge

Makes 195 grams

20 grams Noma Roasted Umami Salt (page 115)
35 grams Celery Reduction*
20 grams Linseed Oil (page 153)
20 grams Cep Oil (page 164)
100 grams Brown Butter (page 198), cut into pieces, at room temperature

When Test Kitchen head Mette Søberg was developing a celeriac dish—our Celeriac Shawarma—for the 2018 Vegetable season, she created a fudge to sandwich between thin slices of the root vegetable. Instead of the standard cucumber reduction, Mette used reduced celery juice to echo the flavour of the celeriac. She then amped up the flavours of the other fudge elements, using linseed and cep oils and brown butter, and adding roasted umami salt for a salty-savory note and roasty flavours.

Place the umami salt in a mortar and crush it with the pestle. Add the celery reduction and muddle it with the crushed salt until smooth, then repeat with the linseed oil and the cep oil. Add the brown butter and pound with the pestle to incorporate it with the mixture. Use a whisk to finish working the butter into the mixture until completely incorporated. Use right away or transfer to an airtight container and reserve in the refrigerator for up to 5 days.

Place the roasted umami salt in a mortar and grind with the pestle until you have a coarse paste.

Add the celery reduction and work it into the salt with the pestle until smooth. Add the linseed oil, followed by the cep oil, blending the ingredients with the pestle.

Pound the brown butter to blend it into the mixture.

Use a whisk to finish working the butter into the mixture until completely incorporated.

Add the brown butter.

Use the linseed fudge right away or refrigerate in an airtight container for up to 5 days.

Elderflower Fudge

Makes 80 grams

35 grams unsalted butter, at room temperature
20 grams Peaso Water Reduction (page 258)
15 grams Elderflower Oil (page 179)
10 grams Cucumber Reduction (page 255)

This fudge uses three of the original four ingredients in Junichi Takahashi's formula (see page 285), but swaps the neutral oil for fragrant elderflower oil.

Bring a saucepan of water to a simmer and set up an ice bath. Combine the butter, peaso water reduction, elderflower oil, and cucumber reduction in a heatproof bowl that will fit over the saucepan. Begin off the heat, whisking thoroughly but gently, without aerating the mixture. If the butter isn't blending well, set the bowl over the simmering water for a few seconds and whisk to soften it; conversely, if the mixture looks too loose and at risk of separating, whisk it over the ice bath. Continue gently whisking until the fudge is thick and creamy but not stiff. Use right away or transfer to an airtight container and reserve in the refrigerator for up to 5 days.

Black Currant Wood Fudge

Makes 80 grams

35 grams unsalted butter, at room temperature
20 grams Peaso Water Reduction (page 258)
15 grams Black Currant Wood Oil (page 193)
10 grams Cucumber Reduction (page 255)

Black currant wood fudge was the first flavoured fudge we developed after Test Kitchen head Junichi Takahashi perfected the foundational ratio for vegetable-based fudges (see page 285). We realized the power of a fudge not just as a singular flavour expression, but as a flexible template for embedding any aromatic fat into a smooth, rich medium. Black currant wood is a particularly important flavour to us, but the real breakthrough was realizing how fudge could act as a carrier, elongating flavour, adding body, and delivering a lasting finish to a dish.

Bring a saucepan of water to a simmer and set up an ice bath. Combine the butter, peaso water reduction, black currant wood oil, and cucumber reduction in a heatproof bowl that will fit over the saucepan. Begin off the heat, whisking thoroughly but gently, without aerating the mixture. If the butter isn't blending well, set the bowl over the simmering water for a few seconds and whisk to soften it; conversely, if the mixture looks too loose and at risk of separating, whisk it over the ice bath. Continue gently whisking until the fudge is thick and creamy but not stiff. Use right away or transfer to an airtight container and reserve in the refrigerator for up to 5 days.

Bear Aebleskiver with Duck Skin and Bearamel, Forest, 2022
A bear consommé-soaked aebleskiver is topped with a delicate duck skin, dotted with bearamel (bear caramel), and served alongside bearamel piped onto an autumn leaf.

Grilled Spring Peas on the Half Shell with Koji Fudge, Vegetable, 2024
Fresh English peas are brushed with smoked butter and lightly grilled, then dressed with koji fudge and horseradish juice and garnished with thyme flowers and pea flowers.

Rose Fudge

Makes 80 grams

35 grams unsalted butter, at room temperature
20 grams Peaso Water Reduction (page 258)
15 grams Rose Oil (page 187)
10 grams Cucumber Reduction (page 255)

One of the most memorable uses of rose fudge was in our dish of Faroese sea urchin, freshly peeled pumpkin seeds, and cold cream. Years ago, we discovered how beautifully the sweet, briny flavour of sea urchin paired with rose oil, but transforming that oil into a fudge gave the combination a new depth. The butter stretches the aromatic quality of the rose, allowing its floral notes to linger long after the dish is finished. Rose fudge is a staple in the Test Kitchen pantry, one we reach for when we want to add nuance, richness, and a lasting finish to a dish.

Bring a saucepan of water to a simmer and set up an ice bath. Combine the butter, peaso water reduction, rose oil, and cucumber reduction in a heatproof bowl that will fit over the saucepan. Begin off the heat, whisking thoroughly but gently, without aerating the mixture. If the butter isn't blending well, set the bowl over the simmering water for a few seconds and whisk to soften it; conversely, if the mixture looks too loose and at risk of separating, whisk it over the ice bath. Continue gently whisking until the fudge is thick and creamy but not stiff. Use right away or transfer to an airtight container and reserve in the refrigerator for up to 5 days.

Morita Chile Fudge

Makes 80 grams

35 grams unsalted butter, at room temperature
20 grams Peaso Water Reduction (page 258)
15 grams Morita Chile Oil*
10 grams Cucumber Reduction (page 255)

This fudge base can be adapted to any flavoured oil, but morita chile became a standout after our work in Mexico. Its name, Spanish for "little blackberry," reflects its dark color and subtle berrylike flavour. When used in this fudge, the oil's smoky heat is extended and softened by the butter, creating a smooth, lingering richness on the palate. We've paired morita chile fudge with grilled peas, but its uses are broad and endlessly adaptable. It would be fantastic, for example, brushed on raw seafood such as sea urchin or shrimp or spread on grilled flatbread and topped with fresh herbs and lightly cooked vegetables—perhaps slices of yellow beet, zucchini, and baby cucumber.

Bring a saucepan of water to a simmer and set up an ice bath. Combine the butter, peaso water reduction, morita chile oil, and cucumber reduction in a heatproof bowl that will fit over the saucepan. Begin off the heat, whisking thoroughly but gently, without aerating the mixture. If the butter isn't blending well, set the bowl over the simmering water for a few seconds and whisk to soften it; conversely, if the mixture looks too loose and at risk of separating, whisk it over the ice bath. Continue gently whisking until the fudge is thick and creamy but not stiff. Use right away or transfer to an airtight container and reserve in the refrigerator for up to 5 days.

Scallop Fudge

Makes about 300 grams

1 kilogram scallops
Neutral oil
Beeswax

At first glance, this fudge looks like an outlier when compared with the Vegetable Fudge (page 288) template. In fact, it was the first fudge we made prior to the Test Kitchen's Junichi Takahashi nailing the base recipe. We don't start by reducing liquid vegetable juice, but instead reduce the scallops themselves through dehydration, which accomplishes the same goal of eliminating water to intensify flavours.

The process came from our efforts to reduce waste. We were serving a dish called Scallop Chips and Ancient Grains; the "chips" were made by freezing raw scallops, slicing them into thin wafers, and dehydrating them until caramelized and crisp. It was impossible to use 100% of each scallop to get properly sized chips, so the chefs were left with nubs of perfectly good scallop. After some experimentation, Noma creative director Thomas Frebel blended the nubs into a puree, thinly spread the puree onto dehydrator trays, and dried it until crisp. And then (because why stop there?) he pulverized the scallop crisps into a powder.

The scallop powder is the equivalent of the reduced vegetable juice called for in the four-ingredient fudge template. Thomas added oil to that scallop "reduction," and instead of butter, he suggested using a small amount of beeswax, which would create a firm though still scoopable consistency when cold. The first dish that featured scallop fudge was grilled ramsons brushed with Smoked Butter (page 196) and then dressed

with warm scallop fudge, a touch more smoked butter, a few drops of horseradish juice, and plenty of flaky salt.

Puree the scallop meat in a Thermomix until smooth, adding water as necessary to ensure the scallops puree evenly (the water will evaporate during dehydration). Spread the puree in a thin layer over nonstick dehydrator mats, covering them from edge to edge, then place the mats on dehydrator trays. Dry in a dehydrator set to 60°C (140°F) until completely crisp. Transfer the scallop crisps to a blender, breaking them into pieces to fit, and blend until powdered. Pass the powder through a fine-mesh nylon sieve, using a whisk to press it through.

Weigh the scallop powder and place it in a Thermomix. Add twice that weight in oil. Set the Thermomix to 60°C (140°F) and begin blending on medium-high speed. When the Thermomix reaches 60°C (140°F), transfer the mixture to a bowl. Measure enough beeswax to equal 3.5% of the total weight of the scallop-oil mixture. Whisk the beeswax into the warm mixture bit by bit, whisking until each addition is fully incorporated before adding the next. Set the bowl over an ice bath and let cool. Use right away, refrigerate in an airtight container for up to 5 days, or freeze for longer-term storage.

Puree the scallops in a Thermomix until smooth, adding water to ensure the scallops puree evenly. Scrape out the scallop puree from the Thermomix, keeping it on ice.

Cover your work surface with plastic wrap. Spread the scallop puree onto nonstick dehydrator mats, covering the mats from edge to edge. Place the mats on dehydrator trays.

Blend the scallop crisps until completely pulverized into a powder. Pass the powder through a fine-mesh nylon sieve, using a whisk to work all the powder through the sieve.

Weigh the scallop powder and place it in a Thermomix. Add twice that weight in oil. Set the Thermomix to 60°C (140°F) and blend on medium-high speed until the mixture reaches 60°C (140°F). Pour into a bowl, keeping it warm.

Dry the puree in a dehydrator set to 60°C (140°F) until completely crisp.

Break the scallop crisps into smaller pieces and place them in a blender.

Measure enough beeswax to equal 3.5% of the total weight of the scallop powder and oil, breaking it into pieces. Whisk the beeswax into the scallop mixture piece by piece until smooth, whisking until each addition is melted before adding the next.

Use the scallop fudge right away, refrigerate in an airtight container for up to 5 days, or freeze.

Suggested Uses

Bread Steak with Cucumber Reduction

Heat some oil in a skillet and fry slices of good bread until lightly browned. Drizzle Cucumber Reduction (page 255) over the bread and cook for a few minutes more so the bread soaks up the reduction and becomes a chewy, savory "steak."

Richer Shrimp Bisque or Cocktail

Add Shrimp Reduction (page 263) to intensify the shellfish flavour of a shrimp bisque, or even add a bit to your favorite cocktail sauce for shrimp cocktail.

Milk Skin "Tacos"

Arrange a few thin slices of char siu or other sliced BBQ pork onto half of a Caramelized Milk Skin (page 268). Add a few fresh tender herbs, maybe some pea tendrils, and lightly dress everything with horseradish juice (see page 237). Fold the milk skin to enclose the fillings and serve like a taco.

Celeriac Glazed with Rabbit Caramel

Toss thick slices or cubes of celeriac with melted butter, season lightly with salt and pepper, and roast in a moderate oven. When it seems close to tender, glaze the celeriac with Rabbit Caramel (page 277) to add a rich layer of savory sweetness.

New Potatoes with Elderflower Fudge

Boil some new potatoes in salted water until tender. Pile into a bowl and top with several slices of Elderflower Fudge (page 292). Serve before the fudge has had a chance to melt.

Grilled Peas with Scallop Fudge

Carefully shuck English peas so that they're "on the half shell": Remove one side of the peapod, leaving the peas attached to the stem. Brush the exterior with a bit of Smoked Butter (page 196) and lightly grill the peas, pod-side down, until they start to blister, then flip them and grill for 10 seconds (taking care that the peas don't fall off). Remove from the grill. Lightly dress the peas with warm Scallop Fudge (page 298), a touch more smoked butter, a few drops of horseradish juice (see page 237), and a sprinkling of salt.

Opposite, top to bottom:
Bread Steak with Cucumber Reduction; Milk Skin "Tacos"; New Potatoes with Elderflower Fudge
Right: Grilled Peas with Scallop Fudge

6.

Pastes

Pastes: Rethinking traditional tools, creating new intensity

Yellow Beet Crisp, Vegetable, 2024
Golden beets are roasted with roasted kelp oil and rested overnight in rose oil. They're thinly sliced and folded across an elderflower peaso crisp dressed with vegetable fudge, crispy seeds, aromatic herbs, ants, and pumpkin bushi paste.

It's November 2003. Noma is about to open. The budget is razor-thin. We are just seven people, front and back of the house combined. I'm twenty-five years old, and apart from Ali Sonko—the veteran in the kitchen—I might be the eldest among us. We are young, hungry to achieve, and desperate for the latest gadgets, like the newest sous-vide machine or a freeze dryer. These tools felt like the key to unlocking something greater . . . tools that were far beyond our reach in those lean early years. Eventually, we acquired more technology, relying for our first decade on high-tech blenders, spice grinders, and the ubiquitous Robot-Coupe.

These tools seemed essential at the time, but in early 2012, everything started to change. I was on one of my trips to Mexico, a country I had visited countless times. But this time, something clicked. I came back to Denmark and told the Test Kitchen team that for the next while, we should use a mortar and pestle for everything that we'd been using a machine to blend. I'd tasted the vibrant flavours in the markets and kitchens of Yucatán so many times before, but on that trip, it dawned on me that it wasn't just the fantastic ingredients in Mexico creating those flavours—it also had to be the mortar and pestle.

There's nothing revolutionary about using a mortar and pestle. It's as ancient as cooking itself, a technique that spans cultures and continents. Here in the Nordics, it was traditionally used to grind grain into flour, but in the Denmark of my youth, we saw the mortar and pestle as something distinctly Southern European, an artifact from a kitchen in Tuscany or Provence, perhaps, where it might be used to make pesto or aioli. Certainly not a tool used in the minimalist, practical kitchens of Scandinavia.

Jellyfish Pie with Caramelized Milk Skin and Green Gooseberry Paste, Ocean, 2025
A pie is made from caramelized milk skin shell spread with green gooseberry paste and topped with a small hosta leaf compressed in marjoram oil and a fresh jellyfish.

But when you hand a mortar and pestle to a group of curious cooks, the world quickly starts to look different. We discovered that pounding fresh herbs in a mortar, rather than blending them, created flavours that were different, more vibrant and alive. We also found out that when the mortar and pestle had been chilled before use, it worked particularly well. That led us to freezing the herbs themselves with liquid nitrogen. Grinding them with the mortar and pestle produced a paste that was unlike anything we had tasted before, so raw and intensely flavourful. The texture was amazing.

We continued experimenting with these herb pastes, adding elements like yeast reductions for a hit of umami, and we stumbled upon flavours that were at once familiar and entirely new—like parsley paste. What was once an ordinary component in our kitchen became a revelation. Now we could capture the flavour of parsley, but ten times more intense. Using the mortar and pestle wasn't just a new way of making a paste or seasoning. It was a new way for us to think about flavour, about tools and how we use them.

In the past decade or so, we've pounded just about anything that can fit into a mortar and pestle or a stone grinder. We've transformed the common Danish wood ant into a powerful seasoning used in savory and sweet applications. We've boiled and then pounded fresh chestnuts until they turn into a mochi-like dough. And now, reflecting on this twenty years on, I find it remarkable how linked this whole category of flavourings—pastes—is to one of the oldest food preparation methods, grinding food between two stones. Our rediscovery of this tool has given us one of the most indispensable techniques in our kitchen, helping push Noma forward.

309

Place the parsley in a mortar and freeze with liquid nitrogen. As the leaves begin to freeze, pound and grind them with the pestle, adding more liquid nitrogen as needed to fully freeze the leaves.

Continue grinding until you have a fine powder. Add the yeast broth reduction and stir until fully blended.

Add the parsley oil and muddle with the pestle until the oil is combined and the paste is emulsified.

Use the paste the same day you make it (refrigerate it in an airtight container if not using immediately).

Parsley Paste

Makes 115 grams

50 grams fresh flat-leaf parsley leaves
Liquid nitrogen
25 grams Yeast Broth Reduction (page 260)
40 grams Parsley Oil (page 178)

The simple parsley paste is a Noma essential. The combination of yeast broth reduction—a liquid form of umami—with fresh parsley and parsley oil results in a workhorse flavouring that delivers an herbaceous punch with a light acidity. Parsley paste can be used to build a dish or finish a dish, or as a condiment on its own. A teaspoon of parsley paste makes the flavours of a freshly roasted langoustine or lobster tail sing. Add a bit to pesto Genovese to deepen the herbal dimension or a small dollop to a freshly shucked oyster to perfectly balance its brininess.

A key step in this recipe is freezing the parsley leaves with liquid nitrogen before grinding them in a mortar, which creates a brittle consistency that allows you to achieve a finer texture than you would if grinding room-temperature parsley.

Place the parsley in a large mortar and freeze with liquid nitrogen. As the leaves begin to freeze, pound and grind them with the pestle, adding more liquid nitrogen as needed to fully freeze the leaves. Grind until the leaves have become a fine powder. Add the yeast broth reduction and muddle it into the parsley powder until thoroughly combined. Add the parsley oil and muddle with the pestle until the oil is combined and the paste is emulsified. Transfer the paste to an airtight container and reserve in the refrigerator until needed. Use the paste the same day you make it.

Parsley Puree

Makes about 1 kilogram

1 kilogram fresh flat-leaf parsley leaves

Not every paste at Noma is made with a mortar and pestle; we choose the tool based on the consistency we want. With parsley puree, for example, we want a smooth, spreadable, almost liquid consistency, unlike the hand-ground texture of Parsley Paste (page 311), so we use a Pacojet (see page 480). The result has a texture like that of tomato paste; it's incredibly flavourful and extremely dense, a consistency you can't achieve with a mortar and pestle alone.

Set up an ice bath and bring a pot of water to a boil. Blanch the parsley until very tender, 5 to 7 minutes, then transfer to the ice bath to stop the cooking. Drain the parsley, then transfer to a superbag and gently wring out excess water. The amount of water that you wring from the parsley will dictate the texture of the finished puree. If you want to yield a very thick paste, wring out more water.

Transfer the wrung-out parsley to a Pacojet container, freeze it, and then spin it until it becomes a fine puree. Pack the puree down using the back of a spoon or a silicone spatula and return the Pacojet to the freezer until the parsley is completely frozen again, then spin it a second time. Repeat this process of freezing and spinning once more. Pass the puree through a tamis lined with a fine-mesh nylon sieve. Use the puree immediately, or return it to a Pacojet container and reserve in the freezer until needed. Spin the puree again to defrost it.

Set up an ice bath. Bring a pot of water to a boil and add the parsley.

Boil the parsley until the leaves are fully tender, 5 to 7 minutes, then transfer it to the ice bath (as Nate French does here).

Transfer the drained parsley to a superbag.

Gently but firmly wring out the parsley to remove most of the moisture.

Leave the parsley in the ice bath until fully cooled.

Drain the cooled parsley.

Transfer the wrung-out parsley to a Pacojet container.
Freeze the parsley and then spin it until it becomes a fine puree.

Pack the parsley down again. Repeat the freezing and spinning twice more. Pass the puree through a tamis lined with a fine-mesh nylon sieve. Use immediately or freeze in a Pacojet container.

Reindeer Sweetbreads Fried in Reindeer Moss with Nordic Pesto, Forest, 2022
Reindeer sweetbreads are cooked in brown butter and then "breaded" with reindeer moss. The sweetbreads are deep-fried until the moss is crisp, dotted with egg yolk paste, sprinkled with sweetbread spice mix, and served with Nordic pesto.

Semi-Dried Tomatoes, Semi-Dried Strawberries, Rabbit Caramel, Pollen Paste, and Parsley Puree, Forest, 2022
Semi-dried tomatoes and strawberries are filled with bee pollen paste and placed on a bowl brushed with parsley paste seasoned with parsley oil and smoked mushroom garum. They are accompanied by black currant shoots and rabbit caramel and finished with a smoked mushroom vinaigrette and Danish curry spice mix.

Corn and Pumpkin Bushi Paste

Makes 53 grams

0.5 gram Madagascar pepper
5 grams semi-dried tomatoes (see page 94)
4 grams Kanzuri Sediment*
6 grams Corn Bushi Powder*
5 grams grated pumpkin bushi (see page 96)
17 grams Black Currant Wood Oil (page 193)
7 grams Red Pepper Tamari*
6 grams Nordic Shoyu*
2 grams Japanese Quince Juice*
1 gram Sake Vinegar*

This intensely flavoured paste is built around two ingredients that we have made for us by a fourth-generation Japanese katsuobushi craftsman named Yusuke Sezaki (learn more about traditional katsuobushi and the journey that brought us to applying the traditional Japanese technique to corn and pumpkin on page 96). The bushis provide umami and an intriguing smokiness that are layered with other ferments, fruit, oils, and spices for a complex flavour that's hard to describe . . . and slightly addictive. We have used the paste on grilled cod jaw, brushed it on steamed baby corn, and added it to roasted reindeer tongue. We use this paste the day we make it. Reserving it until the next day would be okay, but the flavours lose their vibrancy over time.

Place the Madagascar pepper in a mortar and use the pestle to pound it into a powder. Add the dried tomatoes and mix to make a homogenous paste. Add the kanzuri sediment and then the corn bushi powder and pumpkin bushi, mixing to incorporate after each addition. Add the black currant wood oil, tamari, shoyu, quince juice, and vinegar, mixing until well blended. Use right away, keep refrigerated in an airtight container for up to 5 days, or freeze for longer-term storage.

Ant and Morita Chile Paste

Makes 30 grams

12 grams frozen ants
3 grams Pine Salt (page 100)
15 grams Morita Chile Oil*

In several Mexican regional cuisines, ants (including *escamoles*, the larvae and pupae of certain species of ants) are a traditional ingredient. We served *escamoles* during our pop-up in Mexico in 2017; here we use Scandinavian ants, salt made from local citrus-forward pine needles, and a smoky Mexican chile oil to create a beautifully balanced, spreadable, spicy-sour paste. We first developed this flavouring for a skewer of pan-roasted reindeer tongue, and it works well with other fatty cuts of cooked meat, with roasted pumpkin, or even in a taco with some *cochinita pibil*.

Note that you should keep your ants frozen. This is how to humanely kill them, but the cold temperature will also preserve their naturally occurring formic acid, the stuff that actually tastes like lemon juice to us.

Put the ants in a mortar and crush them using the pestle. Add the pine salt and use the pestle to blend it with the ants. Pour in the chile oil and continue working the mixture with the pestle until you have a slightly coarse paste. Use right away, keep refrigerated in an airtight container for up to 5 days, or freeze for longer-term storage.

Nordic Pesto

Makes 410 grams

60 grams unripe sea buckthorn berries
60 grams Black Currant Capers (page 71)
60 grams Green Gooseberry Capers (page 67)
50 grams Black Currant Leaf Oil (page 185)
50 grams Parsley Oil (page 178)
30 grams strained Elderflower Peaso*
20 grams Maitake Garum*
20 grams fresh flat-leaf parsley leaves
20 grams fresh cilantro leaves
20 grams fresh lovage leaves
10 grams fresh basil leaves
10 grams coriander seeds
Salt

In 2020, after the first pandemic lockdown, the Noma team gathered to discuss the next steps. COVID had unceremoniously granted us a brief respite from the constant machinery of feeding guests every day, and while the team missed cooking for others, it didn't feel right to go straight back into fine dining, not to mention that Denmark's borders were still closed. We needed to do something else, but what?

Two ideas rose to the top of the list: a Noma burger place or a Noma wine bar. David Zilber, head of the Fermentation Lab, and sous chefs Stu Stalker and Eoghan Coady took on the burger research, while Mette Søberg headed the wine bar team. Ultimately, David, Stu, and Eoghan's burger became a monthlong burger residency at Noma, during which we offered burgers, a bottle of wine from our cellar, and a spot to enjoy the two in our Piet Oudolf–designed garden.

Nordic pesto came from the research for the wine bar menu. Junichi Takahashi and Riccardo Canella are two Test Kitchen veterans who have never been shy about poking harmless fun at each other's home countries (Japan and Italy, respectively), and it was Jun who created Nordic pesto as an homage to Riccardo. The flavour profile of this chunky pesto is a bit like a Green Goddess dressing, featuring salted preserves with latent acidity, fresh herbs, and flavoured fats. The pesto accompanied a Noma crudité created by Riccardo and was served when Noma reopened in the summer of 2020.

Place the sea buckthorn berries, black currant capers, gooseberry capers, black currant leaf oil, parsley oil, peaso, and garum in a Thermomix. Blend until you have a fairly smooth paste.

Add half the parsley, cilantro, lovage, basil, and coriander seeds to the Thermomix and blend again until incorporated. Scrape down the sides of the Thermomix, add the remaining herbs and coriander seeds, and blend until the pesto is mostly smooth but with a bit of texture remaining. Season with salt.

Transfer the pesto to an airtight container and press a sheet of plastic wrap directly against the surface of the pesto to prevent oxidation. The pesto is best consumed the same day it is made; reserve in the refrigerator until needed.

Sunflower, Rhubarb, and Lingonberry Paste

Makes 105 grams

Sunflower Seed Paste

150 grams Brown Butter (page 198)
150 grams raw hulled sunflower seeds
7 grams Dried Ginger Powder*
7 grams Mustard Seed Spice Mix (page 126)
3 grams Noma Roasted Umami Salt (page 115)
15 grams Celery Reduction*
15 grams Peaso Water Reduction (page 258)
5 grams Nordic Shoyu*

When we were preparing for the first menu at Noma 2.0—after Noma Mexico but before moving to our new home—we set up a test kitchen in a small office building in the courtyard of the apartment complex where my family lives. It was a compact space, but it gave rise to many new ideas and techniques that would go on to define the next era of Noma.

Around that time, the Test Kitchen team was tasked to create new seasonings using a mortar and pestle. Pablo Soto, who is now our head chef, had been experimenting with toasted seeds and spices. He also remembered his mother in Mexico making fried parsley seasoned with citrus and serving it alongside bone marrow. Her treatment transformed delicate parsley into something rich and meaty. Pablo leaned on that memory and fried a mountain of parsley, then got to work with the mortar and pestle. The result was a paste that's appeared on nearly every menu since.

Make the sunflower seed paste: Melt the brown butter in a large skillet over medium-high heat, then add the sunflower seeds and cook, stirring continuously, until the butter is foaming and the seeds are starting to toast. Add the ginger powder, mustard seed spice mix, and roasted umami salt and stir well. Cook for a few minutes to bloom the spices. Stir in the celery reduction, peaso water reduction, and shoyu, then cook until the seeds are deeply caramelized. Remove from the heat and let cool slightly. Transfer the mixture to a mortar

Fried Parsley and Oregano Leaves

Neutral oil, for frying

125 grams fresh flat-leaf parsley leaves

50 grams fresh oregano leaves

Finished Paste

2.5 grams freeze-dried rhubarb

2.5 grams freeze-dried lingonberries

50 grams Cold-Infused Dashi (page 215)

1 gram Mushroom Spice Mix (page 127)

15 grams Koji Oil*

12 grams Fried Parsley Leaves

4 grams Fried Oregano Leaves

18 grams Sunflower Seed Paste

and grind with the pestle until you form a semi-smooth paste. Transfer the sunflower seed paste to an airtight container and reserve in the refrigerator until needed, up to 1 week.

Fry the herbs: Fill a tall pot with about 5 cm (2 inches) oil and heat the oil to 160°C (320°F); arrange a layer of paper towels on a sheet pan near the stove. Drop the parsley leaves into the hot oil and fry until they're translucent and crisp and the bubbling just stops. Use a spider to remove the parsley from the oil and transfer it to paper towels to drain well, changing the towels as necessary to absorb any excess oil. Repeat to fry the oregano leaves.

Make the finished paste: Place the freeze-dried rhubarb and lingonberries in a small container, pour in the dashi, and let stand until the rhubarb and berries are rehydrated. Stir in the mushroom spice mix.

Heat the koji oil in a skillet over medium heat. Add the rhubarb-lingonberry mixture and cook it down until it's evenly caramelized. Meanwhile, place the fried parsley and oregano in a large mortar and grind with the pestle until well mixed. Add the rhubarb-lingonberry mixture to the mortar with the fried herbs, then add the sunflower seed paste. Stir and muddle the ingredients with the pestle until you have a blended but still coarse paste. Transfer to an airtight container and reserve in the refrigerator until ready to use.

Melt the brown butter in a large skillet over medium-high heat.

Add the sunflower seeds and cook, stirring continuously, until the butter is foaming and the seeds are starting to toast.

Fry the parsley and oregano leaves and drain on paper towels.

Soak the freeze-dried lingonberries and rhubarb in the dashi.

Add the ginger powder, mustard seed spice mix, and roasted umami salt. Cook for a few minutes to bloom the spices. Stir in the celery reduction, peaso water reduction, and shoyu.

Cook until the seeds are deeply caramelized. Let cool slightly, then transfer the mixture to a mortar and grind with the pestle until you have a chunky puree.

Heat the koji oil in a skillet. Add the lingonberry-rhubarb mixture and fry until lightly caramelized.

Place the fried parsley and oregano in a mortar. Use the pestle to coarsely grind them. Add the lingonberry-rhubarb mixture and sunflower seed paste. Muddle until blended but still chunky. Use right away or refrigerate in an airtight container.

Pan-Roasted Strawberry Paste

Makes about 300 grams

40 grams Koji Oil*
300 grams ripe strawberries, tops trimmed, halved lengthwise
2 grams Roseroot Spice Mix (page 128)

Strawberries are the national fruit of Denmark, so it only seemed right that Dane Mette Søberg, head of our Test Kitchen, would be the one to experiment with this inherently perfect Danish ingredient.

Mette decided to cook the strawberries until deeply caramelized, bringing out a savory quality along with the sweetness. We've used this velvety paste most often in savory dishes, with ingredients like white asparagus and tomato, though it would work very well with salted dark chocolate, too. You can also spread the paste in a thin layer on a Silpat and dry it to make a chewy fruit leather (see page 427).

Heat the koji oil in a large skillet over high heat until hot. Arrange the strawberries cut-side down and sear until very caramelized and almost burnt. Flip the strawberries and season with the roseroot spice mix. Cook until the second side has caramelized as much as the first, then remove from the heat. Pass the strawberries through a tamis lined with a fine-mesh nylon sieve, pressing them through with a scraper into a bowl. Whisk the resulting paste until any oil that may have separated is reincorporated and the mixture is smooth. Transfer the strawberry paste to an airtight container and reserve in the refrigerator. The paste is best used the same day it's made, but it will keep for up to 5 days.

Trim off the green tops of the strawberries and slice the berries in half lengthwise.

Heat the koji oil in a large skillet until very hot. Arrange the berries cut-side down in the skillet.

Pass the berries through a tamis lined with a fine-mesh nylon sieve, pressing them through with a scraper.

Whisk the strawberry paste until emulsified and smooth.

Sear the berries until deeply caramelized and almost burnt. Flip the berries and sprinkle on the roseroot spice mix. Cook until the second side is also deeply caramelized.

Use the strawberry paste or refrigerate in an airtight container for up to 5 days.

Suggested Uses

Parsley Risotto

Fold a big spoonful of Parsley Puree (page 313) into a classic risotto, adding it just a few minutes before the rice is tender.

Parsley Mashed Potatoes

Make a batch of mashed potatoes enriched with extra-virgin olive oil and season with a dollop of Parsley Paste (page 311). Serve with a grass-fed steak or wild salmon fillet.

Carnitas Tacos with Strawberry Paste

Brush Pan-Roasted Strawberry Paste (page 329) onto one side of a corn tortilla, then top with pork carnitas, fresh herbs (such as cilantro and parsley), chopped onion, and a squeeze of lime.

"Bushi Bolognese"

Gently heat a few spoonfuls of Corn and Pumpkin Bushi Paste (page 319) in a skillet. Cook any pasta shape you like in salted boiling water until al dente, then transfer it to the skillet along with a few big spoonfuls of the pasta cooking water. Toss until the pasta is coated and the sauce is nicely creamy.

Morita Chile Corn on the Cob

Lightly oil a few ears of fresh corn, grill them briefly, and then spread them with Ant and Morita Chile Paste (page 321). Season with a few drops of Morita Chile Oil (page 487) for more fragrant chile heat.

Nordic Chimichurri

Serve Sunflower, Rhubarb, and Lingonberry Paste (page 324) as you would a chimichurri sauce to accompany grilled meats, such as steaks or lamb chops.

Crudités with Pesto

Make a batch of Nordic Pesto (page 322) and serve it with a platter of assorted raw vegetables.

Opposite, top to bottom: Parsley Risotto; "Bushi Bolognese"; Morita Chile Corn on the Cob
Right: Crudités with Pesto

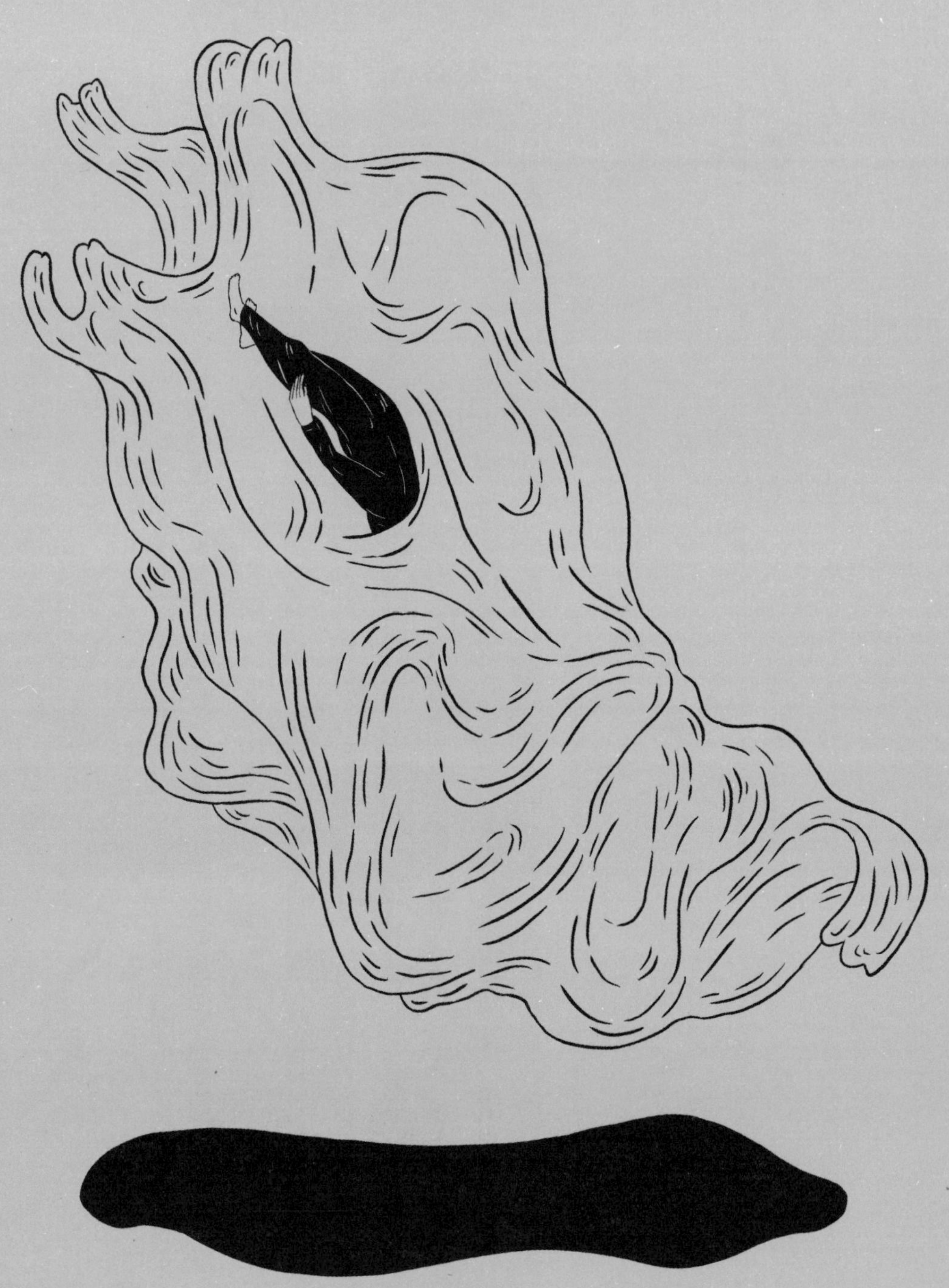

7.

Sauces

Sauces: Completing a dish, inviting you to linger at the table

Grilled Artichoke with Blueberry Vinaigrette, Summer, 2025
Artichoke hearts are split lengthwise and grilled with whisky glaze, then arranged with fresh herbs and flowers dressed with a blueberry vinaigrette. The dish is finished with a sauce made from walnuts and truffle.

When I was growing up, I'd watch my uncle at the table. There'd be a roast chicken in the middle, pan still warm, golden fat and sticky dark bits clinging to the bottom. He'd tear off a piece of bread and use it to soak up the roasting juices. I didn't know it then, but that was sauce. And that's what sauce does. It invites you in.

Of course, that final swipe is nearly universal. In Italy, it's *fare la scarpetta*. In Spain, *rebañar*. In France, *saucer*. The list goes on. Different tables, different languages. Same impulse: Don't let any of it go uneaten.

Earlier in this book, we wrote about broths and reductions. If broths are about clarity and reductions are about intensity, then sauces are something else entirely. Sauces are connectors. They can finish a dish. They soften edges. They tie together flavours that don't belong—but want to. They fill in gaps. And sometimes, they take the lead.

In the world of Western fine dining, sauces have always mattered. Escoffier crowned them royalty, and the rest of us bowed. The French mother sauces still loom large in almost every kitchen. They're complex, technically beautiful.

But if you're looking for seasoned versions of those, you won't find them here. There's no traditional demi-glace. No sauce velouté.

We've spent the past two decades trying to figure out what our mother sauces are. How do we find flavours that reflect where we are, what's in season, and what we believe in?

Of course, we stand on the shoulders of giants. We know the rules—we've just bent them. Like our rose béarnaise, where the tarragon vinegar is replaced with wild roses. Or the grasshopper walnut mole, built on deep tradition, but made with different ingredients. Or the lacto koji butter sauce, which in spirit is a beurre blanc—just without wine, and with a funk that comes from weeks of fermentation.

These are sauces that don't come from textbooks. But they come from knowing what's in the textbooks, and building on that knowledge through exploration.

What follows are some of our favorites, just a few of the dozens we've created over the years. Some are delicate. Some are bold. Some take minutes, others take weeks. But all of them reflect how we see the role of sauces: as one of the great tools we have to complete a dish, and to move the person eating it.

At its most basic, food is about survival. It's about nutrition, calories, getting through the day.

But sauce? A good sauce is a reason to live.

Reindeer Brain Omelet with Pheasant Lacto Rice Koji Butter Sauce, Forest, 2023
A delicate omelet is made by wrapping a thin layer of lightly cooked eggs mixed with pheasant garum and koji oil around a reindeer brain custard. The omelet is then brushed with spiced pheasant oil and accompanied by a foamy koji sauce made from a mix of lacto rice koji water, white peony tea, butter, and spiced pheasant oil.

340

Vinaigrettes

A vinaigrette is an exquisite balancing act, holding opposing flavours in a delicate, satisfying tension. It's also a workhorse in the kitchen, perfect for dressing anything from a piece of raw fish to ripe berries to roast chicken.

In essence, a vinaigrette is made by mixing oil or other liquid fat with an acidic liquid, often vinegar (hence the name), but vinegar isn't mandatory. Fruit juice, a ferment like tamari or garum—any bright, assertive, water-based liquid will work. The oil provides flavour and richness, and the contrasting punch of vinegar (or its friends) balances the fat, creating a complex interplay of flavours and sensations.

Rose vinegar and black currant wood oil join but don't emulsify.

At Noma, we like to leave our vinaigrettes "split," meaning unemulsified (see page 348), so the flavours and textures can be perceived separately. Each bite produces a different flavour experience, which is the goal of the game, right?

Forest Vinaigrette

Makes about 150 grams

20 grams unripe sea buckthorn berries
20 grams pine shoots
5 grams Douglas fir needles
2 grams juniper berries
2 grams angelica seeds
2 grams green coriander seeds
150 grams Mirabelle plum juice
10 grams Larch Wood Oil (page 190)

The title says it all, with the foresty flavours coming from juniper berries, pine shoots, Douglas fir needles, and larch wood oil. In place of an actual vinegar, plum juice contributes a mild, fruity acidity. We first served this sauce as part of a dish we called Forest Ceviche. The "ceviche" element didn't include any seafood, but was instead an arrangement of apples, dried mulberries, blackberries, black currant shoots, Candied Pine Cones (page 450), and salted noble fir cone scales (page 77) dressed with this pine-focused vinaigrette.

Place the sea buckthorn berries, pine shoots, Douglas fir needles, juniper berries, angelica, and coriander in a mortar and pound with the pestle until mostly crushed, then add the plum juice and muddle it in. Let stand for 2 minutes, then strain through a fine-mesh nylon sieve, pressing the solids to extract as much juice and flavour as possible. Transfer this vinaigrette base to an airtight container and reserve in the refrigerator until needed, up to 1 day. When ready to serve, add the larch wood oil; do not emulsify.

Place the sea buckthorn berries, pine shoots, Douglas fir needles, juniper berries, angelica, and coriander in a mortar.

Pound the ingredients with the pestle until mostly crushed, then add the plum juice and muddle to blend.

Let stand for 2 minutes, then strain the mixture through a fine-mesh nylon sieve, pressing the solids to extract the maximum juice and flavour.

Refrigerate the vinaigrette base in an airtight container for up to 1 day. Just before serving, add the larch wood oil; do not emulsify.

Rose Vinaigrette

Makes 225 grams

25 grams fennel flowers, stemmed
150 grams Rose Oil (page 187)
40 grams vinegar from Pickled Wild Beach Roses (page 43)
10 grams smoked Madagascar pepper, crushed
Salt

Rose vinegar became an instant staple the first time we tasted it, a bright and beautiful encapsulation of Danish summer distilled in acetic acid. Rose oil and rose vinegar may seem like they'd be rose overkill, but the flavours are nothing like the cloying "potpourri" scent of store-bought rose water. The two ingredients together can be served on their own or with additional seasonings, as in this recipe. This particular vinaigrette was used with our Vegetable season main course in the summer of 2022 to dress a salad of strawberries, tomatoes, gooseberries, chamomile, and summer flowers.

Quickly chop the fennel flowers. Stir together the rose oil and the rose vinegar in a small bowl (do not emulsify—the vinaigrette must be split), then add the chopped fennel flowers and the crushed pepper. Season the vinaigrette with salt. Use immediately or transfer to an airtight container and reserve in the refrigerator until needed, up to 6 hours.

Warm Mushroom Vinaigrette

Makes 195 grams

30 grams Red Pepper Tamari*, plus more if needed
25 grams Dashi Reduction (page 259), plus more if needed
20 grams Mushroom Garum*, plus more if needed
120 grams Fresh Barley Koji Oil (page 169), plus more if needed
Salt

Not all vinaigrettes need to be served cold on a salad. This one was the sauce for our salt-baked mushroom main course, a warm dish, served in Vegetable season 2024. The dish included salt-baked oyster mushrooms, green rice from Japan, and this vinaigrette. That was it. It's an exceptional example of the power of our larder of ferments, reductions, and flavoured oils, demonstrating that with the right basic ingredients, less can be more. The vinaigrette would be an excellent accompaniment to any mushroom dish, but would also work well over a piece of roasted chicken, steamed asparagus, or grilled eggplant.

Stir together the tamari, dashi reduction, mushroom garum, and koji oil (do not emulsify—the vinaigrette must be split). Taste and season with salt, adjusting the flavour with more of the other ingredients as needed. Transfer to a squeeze bottle or other airtight container and reserve in the refrigerator for up to 2 days. Right before serving, gently warm the vinaigrette by placing the container in a water bath.

Blueberry Vinaigrette

Makes 144 grams

9 grams Noma Roasted Umami Salt (page 115)
39 grams Black Pepper Tamari*
30 grams Blueberry (Bilberry) Reduction (page 262)
54 grams Douglas Fir Oil (page 175)
12 grams Whisky Vinegar*

Fruit-forward vinaigrettes are nothing new, but they're typically built around fruit-based vinegars: white wine, sherry, balsamic. This version flips the formula, using an intense blueberry reduction as the driving force, supported by black pepper tamari, whisky vinegar, and roasted umami salt. The goal was to lean into deep fruit flavour without overwhelming acidity. Originally developed for a dish by sous chef Álvaro de Juan Sánchez featuring grilled artichokes and foraged greens, it pairs particularly well with earthy or bitter vegetables.

Place the roasted umami salt in a mortar and pound it into a paste with the pestle. Add the tamari and mix well. Stir in the blueberry reduction, fir oil, and whisky vinegar (do not emulsify—the vinaigrette must be split). Transfer to an airtight container and reserve in the refrigerator for up to 1 day.

Split Vinaigrettes

At Noma, we deliberately do the wrong thing when we make a vinaigrette (and many of our other sauces), allowing the oil and the sauce base to remain separate, unemulsifed.

With a typical vinaigrette, the goal is to whisk or otherwise agitate the ingredients so that the fat (usually oil) becomes emulsified with the non-fat ingredient, whether that's vinegar, broth, or juice. An emulsified sauce has a slightly thickened, creamy consistency, and each bite contains the flavours of all the ingredients in the sauce.

With our "split" sauces, the flavours—and indeed, the sensation on your tongue—will be different in every bite, allowing you to perceive the flavours in new arrangements, one bite a bit richer, the next a bit sharp.

Keeping your sauce unemulsified also has the advantage of letting you control how much fat to use. When you emulsify a sauce, you need a certain ratio of fat to non-fat ingredients, generally 3 parts fat to 1 part non-fat, in order for emulsification to happen and for the resulting emulsion to remain stable. With a split sauce, you can just float a small amount of oil on top because you're not aiming for a physical blending.

Sometimes, though, we look for a happy medium and give the vinaigrette a quick shake before dressing the food, resulting in a slightly more even, though not fully emulsified, distribution of flavours.

Green Sauces

Not every sauce reveals its flavour through its appearance, but in this category, the vibrant color of the sauce is a definite indication of the deliciousness to come. Whether or not you actually have synesthesia (the phenomenon in which stimulation of one sense activates a different sense), when you see something green on your plate, you can almost taste the fresh, herbaceous flavours, possibly with a hint of spicy, bitter, or acidic as well.

Wild watercress, ready to become sauce.

Noma's green sauces are clean and light-bodied, usually based on herb or green vegetable purees. That plant matter gives the sauces stability and body; spices and sharp ingredients like vinegar and mustard add edges, and a few drops of flavoured oil both brighten and smooth out the sauces.

Parsley Kelp Sauce

Makes 200 grams

100 grams Parsley Paste (page 311)
100 grams Cold-Infused Dashi (page 215)

Perhaps our most intense expression of the flavour of "green," parsley kelp sauce is based on a dense parsley paste (one of our workhorse pastes) that we loosen and season with a bit of dashi. Thanks to the oil content and fine parsley particulates in the paste, the sauce emulsifies well and pairs beautifully with seafood or vegetables. The sauce is also "riffable"—add a bit of raw garlic and chile flake, and you'll have a chimichurri-esque sauce that would perfectly complement grilled meats.

Blend the parsley paste and dashi with an immersion blender until lightly emulsified. Pass the mixture through a fine-mesh nylon sieve and reserve in a container set over an ice bath. Use this sauce the same day you make it.

Ramson Sauce

Makes about 125 grams

Ramson Sauce Base
25 grams ramson leaves
10 grams spinach
55 grams Cold-Infused Dashi (page 215)
27 grams Roasted Kelp Dashi (page 216)
10 grams truffle juice
3 grams Fava Rice Shoyu*
1 gram salt

Ramson Sauce
100 grams Ramson Sauce Base
16 grams Fresh Barley Koji Butter (page 203)
6 grams Parsley Oil (page 178)
Reduced White Wine*
Salt

Ramsons, early signifiers of springtime, are a true representation of the flavour of "spring green." When this wild garlic arrives from our forager, we use as much of it as possible. (Ramsons are native to Europe and Asia, while their cousins, called ramps, are native to parts of North America.) A notable use of this ramson sauce was in our Table-Side Egg, an egg fried in hay oil on a hot plate in front of the guest, then finished with black pepper butter, ramson sauce, and crispy new potato.

Make the sauce base: Blanch the ramson leaves in lightly salted water for 2 minutes and the spinach in lightly salted water for 1 minute. Shock each of the greens in ice water to set the color and stop the cooking. Gently but thoroughly wring out the ramsons and spinach to remove excess water. Place the blanched greens, cold-infused dashi, roasted kelp dashi, truffle juice, fava shoyu, and salt in a Thermomix and blend on high speed for 2 minutes. Strain the sauce base through a fine-mesh nylon sieve into an airtight container set over an ice bath, pressing on the solids well to maximize yield. Reserve over ice in the refrigerator for up to 3 hours.

Make the sauce: Stir together the sauce base, koji butter, and parsley oil in a saucepan and season with reduced white wine and salt. When ready to serve, warm the sauce, but do *not* allow it to boil. If heated above 75°C (165°F), the sauce will lose its vibrant color and flavour.

Grill the asparagus on one side until just about burnt.
Steam in a closed container for 10 minutes.

Juice the asparagus and then strain the asparagus juice through a fine-mesh nylon sieve.

Place the juice in a saucepan and stir in the parsley puree.
Slowly warm the mixture, whisking to incorporate, then add the Douglas fir oil and whisk until emulsified.

Season the sauce with pine vinegar and salt to finish.
Use immediately.

Grilled Green Asparagus Sauce

Makes about 200 grams

20 large stalks green asparagus
30 grams Parsley Puree (page 313)
20 grams Douglas Fir Oil (page 175)
Pine Vinegar (page 39)
Salt

Grilled green asparagus is juiced to produce a liquid that not only flavours the sauce but is also used to adjust its consistency. We grill only one side of the asparagus because we don't want to cook out all the water content. Fresh and citrusy Douglas fir oil is emulsified into the sauce to make it buttery smooth. Take care not to heat the sauce too much, or you will degrade the chlorophyll and lose its fresh quality.

We first served this sauce over a decade ago, in a dish of roasted white asparagus, lightly whipped horseradish-infused cream, and a sprinkling of Pine Salt (page 100).

Grill the asparagus over a charcoal fire on one side until just about burnt. Transfer the grilled asparagus to an airtight 1-liter container, cover, and allow it to steam for 10 minutes. Run the asparagus through a centrifugal juicer and strain the juice through a fine-mesh nylon sieve; you should yield about 150 grams of juice. Immediately transfer the juice to a small saucepan (do not allow it to cool or it will lose a lot of flavour). Stir in the parsley puree. Slowly heat the two together, whisking to incorporate. The puree will melt into the asparagus juice, but will not become fully emulsified. Add the Douglas fir oil and continue to whisk until everything is emulsified and the sauce is silky. Adjust the consistency with water, if necessary. Season with pine vinegar and salt. Use immediately.

Nasturtium Sauce

Makes about 175 grams

Green Anise Oil
10 grams green aniseeds
100 grams neutral oil

Parsley Broth Base
40 grams fresh flat-leaf parsley leaves
Salt
160 grams Roasted Kelp Dashi (page 216)

Nasturtium Sauce
30 grams nasturtium leaves
150 grams Parsley Broth Base
Salt
3 grams Green Anise Oil

Just about every part of the nasturtium plant is edible, from the peppery green leaves to the slightly sweet flower petals to the tiny seeds, which are intensely spicy, reminiscent of wasabi—you can even grind them into a wasabi-like paste.

This sauce is excellent on roasted turbot or other white fish or on roasted celeriac with horseradish cream, to double up on the kick of peppery spice. Note that this recipe makes a lot more green anise oil than you'll use for the sauce, but you need at least this amount of oil to blend properly. Keep the excess oil frozen and use it to season soup, ceviche, or anything where a note of anise would be welcome.

Make the green anise oil: Combine the aniseeds and oil in a Thermomix and blend for 7 minutes on high speed. Transfer to a vacuum bag and let cool, then seal on 100% vacuum. Refrigerate for 24 hours to allow the oil and sediments to infuse. Strain the oil through a fine-mesh nylon sieve. Transfer to a vacuum bag, seal, and reserve in the freezer until needed.

Make the parsley broth base: Blanch the parsley in salted boiling water for 2 minutes, then shock it in ice water. Drain the parsley and squeeze out all the residual water. Combine the parsley and the dashi in a Thermomix and blend for about 30 seconds; season with salt. Immediately strain the broth base through a fine-mesh nylon sieve into an airtight container set over an ice bath and reserve in the refrigerator until needed, up to 3 hours.

Make the nasturtium sauce: Combine the nasturtium leaves and the parsley broth base in a Thermomix and blend for about 30 seconds, then strain the sauce through a fine-mesh nylon sieve into a small saucepan. Gently heat the sauce until warm. Season with salt and top with the green anise oil. Use immediately.

Watercress Sauce

Makes about 300 grams

180 grams watercress leaves and tender stems
6 grams Dijon mustard
15 grams apple balsamic vinegar (see page 483)
30 grams filtered water
110 grams neutral oil
Xanthan gum
Salt
Fresh lemon juice
Horseradish Juice (page 237)

At its core, watercress sauce is a vibrant emulsion—pure, punchy, and notoriously difficult to stabilize due to its lack of protein. The emulsion is primarily held together by the watercress itself: a particulate suspension where the plant matter helps bind water and oil. Mustard adds a secondary layer of emulsification, and a small amount of xanthan gum (or pre-hy) can help fine-tune the texture. The high ratio of fresh greens ensures a clean, intense watercress flavour. Adjust the oil quantity depending on whether you want a thicker or looser consistency. Finished with lemon juice, salt, and a touch of horseradish juice, it's a powerhouse sauce.

Place the watercress, mustard, vinegar, and water in a blender and blend until smooth. Transfer to a bowl and whisk in the oil little by little until creamy and emulsified, adding a small amount of xanthan gum as necessary to stabilize the emulsion. Note that the amount of oil you'll need will vary depending on the moisture in the watercress. Season well with salt and a few drops of lemon juice and horseradish juice (or to taste). Strain the sauce through a fine-mesh nylon sieve into an airtight container set over an ice bath and reserve in the refrigerator until ready to serve, up to a few hours. Use the sauce the same day you make it.

Egg- and Other Protein-Based Sauces

An ideal sauce should taste delicious and it should *feel* delicious, too. Whether fluid and flowing or ethereally light and creamy, the consistency of a sauce needs to seduce.

No category of sauces achieves this texture better than egg sauces, because their mild flavour is coupled with powerful physical skills, namely their ability to thicken and emulsify.

An egg sauce could be something as simple as an egg yolk in Japanese *gyudon*, a dish of hot rice and beef mixed to thicken the entire dish to a creamy texture. Or it could be a French hollandaise, where egg yolks thicken with heat, gather air from the whisk, and, through emulsification and coagulation, hold luxurious amounts of melted butter.

Gently cooked eggs are the base for cured egg yolk sauce.

Other proteins can create luscious textures in sauces, as well. Seafood reductions and raw oysters play the role of egg yolks but contribute their own briny flavours.

Place 20 of the eggs in a water bath heated to 68°C (155°F) with an immersion circulator; cook for 20 minutes. Separate the remaining 10 eggs and place the yolks in the garum to cure for 20 minutes.

Transfer the cured raw yolks to a bowl; reserve the garum. Shock the cooked eggs in ice water until cool, then separate the yolks and place them in the garum to cure for 20 minutes.

Transfer the cured cooked egg yolks to the bowl with the raw cured yolks and gently whisk to combine. Season with smoked butter, smoked butter whey, a bit of the garum, if you like, and salt. Whisk to incorporate.

Strain the sauce through a tamis lined with a fine-mesh nylon sieve so it's perfectly smooth. Use immediately or refrigerate in a squeeze bottle or airtight container until needed, up to 6 hours.

Cured Egg Yolk Sauce

Makes about 600 grams

30 large eggs
1 kilogram Beef Garum*
Clarified Smoked Butter (reserved from making Smoked Butter Whey, page 197)
Smoked Butter Whey (page 197)
Salt

We've served many iterations of this luxuriously textured golden sauce. The concept was initially developed by Junichi Takahashi. Jun built upon *shoyuzuke*, the Japanese method of pickling in soy sauce, and (no surprise) made it more complex by using egg yolks, both lightly cooked and raw, and curing them in our beef garum rather than soy sauce. We almost always use beef garum because we think the flavour combo is ideal—think steak and eggs—but any garum will work. One of the first iterations of this sauce was served at our Noma Australia pop-up, when we served it with freshly steamed Western Australia snow crab.

This recipe yields a sauce that slowly drips off a spoon—not quite as thick as a hollandaise, but not as thin as a beurre blanc. You can adjust the texture in a few ways: by adjusting the cooking time for the eggs (more time will yield a thicker sauce), or by changing the ratio of cooked and cured yolks to raw cured yolks. More cooked yolks will yield a thicker sauce, and vice versa. The smoked clarified butter will also make the sauce a bit thicker as it emulsifies, while the smoked butter whey will thin it due to the whey's water content.

Temper the eggs at room temperature for 30 minutes. Set up a water bath with an immersion circulator set to 68°C (155°F). Place 20 of the eggs in the water bath and cook for 20 minutes. *(Recipe continues)*

Separate the remaining 10 eggs, keeping the yolks whole. Place the raw yolks in a plastic container and cover them with the garum. Let the yolks cure in the garum for 20 minutes, then transfer them to a bowl, cover, and set aside. Reserve the garum.

Remove the cooked eggs from the water bath and shock them in ice water. Let cool, then crack the eggs and separate the yolks from the whites (you may need to rinse the yolks gently with cold water to remove any remaining egg white). Place the yolks in the garum and let them cure for 20 minutes, then transfer all but one or two of them to a large bowl. Add the cured raw yolks to the bowl as well, reserving one or two. Gently whisk the cooked and raw yolks to combine (you are not trying to whip them, just mix them thoroughly), adding the reserved yolks as needed to achieve the desired consistency. Season to taste with clarified smoked butter, smoked butter whey, some of the garum, if you like, and a bit of salt; whisk to incorporate.

Strain the egg yolk sauce though a tamis lined with fine-mesh nylon sieve. (The sauce can be used at this point, but to make it ultra-smooth, we cycle it through the vacuum machine until all the air bubbles are compressed and we can run a full cycle without stopping the machine.) Transfer the finished egg yolk sauce to a bowl and serve immediately, or transfer to an airtight container and reserve in the refrigerator until needed, up to 6 hours.

Whisky Egg Yolk Sauce

Makes about 150 grams

6 large eggs
Beef Garum*
15 grams Smoked Butter (page 196), melted
20 grams Whisky Vinegar*
4 grams Danish whisky
0.5 gram salt

This is a tasty variation on the basic Cured Egg Yolk Sauce (page 363) that uses gently cooked yolks for body and both whisky vinegar and actual whisky for flavour.

Temper the eggs at room temperature for 30 minutes. Set up a water bath with an immersion circulator set to 68°C (155°F). Cook the eggs in the water bath for 20 minutes. Remove the eggs and shock them in ice water. Let cool, then crack the eggs and separate the yolks from the whites (you may need to rinse the yolks gently with cold water to wash off any remaining egg white). Place the yolks in a plastic container, cover with garum, and cure for 20 minutes. Transfer the cured yolks to a medium bowl and gently whisk them to combine (you are not trying to whip them, just mix them thoroughly). Season with the melted butter, whisky vinegar, Danish whisky, 3.5 grams of the garum, and the salt; whisk to incorporate. Transfer the sauce to a small bowl and serve immediately, or transfer to an airtight container and reserve in the refrigerator until needed, up to 6 hours.

Rose Béarnaise

Makes about 780 grams

6 large egg yolks
36 grams Noma Umami Salt (page 113)
30 grams vinegar from Pickled Wild Beach Roses (page 43), plus more if needed
10 grams filtered water
500 grams unsalted butter, melted, plus more if needed
100 grams Rose Oil (page 187)
Salt

Look at the menu at an old-school French restaurant and you're likely to see some type of beef served with béarnaise sauce, because even though this cousin of hollandaise sauce has a delicate texture, the flavour is punchy enough to pair well with meats. At Noma, we pair béarnaise sauce with a "steak" of lion's mane mushroom, a stand-in for beef. We slice the mushroom into slabs, confit them in koji oil, press them to tighten the texture, smoke them, and finally grill them, creating a beautiful caramelized crust like you'd find on a perfect steak. A béarnaise was a logical accompaniment, though instead of the classic white wine, shallot, and tarragon reduction, we flavour ours with rose vinegar and rose oil. The béarnaise formula is a perfect template for variation; we've made béarnaise flavoured with whisky, pine, and even one with sencha tea, which we serve with grilled bamboo poached in koji butter.

Just before serving, bring a saucepan of water to a simmer over low heat. Combine the yolks, umami salt, rose vinegar, and filtered water in a large heatproof bowl and set it over the simmering water. Whisk until the mixture has quadrupled in volume. Slowly whisk in the melted butter, including the whey, until emulsified. Whisk in the rose oil, then taste and adjust the seasoning; this sauce will take a good amount of salt and potentially a bit more vinegar. Whisk in additional melted butter, if needed, to adjust the viscosity. Use immediately.

Combine the egg yolks, umami salt, rose vinegar, and water in a heatproof bowl.

Set the bowl over a saucepan of simmering water and whisk until the egg mixture has quadrupled in volume (as Mirek Anderson does here).

Whisk in the melted butter and then the rose oil.

Taste the sauce and adjust the seasoning with salt and possibly more vinegar. Use immediately.

Brown Butter Emulsion

Makes about 680 grams

300 grams Brown Butter (page 198)
4 large eggs
100 grams filtered water, plus more as needed
80 grams fresh lemon juice
Salt

This is essentially a brown butter hollandaise, but instead of using raw egg yolks, we soft-boil whole eggs and then emulsify everything with warm melted brown butter. We adjust the consistency and add flavour with lemon juice, sometimes working in green gooseberry capers and some lacto koji water, both sources of salt and acid that give the sauce an even more complex flavour. This sauce has been a consistent favorite at Noma, where we serve it numerous ways, including with raw shrimp or on flatbread with grilled rose petals.

Melt the brown butter and keep it warm (about 35°C/95°F). Bring a medium pot of water to a boil. Add the eggs and cook for 4 minutes, then transfer to an ice water bath to cool. Peel the eggs, place them in a small container, and add half the filtered water. Using an immersion blender, puree the eggs into a smooth paste. With the blender running, stream in the melted brown butter and blend until you have a smooth, homogeneous emulsion. Blend the lemon juice into the emulsion and add more filtered water as needed to adjust the consistency. Season with salt. This emulsion is best used immediately and should not be refrigerated because of the butter content, which will cause the sauce to become too thick if chilled.

"À la Crème" Sauce

Makes about 220 grams

40 grams Shrimp Stock (page 227), plus more as needed
30 grams Shrimp Reduction (page 263)
15 grams Umami Salt Shrimp Garum*
3 grams pre-hy (diluted to 3%)
100 grams Fresh Barley Koji Oil (page 169)
30 grams Douglas Fir Oil (page 175)

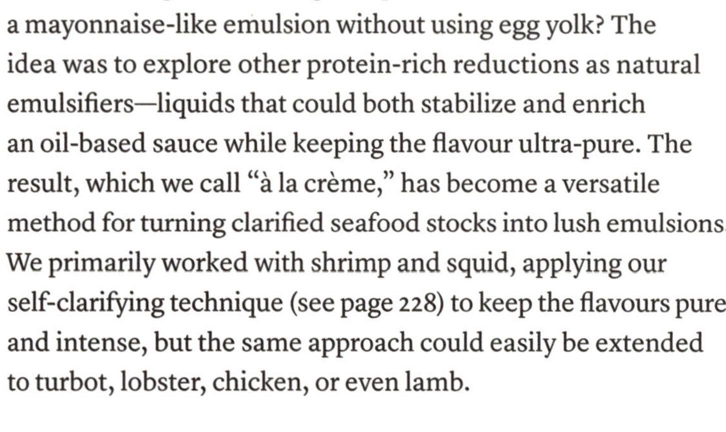

This sauce began as a thought experiment: Could we build a mayonnaise-like emulsion without using egg yolk? The idea was to explore other protein-rich reductions as natural emulsifiers—liquids that could both stabilize and enrich an oil-based sauce while keeping the flavour ultra-pure. The result, which we call "à la crème," has become a versatile method for turning clarified seafood stocks into lush emulsions. We primarily worked with shrimp and squid, applying our self-clarifying technique (see page 228) to keep the flavours pure and intense, but the same approach could easily be extended to turbot, lobster, chicken, or even lamb.

Combine the shrimp stock, shrimp reduction, shrimp garum, and pre-hy in a bowl set over an ice bath and whisk until the mixture is slightly thickened. Slowly whisk in the koji oil and Douglas fir oil until the sauce is emulsified. Adjust the consistency as needed with more shrimp stock. Reserve over ice until needed, up to 2 hours.

Combine the shrimp stock, reduction, garum, and pre-hy in a bowl set over ice (as Pablo Soto does here).

Whisk until the mixture is slightly thickened.

Slowly whisk in the koji oil and Douglas fir oil until the sauce is emulsified.

Adjust the consistency of the sauce with more shrimp stock, if needed. Reserve over ice until needed, up to 2 hours.

Oyster Emulsion

Makes about 325 grams

150 grams shucked oysters, rinsed in strained oyster liquor (reserve some of the liquor)
17 grams fresh flat-leaf parsley leaves
150 grams neutral oil
10 grams Parsley Oil (page 178)
Fresh lemon juice
Salt

Oyster emulsion is essentially a mayonnaise made with raw oyster as the protein component (the emulsifier) instead of egg yolk. The sauce evolved from a Test Kitchen exploration by Torsten Vildgaard and Søren Westh, when they were working on a dish of langoustine stuffed with oyster, parsley, and rye bread crumbs. Through the process of paring down the flavours and simplifying the execution, the chefs arrived at a pure seafood-flavoured emulsion, with parsley reflecting the mineral tones of the oysters. Oyster emulsion is fairly loose at room temperature after it's first made but will set up well after an hour in the refrigerator. The looser consistency can be desirable in some contexts, but we typically store the emulsion over ice to keep it "stiff." Choose super-fresh oysters that are briny and nutty, with a creamy texture.

Using an immersion blender, blend the oysters with the parsley leaves to combine. Slowly blend in the neutral oil until emulsified. Blend in the parsley oil until fully emulsified, then season with lemon juice (the emulsion should not taste lemony, per se—use the lemon simply to enhance the freshness) and salt. Pass the emulsion though a tamis lined with a fine-mesh nylon sieve. Transfer to an airtight container set over an ice bath and reserve in the refrigerator until needed. Use the oyster emulsion the day you make it; mix well before using, adjusting the consistency with some of the reserved oyster liquor, if needed.

Lobster Head Sauce

Makes about 100 grams

12 grams pine shoots
9 grams Noma Umami Salt (page 113)
40 grams lobster tomalley
16 grams Truffle Tamari*
16 grams Umami Salt Shrimp Garum*
Rose Oil (page 187)
Pine Vinegar (page 39)
Cold-Infused Dashi (page 215; optional)
Salt

Over the years, we've found countless uses for lobster tomalley, the rich, green substance often mistakenly called the brain (it's actually the lobster's liver and pancreas). During our first pop-up in Kyoto, we served ise ebi (Japanese spiny lobster) as a main course, preceded by a dish of sansai, wild mountain vegetables that mark the arrival of spring. To balance the bitter, herbal notes of the greens, we created a smooth, deeply savory sauce using the lobster tomalley. We've since adapted that technique in Copenhagen, using Danish blue lobster and seasoning it with tools from our Nordic pantry: pine vinegar, rose oil, and umami salt. While lobster tail and claw meat gets most of the attention, some of its boldest, most complex flavour lies hidden in the head.

Pound the shoots and the umami salt to a paste in a mortar and pestle. Add the lobster tomalley and mash to incorporate. Add the tamari and garum and muddle until the mixture is creamy. Strain through a fine-mesh nylon sieve.

Transfer to a heatproof bowl set over a saucepan of simmering water and cook gently until thickened; the sauce may change color from green to orange (but if it doesn't, that's fine). Whisk in a bit of rose oil and pine vinegar to taste. Loosen the consistency of the sauce with dashi, if needed; you want a richly napping but not thick consistency. Season lightly with salt. Use immediately.

Pound the pine shoots and umami salt until you form a paste. Add the lobster tomalley (as Álvaro de Juan Sánchez does here) and pound until creamy.

Add the tamari and garum and muddle until blended. Pass the mixture through a fine-mesh nylon sieve.

Gently cook the mixture over simmering water until slightly thickened and the color has changed from green to orange.

Season to taste with rose oil, pine vinegar, and salt. Use immediately.

Celeriac Kebab with Kelp Mushroom Truffle Sauce, Vegetable, 2024
A skewer is made from tree sap hydrated and cooked in truffle juice, slow-roasted kohlrabi dried with mushroom kelp reduction, and pieces of a celeriac and truffle terrine. The skewer is brushed with linseed fudge and grilled and then served with kelp mushroom truffle sauce.

Kokotxas with Grilled Ramson and Parsley Kelp Sauce, Ocean, 2024
Cod throats (kokotxas) are cooked with barley koji oil and served with parsley kelp sauce and fig leaf oil along with grilled ramson leaves and a sprinkle of "Jun spice mix."

Butter Sauces

A beurre blanc in its traditional form—loads of fresh butter emulsified into reduced white wine, vinegar, and chopped shallots—may have found its way onto Noma menus in our early years, but once we opened the door to fermentation, we began to reimagine this classic sauce in our own context. Instead of a crisp sauvignon blanc as the main acidic ingredient, lacto-fermented koji water became the nervy contrast to all that butter.

The simple structure of a beurre blanc begs for improvisation, and over the years, our butter sauces have become more expressive, using ingredients such as various kojis, flavoured oils, teas, and juices.

Danish butter is renowned for its high butterfat content.

In this section, we go beyond the classic butter sauce to include other sauces. Some are simple, some more complex, but all with distinct personalities, and, of course, drenched in butter.

Keeping a Butter Sauce Together

Beurre blancs and other butter-based emulsions are pretty good at maintaining their rich, creamy texture thanks to the proteins in the milk solids. These proteins act as emulsifiers, coating the tiny droplets of butterfat dispersed into the sauce base through the cook's vigorous whisking; the coating makes it harder for the fat droplets to coalesce again.

In addition, the acidic ingredients in a beurre blanc—white wine, vinegar, lemon juice, lacto koji water, tomato water, to name a few—help the proteins keep the fat droplets separated from each other by allowing the milk proteins to carry more positive charge. This means the proteins can easily interact with both types of molecule in the sauce: the water (wine, lemon juice, lacto koji water . . .) and the fat, which don't normally want to mingle. The proteins form a barrier that also encourages the fat droplets to remain dispersed.

An immersion blender is an excellent tool for making butter sauces.

Temperature also matters to the stability of the sauce. If you've ever tried to make a butter sauce ahead of time and hold it while you finish the rest of your dish, you know that they can be fickle and will easily break or split if they get too warm or too cool. A butter-based emulsion remains stable between 30° and 60°C (86° and 140°F). Below 30°C (86°F), the butterfat begins to crystallize and solidify. Above 60°C (140°F), the water molecules in the sauce begin to move more rapidly, which destabilizes the suspension of fat molecules in the emulsion and can therefore cause the sauce to split. You can hold your butter sauce for up to 2 hours in the best temperature zone by using a water bath or pouring the sauce into a thermal vessel.

Lacto Koji Butter Sauce

Makes 250 grams

200 grams Lacto Koji Water*
  (made with barley koji)
50 grams cold unsalted butter, cubed
Salt
Filtered water

This sauce is our standard butter sauce—Noma's beurre blanc—built on lacto koji water, a complex, acidic, lightly fruity liquid made from lacto-fermenting koji (see opposite) and then clarifying the liquid (see page 240). When this lively liquid is ice-clarified and then emulsified with butter, the result provides the same palate-satisfying sensation of a beurre blanc but with a completely different flavour profile than you might expect—mouthwatering umami delicately balanced with notes of citrus zest and deeper undertones of roasted chicken. Such complexity in flavour can be directly attributed to the lacto koji water itself, but the added richness from the butter helps round out the sauce.

The simple construction of this sauce—lacto koji water, butter, and salt—allows for endless variation: Change the flavour profile by adding flavoured oils or tea infusions, for example. Or make a bigger adjustment by changing the substrate of the koji; we typically use pearl barley, which has a light cheesiness, but you could use rice koji instead, which is fruitier. (See the chart on page 389 for inspiration.)

This sauce should be treated just like a beurre blanc. It's best made fresh; it can keep for a bit, but temperature fluctuations can destabilize the emulsion and cause the sauce to separate. You can reemulsify the sauce, of course, but that would require reseasoning, so it's best made just before you need it.

The overall ratio here is 4 parts koji water to 1 part butter, but this can be adjusted based on specific uses.

Bring the koji water to a boil in a small saucepan. With an immersion blender, gradually blend in the butter to emulsify and fully incorporate. Season with salt and filtered water to taste. The sauce is best served immediately, but can be reserved for up to 2 hours; keep the emulsion slightly warm (around 50°C/120°F) to prevent it from breaking.

What Is Lacto Fermentation?

Lacto fermentation is a seemingly magical method of molecular transformation using a basic ingredient—salt—to control the environment of the ingredient being fermented. We wrote about this process in *The Noma Guide to Fermentation*. Making lacto koji water ("koji water" for short) involves a double fermentation. The first is to make the koji itself using a grain; we mostly use pearl barley as our substrate for the *Aspergillus oryzae* spores to do their magic, but we have also used rice and wheat. Once the koji is made, it is then blended with twice its weight in water, the total weight is combined with 2% salt, then vacuum sealed and allowed to ferment a second time at 28° to 32°C (82° to 90°F) for two to three days, until the bag has expanded with carbon dioxide. The resulting liquid—lacto koji water—now has a pleasing sourness, thanks to another magical organism, lactobacillus bacteria.

Koji Jasmine Sauce

Makes 450 grams

200 grams Lacto Koji Water*
(made with Øland wheat koji)
80 grams jasmine tea
60 grams Tomato Water*
100 grams cold unsalted butter, cubed
10 grams Fresh Barley Koji Oil (page 169)
Salt

This sauce illustrates ways to layer more flavours onto the basic butter sauce (page 384). Tea and tomato water add floral and fruity notes; fresh koji oil adds a bit more umami.

Place the lacto koji water, tea, and tomato water into a small saucepan. Bring to a simmer over medium heat, then, using an immersion blender, begin blending in the cubed butter one piece at a time to emulsify. When the butter has been fully incorporated, drizzle in the koji oil and blend until emulsified. Season the sauce with salt. The sauce is best served immediately, but can be reserved for up to 2 hours; keep the emulsion slightly warm (around 50°C/120°F) to prevent it from breaking.

Smoked Tomato Koji Sauce

Makes 300 grams

100 grams Lacto Koji Water*
(made with rice koji)
100 grams Tomato Water*
100 grams Smoked Butter
(page 196), cubed
Salt

This sauce uses a koji water made with rice koji, which is sweeter and lighter than wheat koji. Rice koji tends to exhibit more tropical fruit flavours, whereas wheat or pearl barley kojis have a deeper, nutty, cheesy flavour. The combination of tomato and lacto koji water has become a favorite of ours, especially in the summertime as a sauce for vegetables picked from the farm in the morning on the day they are served.

Place the lacto koji water and tomato water in a small saucepan. Bring to a simmer over medium heat, then, using an immersion blender, begin blending in the smoked butter one piece at a time to emulsify. When the butter has been fully incorporated, season the sauce with salt. The sauce is best served immediately, but can be reserved for up to 2 hours; keep the emulsion slightly warm (around 50°C/120°F) to prevent it from breaking.

Rose and Yeast Sauce

Makes 305 grams

100 grams Lacto Koji Water*
(made with rice koji)
100 grams Yeast Broth (page 218)
80 grams cold unsalted butter, cubed
25 grams Rose Oil (page 187)
Salt

The Test Kitchen is often asked to research problems that don't have clear answers, which allows the team members the freedom to explore conceptual hypotheses, express their own creativity, and hold each other accountable. During the Danish pandemic shutdowns of 2020 and 2021, for example, the team spent their time working on the concepts of "crispy" or "folded foods."

Back in 2012, the Test Kitchen focused on the concept of "umami broths," and yeast broth was created. The broth is a mixture of roasted fresh yeast (full of glutamic acid) and peaso, Noma's version of miso, made with Scandinavian yellow split peas—a double dose of umami. Paired with the pleasantly acidic, fruity lacto rice koji water, it's a winning combination. Rose oil adds a floral top note that lingers on the palate and ties the whole sauce together.

Place the lacto koji water and yeast broth in a small saucepan. Bring to a simmer over medium heat, then, using an immersion blender, begin blending in the cubed butter one piece at a time to emulsify. When the butter has been fully incorporated, drizzle in the rose oil and blend until emulsified. Season the sauce with salt. The sauce is best served immediately, but can be reserved for up to 2 hours; keep the emulsion slightly warm (around 50°C/120°F) to prevent it from breaking.

Lacto Koji Butter Sauce Variations

When we craft a new menu at the restaurant, we aim for eighteen to twenty-three small courses that convey the sentiment of the season, without repeating flavours. This constraint has limited the sheer quantity of lacto butter sauces that we have featured on menus, but during testing, we have worked with literally thousands of combinations, sometimes changing one lacto koji water and one butter variation, other times adding an additional broth or flavoured oil—more combinations are possible by adding more than one item from each category. Here's a chart that expresses the possibilities.

Lacto Koji Waters	Butter Variations	Additional Broths	Flavoured Oils	Additional Seasonings	Spice Mixes
Lacto Barley Koji Water	Butter	Cold-Infused Dashi	Rose Oil	Noma Umami Salt	Danish Curry Powder
Lacto Øland Wheat Koji Water	Smoked Butter	Tomato Water	Elderflower Oil	Noma Roasted Umami Salt	Berry Spice Mix
Lacto Rice Koji Water	Fresh Barley Koji Butter	Smoked Tomato Water	Pine Oil	Nordic Shoyu	Nordic Punch Spice Mix
		Yeast Broth	Pheasant Spice Oil	Dashi Reduction	Jun Spice Mix
		Jasmine Tea	Black Currant Wood Oil	Umami Salt Shrimp Garum	Saffron Spice Mix
		White Currant Juice	Larch Wood Oil	Blue Mussel Garum	
		Pine Dashi	Parsley Oil	Chicken Wing Garum	
		Mussel Broth	Mustard Seed Oil	Mushroom Garum	
			Lemon Thyme Oil	Black Pepper Tamari	
			Hazelnut Oil	Fava Rice Shoyu	
			Plum Kernel Oil	Peaso Reduction	
			Sunflower Seed and Beef Garum Oil	Yeast Reduction	
			Cep Oil	Smoked Seaweed Shoyu	
			Morita Chile Oil	Truffle Tamari	

Roasted Kelp Butter Sauce

Makes 140 grams

40 grams Noma Roasted Umami Salt (page 115)
20 grams filtered water, plus more if needed
80 grams cold unsalted butter, cubed

This three-ingredient sauce is essentially pure umami cloaked in butter. Raw kelp is full of glutamates, and roasting it makes those savory flavours deeper and richer. The sauce was originally used for a warm squid dish in the first Ocean season menu in 2018, but it's now a versatile menu staple that works well in any season.

Similar to Lacto Koji Butter Sauce (page 384), this sauce is open to limitless variation, but the ratio of butter to water makes it more fickle than your typical butter sauce. The particulates in the roasted umami salt help stabilize the emulsion, but it's not bulletproof; you need to pay attention to the temperature at which you hold it during service. We often season the sauce with different shoyus, tamaris, or other intense reductions and ferments, and a spice mix would certainly work wonders in this sauce. It is excellent with squid, scallops, red shellfish, white fish, and crab. It is also a perfect complement to grilled artichokes, mushrooms, an assortment of root vegetables, and game meats. As we said—versatile.

In a small saucepan, combine the roasted umami salt and the filtered water. Heat over medium-low heat, stirring to dissolve the umami salt, then, using an immersion blender, begin blending in the cubed butter one piece at a time to emulsify. Add a bit more water, if necessary, to maintain the emulsion. Keep the sauce warm and use right away.

Wild seaweeds.

Wild mushrooms.

Kelp Mushroom Truffle Sauce

Makes about 250 grams

50 grams reduced Mushroom Kelp Broth (page 221, reduced to 43°Bx), plus more if needed
100 grams truffle juice, plus more if needed
White wine vinegar
Reduced White Wine*
100 grams Brown Butter (page 198), melted
Chopped black truffle, to taste (about 2 grams per person)

This deeply flavoured sauce gets its backbone from umami-rich reduced mushroom kelp broth, with black truffle and truffle juice added for extra aroma and flavour. Unlike the previous butter sauces in this chapter, we take care to *avoid* emulsifying this sauce with the butter. The idea is to have little pockets of toasty, nutty brown butter floating on top of the sauce, so that the flavours in each bite are distributed randomly, creating a different experience from one spoonful to the next. Torsten Vildgaard is the chef behind many of Noma's most impressive sauces, including this one, which was originally created to accompany our Celeriac Shawarma main course for the first Vegetable season in 2018.

Place the reduced mushroom kelp broth in a small saucepan, add the truffle juice, and bring to a simmer over medium heat. Cook until the sauce is just able to coat the back of a spoon; the consistency should be much thinner than a demi-glace but thicker than a broth, so adjust with more truffle juice or kelp broth if needed. Season the sauce lightly with white wine vinegar and reduced white wine. Slowly add the brown butter, stirring to incorporate but not emulsify; to avoid emulsification, do not boil or whisk the sauce once the butter has been added. Just before serving, add the chopped truffle to the warm sauce. Use immediately.

Place the reduced mushroom kelp broth in a saucepan.

Add the truffle juice, bring the mixture to a simmer, and reduce to a light napping consistency. Season lightly with white wine vinegar and reduced white wine.

Add the brown butter, stirring to incorporate but not emulsify.

Just before serving, add the chopped black truffle. Use immediately.

Celeriac Shawarma, Vegetable, 2018
Thin slices of celeriac are cooked in brown butter and truffle juice and then layered with truffle puree, celeriac puree, and linseed fudge. The celeriac is slowly grilled and served with steamed greens, white currants, and kelp mushroom truffle sauce.

Cheese Sauce

Makes about 400 grams

Jasmine Tea

1.5 grams loose jasmine tea leaves
220 grams filtered water

Cheese Sauce

200 grams Vesterhavs cheese, chopped into small pieces
200 grams Jasmine Tea, plus more if needed
Cold unsalted butter, cubed

When we first developed this recipe almost fifteen years ago, it was a simple combination of cheese and water blended together, seasoned, and then foamed. The popularity of "foamy" sauces sprang from late-twentieth-century modernist cuisine spearheaded by Ferran Adrià, but of course a foamy texture in food is timeless—think sabayon, meringue, soufflé, or even the foam on a well-made matcha.

A sauce can foam when your ingredients emulsify and then capture air bubbles; the air, however, presents a stability issue because of the difference in density between air and water. This just means that a foamy sauce is less structurally stable than an emulsified liquid. In other words, bubbles will pop.

Vesterhavs cheese (also known as North Sea cheese) is a semi-hard cow's-milk cheese from an area in North Jutland close to the sea. This Gouda-style cheese has excellent saltiness and nuttiness, and is rich in protein, which makes it ideal for a foamy sauce. Cold-infused jasmine tea is added for floral notes, and cold butter can help create more foam.

Make the jasmine tea: Combine the tea leaves and water in a container. Refrigerate overnight to infuse. Strain through a fine-mesh nylon sieve.

Make the cheese sauce: Place the cheese and the tea in a Thermomix and blend on speed 5 for 15 minutes. Strain the sauce through a fine-mesh nylon sieve and reserve in an airtight container in the refrigerator until ready to serve.

Just before serving, warm the sauce in a medium saucepan over medium heat, but do not let it boil. Tip the saucepan and, using an immersion blender, buzz the surface of the sauce to aerate and foam. Add cold butter piece by piece as needed to help the sauce foam more easily. Add a bit more jasmine tea to adjust the consistency, if needed. Serve immediately; this sauce does not reheat well.

Grasshopper Walnut Mole

Makes about 200 grams

Grasshopper Butter
80 grams unsalted butter
80 grams grasshoppers
3 grams Berry Spice Mix (page 132)

Mole
40 grams Grasshopper Butter
100 grams Walnut Butter*
25 grams Roasted Kelp Oil (page 170)
20 grams Cucumber Reduction (page 255)
Peaso Water Reduction (page 258)
Salt
Xanthan gum (optional)

This mole first appeared on our 2018 Vegetable menu. We've long admired Mexican moles, having spent time in Mexico for our pop-up in Tulum; we were also experimenting with insects. Test Kitchen head Mette Søberg was developing a grasshopper butter as well as a reduction of walnut milk that we also called a "butter." She combined the two, resulting in a creamy, rich, and nutty "mole," a key component in an iconic dish called Pumpkin Seed Tofu and Walnut Mole. The tofu was lightly cooked, dotted with Pumpkin Seed Oil (page 487), and served with grasshopper walnut mole and grilled rose petals.

Make the grasshopper butter: Melt the butter in a large skillet over medium heat. When it starts to bubble, add the grasshoppers, followed by the berry spice mix. Reduce the heat to low and cook for about an hour, until the grasshoppers begin to crisp. Transfer the mixture to a mortar and use the pestle to crush the grasshoppers. Let cool slightly, then pass through a tamis lined with a fine-mesh nylon sieve, squeezing the solids to extract as much flavour as possible. Reserve the butter.

Make the mole: Place the grasshopper butter, walnut butter, kelp oil, and cucumber reduction in a medium saucepan and whisk over low heat. Season to taste with peaso water reduction and salt and whisk until smooth. This sauce has a tendency to split; if you need to reemulsify it, heat it gently, add a splash of water and a knifetip of xanthan gum, and blend with an immersion blender to bring it back together. Use immediately.

Make the Berry Spice Mix.

Melt the butter in a large skillet over medium heat, then add the grasshoppers.

Strain the grasshopper butter through a tamis lined with a fine-mesh nylon sieve, squeezing to extract as much flavour as possible.

Place the walnut butter in a medium saucepan. Use immediately.

Add the berry spice mix and cook until the grasshoppers and butter are both nicely toasted, about 1 hour.

Transfer the mixture to a mortar and crush the grasshoppers with the pestle.

Add the grasshopper butter, roasted kelp oil, and cucumber reduction and whisk over low heat to combine.

Season with the peaso water reduction and salt to taste; whisk until smooth. Use immediately.

Suggested Uses

Roasted Eggplant in Watercress Sauce

Cut an eggplant in half and score the flesh to help the eggplant cook evenly. Brush with clarified butter, season with salt, and roast in a hot oven until the exterior is nicely browned and the interior is creamy and tender. Serve on a pool of Watercress Sauce (page 359).

New Potatoes with Cheese Sauce

Boil new potatoes and a few lovage stems until the potatoes are tender. Drain and serve the potatoes with Cheese Sauce (page 398), a sprinkling of chopped fresh parsley and lovage leaves, and a few pan-fried lardons.

Grilled Artichokes Glazed with Roasted Kelp Butter Sauce

Pare a few artichokes down to the base and tender inner leaves. Brush lightly with oil and grill until tender and just slightly crisp around the edges. Remove from the grill and brush generously with Roasted Kelp Butter Sauce (page 391).

A Twist on Seafood Cocktail

Replace your tomato-based seafood cocktail sauce with Oyster Emulsion (page 375).

Roasted Turbot with Lacto Koji Butter Sauce

Simply season a fillet of turbot or halibut with salt and freshly ground black pepper, then roast or sauté. Dress the fish with a generous spoonful of Lacto Koji Butter Sauce (page 384).

Lobster in Lobster Head Sauce

Split the lobster in half lengthwise. Remove half the tomalley and use it to make Lobster Head Sauce (page 376). Boil the claws, crack one open, and extract the meat. Finely chop and combine with the remaining tomalley and some chopped fresh tarragon. Stuff this mixture into one half of the lobster head. Gently sear the head cut-side down in foaming butter until lightly caramelized. Sear the tail in foaming butter until just cooked through. Gently warm the remaining claw in the same butter. Serve with the Lobster Head Sauce.

Opposite, top to bottom: Roasted Eggplant in Watercress Sauce; Grilled Artichokes Glazed with Roasted Kelp Butter Sauce; Roasted Turbot with Lacto Koji Butter Sauce
Right: Lobster in Lobster Head Sauce

Grasshopper Walnut Mole with Flatbread

Make a simple flatbread, such as naan or chapati, or a flour tortilla, and serve with a bowl of warm Grasshopper Walnut Mole (page 401) for dipping.

Brown Butter Emulsion on Roast Beef Toasts

Toast sliced sourdough bread and brush generously with Brown Butter Emulsion (page 371). Top the toasts with thinly sliced rare roast beef and a small handful of spicy mustard greens.

Grilled Vegetables with Ramson Sauce

Grill green asparagus spears and some cabbage leaves. Season the vegetables with Smoked Butter (page 196) and horseradish juice (see page 237) and then serve with Ramson Sauce (page 353).

Fried Eggs in Kelp Mushroom Truffle Sauce

Fry a few eggs to your desired doneness and dress with a few spoonfuls of Kelp Mushroom Truffle Sauce (page 395). Serve with good toast for sopping up the sauce.

Tempura Vegetables with Whisky Egg Yolk Sauce

Fry an assortment of vegetables in a tempura batter; pumpkin or other winter squash, white asparagus, or baby corn work well. Serve the tempura vegetables with Whisky Egg Yolk Sauce (page 365) for dipping.

Rose Béarnaise on Grilled Mushroom Steak

Brush large mushrooms (such as oyster, maitake, or lion's mane mushrooms) with olive oil and roast in a hot oven until just tender. Press under a weight to remove most of the remaining juices, then brush with soy sauce and butter and grill. Serve the mushroom steak with Rose Béarnaise (page 367).

Blackened Padrón Peppers with Warm Mushroom Vinaigrette

Heat a grill or cast-iron skillet, toss in some Padrón peppers, and cook until they're nicely blackened on several sides. Arrange them on a serving plate and dress the plate with Warm Mushroom Vinaigrette (page 345).

Opposite, top to bottom: Grasshopper Walnut Mole with Flatbread; Fried Eggs in Kelp Mushroom Truffle Sauce
Right: Blackened Padrón Peppers with Warm Mushroom Vinaigrette

8.

Sweet Flavours

Sweet Flavours: Refining and rebalancing with restraint

Tree Sap Pie, Forest, 2023
Tree sap is simmered in orange wine, sugar, bergamot, roseroot, and rose petals until tender. The sap is embedded with ants and served on a tart shell made from frozen cream.

Dessert is probably the most unnecessary part of a meal—which is exactly what makes it special. A final pleasure. A moment made only to be enjoyed.

But I've always questioned how desserts fit into a menu. So often, they come at the end like a heavy curtain. Dense, sugary, final. They close the experience, instead of leaving you curious, alert, wanting more.

Is this because desserts are too sweet? How sweet is sweet enough? We've been asking that for years, and the answer keeps changing.

When I was an apprentice, as much as 300 grams of sugar per liter of ice cream was standard. Today, that kind of sweetness feels unthinkable. We've spent years reducing the sugar in our desserts. Not to make them healthier—but to make them better. Because sugar shouldn't be the point. It should be the support.

That's where we've focused most of our work: searching for sweetness in other places. In fruit, in time, in technique. In a syrup made from berries at their peak, in fermented plums, birch sap, even seaweed. With fruity aromas that enhance sweetness without adding sugar (thank you, Dr. Arielle Johnson, who, over the course of five years, helped us understand flavour).

And salt is essential to sweet. It doesn't make desserts salty—it makes them better. A pinch in vanilla ice cream makes the vanilla stronger. A sprinkle in chocolate ganache rounds off the bitterness.

411

Candied Pine Cone, Forest, 2023
Candied pine cones are dressed with an ant paste and juniper skin, served with wild sumac dipped in chocolate sauce.

In our perpetual efforts to refine and rebalance, we've had many missteps over the years. (There was a certain celery dessert that didn't go down well.) Some ideas stayed, most didn't. But the work mattered. It forced us to question everything.

Thankfully, we've been lucky with the pastry chefs who've passed through Noma—Rosio Sanchez and Malcolm Livingston II, among others. All of them left a mark. Their ideas still echo in the way we think, in the textures and the details of the pastry kitchen.

I once cooked a dinner with Albert Adrià—maybe the greatest pastry chef of his generation. He was focused, moving fast, trying to get everything just right. He turned to me with a drop of sweat hanging from the tip of his nose and said, "You know what? In the end, people want a break. They've had drinks. They've had a full menu. Dessert's just an afterthought."

He may have been right, which is why we work extra hard to reimagine the end of a meal at Noma.

The best way to make dessert more than an afterthought, I believe, is to make the flavour matter more than the sugar.

Syrups

Making a syrup from fruit or flowers at their peak is a brilliant way to capture the seasons, an ongoing pursuit for us at Noma, especially given our short Danish summers. We use our syrups to sweeten juices served as beverages and to balance flavours in our sweet dishes.

Most of our syrups begin with equal parts sugar and water—simple syrup. This solution is "polar," meaning it loves water and readily mixes with other polar molecules (for more on polarity, see page 12). Many of the enchanting aromas from fruit and flowers—aromas that are responsible for our sensation of "tasting" them (see page 11)—come from compounds called volatile esters, which are also polar compounds, so they blend easily into a simple syrup. The viscosity of a simple syrup also reduces the rate of evaporation of these delicate aroma compounds, trapping them in the thick syrup, one more reason simple syrup is an ideal medium for expressing flavour.

Syrups capture the flavours of summer.

Elderflower Syrup

Makes about 1.5 kilograms

750 grams filtered water
750 grams sugar
250 grams picked elderflower umbels (flower clusters)
80 grams lemon slices

Elderflower grows wild all over Denmark, and Danes are crazy about this fragrant early-summer flower. You will find elderflower syrup, elderflower cordial, and various commercially available elderflower-spiked juices in all the supermarkets, and many home cooks make their own elderflower syrup to use in cocktails, to add to soda water for a soft drink, and to sweeten desserts. At Noma, we make this seasonal syrup as well, adding it to various sauces and other concoctions, including our elderflower kombucha.

Place the water and sugar in a saucepan and bring to a boil, stirring to dissolve the sugar. Place the elderflowers in a heatproof airtight container and pour the hot syrup over them; the flowers will float. Lay the lemon slices on top of the floating flowers and place a sheet of plastic wrap directly against the surface of the syrup. Let cool to room temperature, then cover and refrigerate for 2 weeks to infuse.

Strain the syrup through a conical strainer, pressing on the solids for maximum extraction, then strain again through a fine-mesh nylon sieve. Use right away, keep refrigerated in an airtight container for up to 5 days, or freeze for longer-term storage.

Beeswax Syrup

Makes about 1.4 kilograms

250 grams beeswax
1 kilogram filtered water
1 kilogram sugar

Beeswax is special to us at Noma. We use this enchanting material to fashion bowls and other servingware, and we also use it to age game meats, flavour desserts, and season juices. Here we infuse beeswax into water using an ultrasonic homogenizer, or sonicator for short. Through intense sound waves that create microscopic bubbles, a sonicator agitates and breaks down the cell walls of ingredients to release flavour molecules. Beeswax is a fat, and fat and water don't mix. However, using a sonicator, we can disperse the flavour molecules into all sorts of liquids, allowing us to combine previously incompatible flavours.

You could simply steep the beeswax in water or heat the wax and water together, but this would alter the flavour of the wax. Beeswax syrup is a simple illustration of the power of a sonicator, but we have also used this technology to create infusions for beverage pairings, including beeswax sonicated into pumpkin juice, quince juice, and saffron kombucha.

Sonicate the beeswax into the water at 30% amplitude until the mixture reaches a temperature of 60°C (140°F). Strain the water through a fine-mesh nylon sieve into a saucepan. Add the sugar and bring the mixture to a boil, stirring to dissolve the sugar, then reduce the heat to maintain a simmer and cook until the syrup reaches 72°Bx (as measured by a refractometer). Remove from the heat and let cool. Use right away, keep refrigerated in an airtight container for up to 5 days, or freeze for longer-term storage.

Lemon Thyme Syrup

Makes 900 grams

600 grams filtered water
300 grams sugar
5 grams lemon thyme sprigs
5 juniper berries

Lemon thyme has been a staple ingredient at Noma for decades. It offers the earthy, slightly peppery character of classic thyme, with a bright citrus note that's more subtle and nuanced than lemon zest. Infused into a light syrup alongside piney juniper berries, the result is fragrant and herbaceous—balanced rather than overpowering.

Place the water and sugar in a saucepan and bring to a boil, stirring to dissolve the sugar. Remove from the heat and add the lemon thyme and juniper berries. Let stand at room temperature for 3 hours to infuse, then strain the syrup through a fine-mesh nylon sieve. Use right away, keep refrigerated in an airtight container for up to 5 days, or freeze for longer-term storage.

Gaute Schartau Berrefjord adds Gammel Dansk to glucose syrup.

Gammel Dansk Blueberry Syrup

Makes about 400 grams

300 grams glucose syrup
200 grams Gammel Dansk liqueur (Fernet-Branca is an acceptable substitute)
100 grams freeze-dried blueberries

In the Test Kitchen, ideas often start with a passing comment—in this case, a curiosity about a dessert made with Gammel Dansk, a beloved bitters made from a blend of twenty-nine herbs, spices, and roots. Rosio Sanchez, Noma's pastry chef from 2012 to 2017, took up the challenge. With experience at the restaurant wd-50 in New York, she had previously worked with bitters in sweet contexts and knew instinctively that bitterness didn't just pair well with sugar—it also played beautifully against fat, like cream or dairy. Cooking out the alcohol in the Gammel Dansk helped mellow the bitterness, and the berries brought a faint fruitiness with just a touch of color. Blend the syrup with a milk ice cream base to act as both a flavouring and a stabilizer (the glucose prevents crystallization), or simply drizzle it over a scoop of rich vanilla ice cream, or use it anywhere you'd reach for a bittersweet syrup with depth. This syrup recipe is a template, one that can be adapted for use with other herbal spirits.

Using wet hands, scoop the glucose syrup into a small saucepan. Add the Gammel Dansk and stir to combine. Bring to a simmer over medium heat. Simmer until reduced to 65°Bx (as measured by a refractometer), then remove from the heat. Add the blueberries and let stand for 5 minutes to infuse. Strain the syrup through a fine-mesh nylon sieve; do not press on the blueberries, as you don't want the syrup to acquire too much color. Let cool. Use right away, keep refrigerated in an airtight container for up to 5 days, or freeze for longer-term storage.

Pine Syrup

Makes about 400 grams

200 grams sugar
200 grams filtered water
25 grams Douglas fir needles

Pine (which we use as a catchall name for various conifers) is one of Noma's "mother flavours," and is extremely versatile and useful in our kitchen. Emblematic of our Scandinavian geography, pine's flavour and aroma are rich with two terpenes in particular: pinene (resinous and woody) and limonene (citrusy and bright). This "foresty" fragrance is excellent for balancing anything rich, fatty, or sweet. We most commonly use pine syrup in our nonalcoholic beverage pairing, but will also use it as a general seasoning tool for desserts.

Combine the sugar and water in a saucepan and bring to a boil over medium heat, stirring to dissolve the sugar. Remove from the heat and let cool to room temperature. Transfer the syrup to a Thermomix, add the Douglas fir needles, and blend until well combined. Pass the mixture through a fine-mesh nylon sieve, pressing on the solids well to maximize your yield. Use right away, keep refrigerated in an airtight container for up to 5 days, or freeze for longer-term storage.

Place the cleaned ants in a mortar.

Freeze the ants with liquid nitrogen and crush with the pestle until they are powdered.

Add the elderflower oil and the honey.

Blend with the pestle until well combined.
Use right away, refrigerate in an airtight container for up to 5 days, or freeze.

Ant Honey

Makes 65 grams

10 grams frozen ants
Liquid nitrogen
15 grams Elderflower Oil (page 179)
40 grams honey

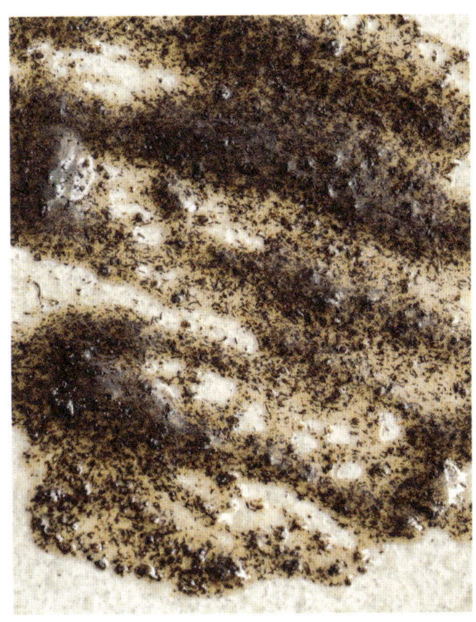

Honey is a polar substance that dissolves easily in other polar liquids (see page 12 for more on polarity), in this case, the formic acid produced by the wood ants that we forage in our region. The formic acid has a white vinegar aroma and a purely lemon juice flavour. The coniferous forests near Copenhagen have a limitless supply of dried pine needles available for anthill construction, and the ants adopt the limonene-terpene aromas common to pine. Lemon and honey is a winning combination, and we elevate the syrup further by adding an extra layer of flavour with elderflower oil. We have served this seasoned honey in a Honeycomb Chew petit four, but it can be used anywhere you would normally use honey.

Place the ants in a mortar, freeze them with liquid nitrogen, and use the pestle to crush them until fully pulverized into a powder. Add the elderflower oil and the honey and mix with the pestle until well combined. Use right away, keep refrigerated in an airtight container for up to 5 days, or freeze for longer-term storage.

Fruit Leathers and Compotes

Walk through the markets in Georgia, the Balkans, or other places in Eastern Europe and you'll see vendors offering fruit leathers in a kaleidoscope of colors, some folded, others shaped into large discs, all tempting. Fruit has been dried through the evaporative power of the sun for ages, and it's an ingenious way to preserve seasonal fruit for use later in the year. The fruit can be dried when ripe and sweet to enjoy as a snack, or unripe and tart to use in savory dishes when you want a hint of sour.

Fruit leathers can be used in both sweet and savory dishes.

At Noma, we make fruit leather to use in similar ways, and we also focus on the leather as a wrapper for other elements of a dish. Maybe a blackberry, black currant, and aronia leather to wrap around smoked and roasted beets, or a white currant leather to encapsulate rose hip puree. The beauty of working with fruit leathers is that the puree is extremely malleable before it fully dries, so by using molds, we can shape the leathers to look like insects,

Pages 430–431:
Fruit leathers air-drying.

as in our Ice-Cold Beet Juice and Ladybug dish from Vegetable season 2021.

Making fruit compote is another way to preserve the flavours of the season, though our Noma compotes are meant to be eaten in the near term rather than canned for longer storage. Unlike a rustic homestyle fruit compote, where the fruit, sugar, and seasonings are stewed together, we like to preserve the shape of the fruit, simmering them in syrups until imbued with sweetness, then chopping and enrobing them in just enough reduced syrup to give them a sparkling, gem-like appearance.

White Currant Leather

Makes about five 42 by 30 cm (16¾ by 12-inch) sheets

1 kilogram White Currant Juice*
80 grams sugar
30 grams honey

Fruit leather is a perfect destination for white currant juice, but the method we use here is appropriate for most fruit. Use a dehydrator to jump-start the drying process, or simply cook the sweetened fruit juice until it has thickened to a spreadable consistency, thanks to the pectin in the currants.

Place the white currant juice, sugar, and honey in a saucepan and bring to a boil, stirring to dissolve the sugar and honey. Transfer the liquid to a shallow container and place in a dehydrator or oven set to 60°C (140°F)—no higher than this temperature, or the flavour will change. Reduce the mixture overnight. Blend the mixture with an immersion blender so it's fully homogeneous, then measure the sugar content with a refractometer. If it has not reached 64°Bx, return it to the dehydrator or oven and continue to reduce. Using a pastry card, pass the mixture through a tamis lined with a fine-mesh nylon sieve, then transfer the mixture to a vacuum machine and compress it until all the air is removed from the leather base. (If you don't have a vacuum machine, you can skip this step.)

Spread some of the mixture over a Silpat to your desired thickness; repeat with the remaining mixture and more Silpats. Let stand at room temperature for at least 2 days, or until set and no longer tacky. Use right away, reserve in an airtight container in the refrigerator for up to 2 weeks, or stack between sheets of oiled parchment paper to prevent sticking and freeze for up to 6 months.

Lacto Plum Leather

Makes about five 42 by 30 cm (16¾ by 12-inch) sheets

1 kilogram plums, halved and pitted
Salt
Freeze-dried lingonberries
Freeze-dried blueberries

Lacto fermentation is an easy technique that gives plums, and many other ingredients, a more complex flavour profile, adding acidic and umami notes without overwhelming the natural sweet-tangy fruitiness of the plums. We most often use this lacto plum leather as a crisp: Once dried, we bake it until snappy. The result is a tangy, fermented crisp we've served with everything from trout roe and Cured Egg Yolk Sauce (page 363) to spring peas and roses.

Place the plums in large vacuum bags and add 2% salt by weight. Seal on 100% vacuum, then let stand at 28°C (82°F) for 5 to 6 days, until sour.

Drain the lacto-fermented plums, reserving their juice. Weigh the plum flesh and transfer to a Thermomix. Add 2% freeze-dried lingonberries and 3% freeze-dried blueberries by weight and blend until pureed, adjusting the consistency with some of the reserved plum juice, if needed. Pass the puree through a conical strainer. Spread some of the puree over a Silpat in a thin layer; repeat with the remaining puree and more Silpats. Let stand at room temperature for at least 2 days, or until set and no longer tacky, or dry in a dehydrator set to 60°C (140°F). (If desired, this leather can be further dried in the oven at 80°C/176°F until it forms a crisp.) Use right away, reserve in an airtight container in the refrigerator for up to 2 weeks, or stack between sheets of oiled parchment paper to prevent sticking and freeze for up to 6 months.

Place the lacto-fermented plums in a Thermomix with 2% freeze-dried lingonberries and 3% freeze-dried blueberries by weight. Blend until smooth. Adjust the consistency with reserved juice, if needed.

Strain the plum puree through a conical strainer, then spread it over a Silpat in a thin layer.

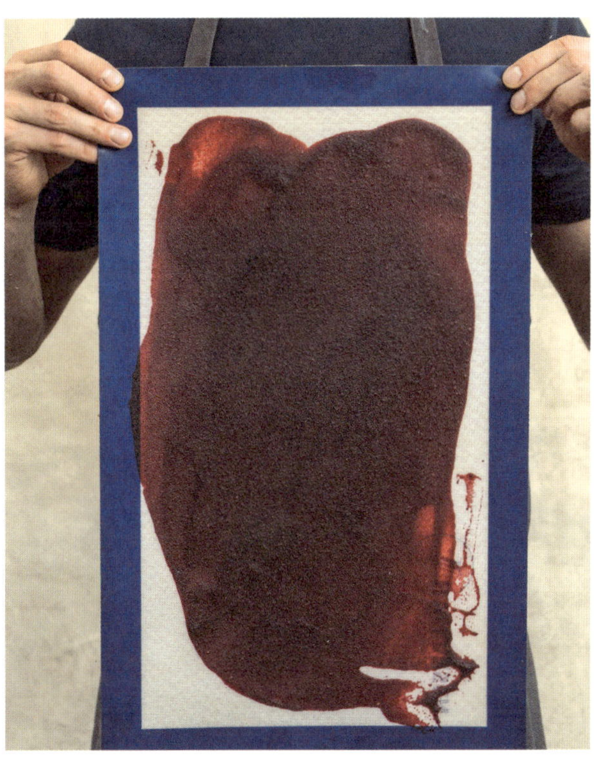

Let stand at room temperature for at least 2 days, or until no longer tacky but not so dry that it becomes crisp.

Gently peel the plum leather from the Silpat and refrigerate in an airtight container for up to 2 weeks, or stack between sheets of oiled parchment paper and freeze for up to 6 months.

Rose Hip Leather

Makes about three 42 by 30 cm (16¾ by 12-inch) sheets

1 kilogram rose hips
15 grams Chamomile Oil*
1.5 grams dried angelica seeds
1 gram dried meadowsweet
150 grams red gooseberries

After the petals fall off the *Rosa rugosa* bushes that grow along the coastlines of Denmark, rose hips emerge. The fruit can be difficult to process because it's quite seedy, but the flavour is tangy—it's full of vitamin C—lightly floral, sweet, and very popular in Scandinavia for use in juices, jams, and other preserves.

Pass the rose hips through a tamis to separate the seeds from the flesh. Reserve.

Heat the chamomile oil in a sauté pan over medium-low heat. Add the angelica and meadowsweet and sweat them briefly, then add the gooseberries, allowing them to break down and sweat. Add 300 grams of the rose hip flesh (reserve the rest for another use) and cook until the mixture has thickened a bit (it can't be too wet), about 30 minutes. Strain the mixture through a fine-mesh nylon sieve. Spread some of the puree over a Silpat in an even layer; repeat with the remaining puree and more Silpats. Let stand at room temperature for at least 2 days, or until set and no longer tacky, or dry in a dehydrator set to 60°C (140°F). Use right away, reserve in an airtight container in the refrigerator for up to 2 weeks, or stack between sheets of oiled parchment paper to prevent sticking and freeze for up to 6 months.

Sea Buckthorn and Carrot Leather

Makes about three 42 by 30 cm (16¾ by 12-inch) sheets

300 grams Sea Buckthorn Juice*
700 grams Carrot Juice*
45 grams honey
20 grams pectin powder

Sea buckthorn is a hardy plant that survives well in sandy soil near the Danish coast. This spiny shrub produces tiny, extremely tart orange berries that are the size of a pill and contain a large seed. They are packed with vitamin C—one sea buckthorn berry has more vitamin C than an entire orange. Sea buckthorn has been used in Scandinavia for thousands of years, and given our desire to find naturally acidic ingredients in our landscape, the plant was an early (and welcome) discovery for Noma.

Sea buckthorn is not rich in pectin, so we add a bit to ensure that everything binds together to make a chewy leather. This recipe dates back more than a decade but represents Noma's early dive into the preservation of the native flavours of Scandinavia.

Stir together the sea buckthorn juice, carrot juice, and honey in a bowl. Transfer a third of the juice mixture to a saucepan and sift in the pectin. While whisking, bring the mixture to a boil, then pour it into the bowl with the remaining juice and stir well to combine. Strain the juice through a fine-mesh nylon sieve. Line three flat sheet pans with Silpats and divide the juice among the prepared pans. Let stand at room temperature (if space allows) for at least 2 days, or until set and no longer tacky, or dry in the oven at 60°C (140°F), watching it carefully. Use right away, reserve in an airtight container in the refrigerator for up to 2 weeks, or stack between sheets of oiled parchment paper to prevent sticking and freeze for up to 6 months.

Aronia Kelp

Makes about 250 grams

250 grams kelp (thick center-cut pieces only)
3.5 kilograms aronia juice
1 kilogram filtered water
70 grams muscovado sugar
30 grams dried ceps
25 grams dried morels
20 grams freeze-dried lingonberries
10 grams roasted juniper wood
8 grams quince tea
Flavoured oil of your choice, for brushing (optional)

Unlike our other fruit leathers, which begin with fresh fruit blended into a puree that's spread thin and dried, this "fruit leather" is actually kelp that has been slowly simmered in a tart broth of aronia berry juice, dried mushrooms, and juniper wood until meltingly tender, then dried for three days until tacky and chewy, like a fruit leather. It's the perfect blend of earthy fruitiness and umami, and can be rolled thin like a sheet of pasta.

About twelve years ago, this unlikely marriage of aronia and kelp found harmony in our Test Kitchen thanks to Thomas Frebel and his love for long-duration cooking techniques. Aronia berries are blue-black berries that grow on shrubs and have more than three times the antioxidants of blueberries. The flavour of a raw aronia berry is extremely astringent, but when stewed with kelp, a touch of sugar, and other forest aromatics, the broth develops beautiful depth and roundness, and is an excellent counterpoint to the mineral-umami flavours of the kelp. Our black currant wood farmer has an affinity for the not-very-well known aronia berry and its health benefits, which is how we first discovered the fruit.

We've used aronia kelp in both savory and sweet preparations, including a carrot terrine, a plum snack in which the aronia kelp mimics plum skin, and a sheep's-milk mousse with semi-dried fruits (see page 94).

Place the kelp, 2 kilograms of the aronia juice, the water, sugar, ceps, morels, lingonberries, juniper wood, and quince tea in a large pot and bring to a boil. Reduce the heat to low and simmer for 24 hours. Remove the kelp and set aside. Strain the broth through a superbag, squeezing the solids to maximize your yield. Transfer the broth to a clean pot and add the remaining 1.5 kilograms aronia juice. Return the kelp to the broth and simmer for 72 hours more, until the liquid has reduced to a syrupy consistency. Remove from the heat.

Transfer the kelp to Silpat-lined perforated trays (the broth is also excellent and can be further reduced into a tart, fruity, umami-laden syrup). Let stand at room temperature for 24 to 36 hours, flipping the kelp every few hours, until it is tacky but no longer wet to the touch; it should have the texture of a gummy candy. As the kelp dries, brush it with a flavoured oil of your choice, if you like (Larch Wood Oil, page 190, is a favorite of ours), brushing each side when you flip the kelp.

If you want a thinner product to use as a wrapper, sandwich the kelp between two pieces of parchment paper and pass it through a pasta roller (or simply roll it with a rolling pin). Use right away, reserve in an airtight container in the refrigerator for up to 2 weeks, or stack between sheets of oiled parchment paper to prevent sticking and freeze for up to 6 months.

Combine the kelp, 2 kilograms of the aronia juice, the water, sugar, ceps, morels, lingonberries, juniper wood, and quince tea in a large pot. Bring to a boil, then simmer for 24 hours.

Remove the kelp from the juice and set aside.

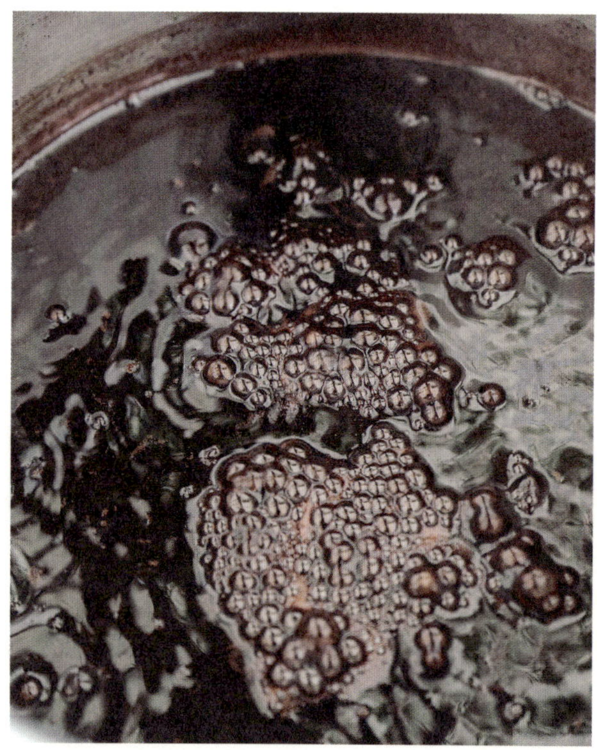

Simmer for 72 hours more, until the broth is syrupy.

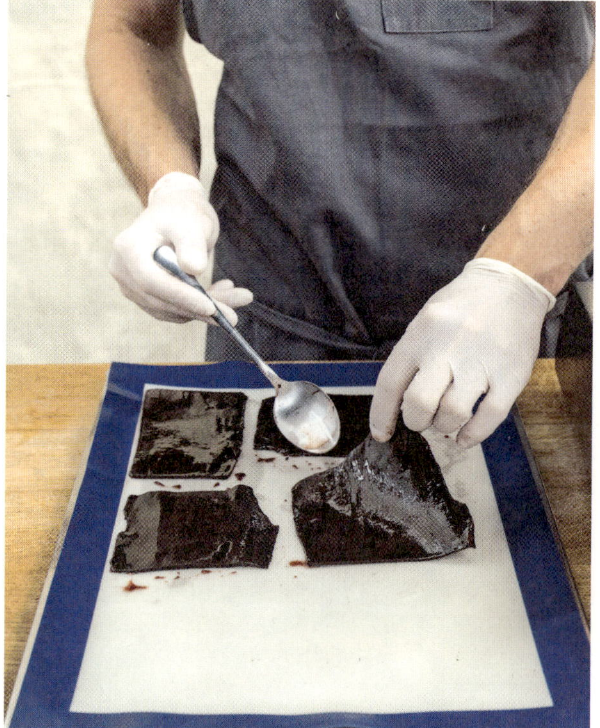

Remove the kelp from the broth and arrange it on a Silpat.
Let dry at room temperature, flipping it frequently for even drying.

Strain through a conical strainer and pass the juice through a superbag. Return the strained juice to a clean rondeau and add the remaining 1.5 kilograms aronia juice.

Return the kelp to the broth.

As the kelp dries, brush it with a flavoured oil, if you like, brushing each side as you flip the kelp. Dry until the kelp is tacky but no longer wet to the touch and has the texture of a gummy candy.

For even thinner kelp, sandwich between two squares of parchment and pass through a pasta roller. Use right away, refrigerate in an airtight container for up to 2 weeks, or stack between sheets of oiled parchment and freeze.

Kelp Fruit Leather, Ocean, 2025
A leather of black currant, blackberry, and lingonberry is dried on a piece of sugar kelp and seasoned with apple balsamic vinegar, black currant wood oil, and Japanese red sansho. The leather is then peeled off the seaweed by the guest.

Sea Star Caramel, Ocean, 2025
A sea star shell is made from sea buckthorn and carrot leather mixed with black currant leather. The shell is filled with a cardamom-saffron caramel and glazed with a saffron and black yuzu glaze.

Rhubarb Compote

Makes about 200 grams

Sweet Rhubarb Reduction
2 kilograms rhubarb stalks, trimmed and cut into 2.5 cm (1-inch) pieces
Birch syrup

Aronia Juice Reduction
1 kilogram aronia juice

Chewy Rhubarb Compote
200 grams rhubarb stalks (only the reddest parts)
30 grams birch syrup
4 grams Aronia Juice Reduction
Sweet Rhubarb Reduction, to taste

This compote uses layering and intensifying flavour through slow dehydration. Though labor-intensive, the result is a pleasingly chewy, sticky-sweet compote that we've served alongside sheep's-milk mousse and fresh sorrel.

Make the sweet rhubarb reduction: Run the rhubarb through a centrifugal juicer, then pass the pulp through the juicer twice more. Transfer the juice to a pot and bring it to a boil, skimming off the residue. Strain the juice through a tamis lined with a fine-mesh nylon sieve and let cool to room temperature. Reserve a small amount of the fresh rhubarb juice and transfer the rest to a shallow container. Place in a dehydrator set to 60°C (140°F) and reduce slowly until the juice has a sugar content of 30°Bx (as measured by a refractometer). Mix the reduced rhubarb juice with birch syrup at a ratio of 5 parts rhubarb juice to 1 part birch syrup. Reserve in an airtight container in the refrigerator until needed.

Make the aronia juice reduction: Heat the aronia juice in a saucepan over low heat until steaming. Transfer to a shallow container and place in a dehydrator set to 60°C (140°F). Reduce slowly until the juice has a sugar content of 30°Bx. Refrigerate in an airtight container until needed.

Make the compote: Place the rhubarb stalks into a vacuum bag with the birch syrup and aronia juice reduction and seal on 100% vacuum. Steam in a combi oven set to 70°C (160°F) for

18 minutes. Remove the rhubarb from the bag and reserve the liquid. Cut the cooked rhubarb into smaller strips, place them in a 1-liter container and add enough of the reserved cooking liquid to cover. Place in a dehydrator set to 60°C (140°F). Dry for 3 hours, flipping the strips and basting with the cooking liquid every 45 minutes, then dry for 2 hours more, flipping and basting every 20 minutes and adding sweet rhubarb reduction as necessary if the liquid becomes too thick. The goal is chewy rhubarb strips that retain their shape. Remove the rhubarb strips from the cooking liquid and dice them into 1 cm (½-inch) pieces. Season with more sweet rhubarb reduction and reserved fresh rhubarb juice to taste. The chewy rhubarb mixed with the sweet rhubarb reduction should be quite tacky in texture, like a compote. Reserve in an airtight container in the refrigerator for up to 3 days.

Japanese Quince Compote

Makes about 200 grams

About 200 grams frozen Japanese quince
100 grams orange wine
150 grams sugar
100 grams filtered water
75 grams Elderflower Syrup (page 417)
3 grams dried roseroot
2 grams dried marigold flowers

For the Ocean season in 2022, Test Kitchen head Junichi Takahashi was working on a rather unconventional dessert: Quince Amazake and Oyster, complete with quince amazake ice cream, an oyster and kelp caramel, quince-honey gel, and elderflower oil, all served in an oyster shell. We thought it was a brilliant dessert (though the psychological impact of eating ice cream from a rather large oyster shell was a bit too much for some of our diners!).

In 2024, Mette Søberg, Jun's colleague in the Test Kitchen, took that psychological game a step further. Our Oyster Dessert entailed a very detailed "oyster shell" made of frozen cream tinted with natural food colorings—charcoal, spirulina, Poppy Seed Praline (page 465)—to make an edible shell. She filled it with milk ice cream and then topped it with this Japanese quince compote. It's one of the best desserts we have ever produced at the restaurant.

Halve the quince and remove the seeds and white pith. Weigh 130 grams of the quince and place them in a saucepan. Add the wine, sugar, water, elderflower syrup, roseroot, and marigold flowers and simmer for 1 hour. Remove from the heat and let cool. Strain the syrup and reserve. Transfer the quince to a cutting board and dice into 5 mm (¼-inch) cubes. Place the diced quince in a bowl and fold in enough of the reserved syrup to lightly coat; the mixture should be compote-like. Reserve the compote in an airtight container in the refrigerator for up to 3 days.

Kevin Jeung prepares milk crumb for baking.

Milk Crumb

Makes about 350 grams

100 grams milk powder
75 grams tipo 00 flour
75 grams sugar
40 grams cornstarch
5 grams crushed salt
75 grams unsalted butter, melted

Inspired by pastry chef Christina Tosi's iconic Milk Crumb from Milk Bar, this version was born out of a Test Kitchen investigation into milk powder and its possibilities. The team had previously explored adding milk powder to hot brown butter to intensify the caramelized flavours. Rosio Sanchez recalled tasting Tosi's creation years earlier during her formative time in New York. Drawing from that memory, she removed the white chocolate to reduce sweetness and adjusted the baking method to produce a finer crumble. The first use of this crumb was in a dessert themed around bitters: milk ice cream spun with Gammel Dansk Blueberry Syrup (page 421), milk chips, baked milk crumb, and a bright sorrel juice. Unlike many common crumbles that dominate a dish with sweetness, this one is more restrained—slightly savory, texturally crisp, and quietly supportive of the flavours around it.

Whisk together the milk powder, flour, sugar, cornstarch, and salt in a large bowl to combine. Pour in the melted butter and work the mixture until the ingredients are evenly moistened and the mixture has formed a crumbly dough.

Transfer the dough to a large vacuum bag. Roll it to a thickness of 5 mm (¼ inch) and seal at 100% vacuum, then freeze. Once frozen, break the dough into small pieces and spread them over a sheet pan. Bake at 160°C (320°F; 40% fan) for 6 to 7 minutes, until very light brown. Remove from the oven and let cool. Refrigerate in an airtight container for up to 3 days.

Tree Sweets

At Noma, we love eating trees. We flavour oil with tree leaves, buds, and branches. We make salts and sugars with fragrant needles from evergreen trees. And of course we love to eat the sweet fruits that so many trees offer us.

But fruit is not the only sweet ingredient that comes from a tree. Scandinavians boil the watery sap from birch trees to make birch syrup, much like North Americans do with maple trees, and at Noma, we use other parts of trees to make sweet confections—tender tiny pine cones from dwarf mountain pine trees, the amber-like hardened sap from peach trees, the potently flavoured kernels from ripe plums. We find flavour in unexpected places, including orchards and forests.

Tree sap becomes tender when fully hydrated.

Candied Pine Cones

Makes about 500 grams pine cones, plus syrup

500 grams dwarf mountain pine cones (*Pinus mugo*)
1.5 kilograms sugar
2 kilograms filtered water

These delectable mouthfuls are common in Russia, Eastern Europe, and the rugged terrain of northern Asia, where they're called "pine cone jam" in the various languages. Traditionally, the pine-flavoured sweet syrup is more valued than the pine cones themselves, but we think the pine cones are insanely good, so we started making our own. Glimmering with sugar, they're like a perfect petit four. We do use the syrup as well, to flavour juices and in seasonal cocktails.

Blanch the pine cones in boiling water for 20 seconds, then shock them in ice water. Repeat until you've blanched and shocked the pine cones ten times, using a fresh pot of water for each blanching, then place them in a clean pot and add the sugar and filtered water. Bring to a boil, stirring to dissolve the sugar, then reduce the heat to maintain a simmer and cook the pine cones in the syrup until tender, 5½ to 6½ hours.

Carefully remove the pine cones from the syrup and transfer them to a clean glass jar. Continue to reduce the syrup until the sugar content is about 80°Bx (as measured by a refractometer). Remove from the heat and let cool slightly, then pour the reduced syrup over the pine cones (make sure they are fully submerged). Let the pine cones cool to room temperature, then seal the jar. Reserve in the refrigerator; because of the sugar content, they will keep indefinitely.

Blanch the pine cones in boiling water for 20 seconds, then shock them in ice water. Repeat the blanching and shocking nine more times, using a fresh pot of boiling water each time.

Place the blanched pine cones in a large pot and add the sugar and filtered water. Bring to a simmer, stirring to dissolve the sugar, then simmer for 5½ to 6½ hours.

Transfer the pine cones to a jar and continue to simmer the syrup until it reaches 80°Bx.

Pour the reduced syrup over the pine cones. Let cool, then seal the jar and reserve in the refrigerator.

Soak the tree sap in filtered water until rehydrated and soft, 3 to 4 days. Sort the rehydrated sap into softer, translucent pieces and harder, more opaque pieces.

Transfer the softer pieces of rehydrated sap to a saucepan with the water and wine.

Add the sugar, roseroot, rose petals, and dried bergamot skin. Bring to a simmer and cook for 30 minutes.

Let cool, then lift out the candied sap with a spider and trim as desired. Reserve the sap in the syrup in an airtight container in the refrigerator until needed.

Candied Tree Sap

Makes about 500 grams

Hydrated Tree Sap
300 grams tree sap
Filtered water

Candied Tree Sap
400 grams Hydrated Tree Sap
350 grams filtered water
150 grams orange wine
100 grams sugar
10 grams dried roseroot
2 grams dried rose petals
1.5 grams Dried Bergamot Skin*

Tree sap (also called gum or resin) is the result of a natural occurrence on many stone fruit trees known as gummosis; translucent, amber sap oozes from tree branches, then hardens and is plucked from the tree. In traditional Chinese culture, tree sap is used as both a medicine and a food.

We source tree sap from a local seed bank that specializes in preserving stone fruit varietals. We use the sap, which becomes gelatinous after hydrating, in both savory and sweet dishes. For the Vegetable season in 2024, it was served as a vegan "fat" in our Kohlrabi Kebab, which included roasted kohlrabi, grilled celeriac, and peach tree sap soaked in truffle juice. In 2023, we served a Tree Sap Pie for the Forest season, which used candied tree sap, ants, and a frozen cream pie shell.

Hydrate the tree sap: Soak the tree sap in filtered water for 3 to 4 days until rehydrated. Sort the sap into soft, translucent pieces and harder, more opaque pieces; reserve the harder pieces for another use.

Make the candied tree sap: Combine the softer sap, water, wine, sugar, roseroot, rose petals, and dried bergamot skin in a saucepan and bring to a simmer over medium heat. Cook for 30 minutes, then remove from the heat and let cool. Lift the sap pieces out of the syrup and trim them to suit your final use. Transfer the syrup to an airtight container, return the sap to the syrup, and reserve in the refrigerator for up to several weeks.

Plum Kernel Cream

Makes about 1 kilogram

360 grams plum pits (about 180 pits)
200 grams milk
80 grams sugar
800 grams heavy cream

Former Noma pastry chef Rosio Sanchez had worked with apricot kernels before and loved their deep bitter-almond aromas. Apricots aren't common in Denmark, but plums are, so Rosio began cracking open plum pits to harvest their kernels.

Plum kernels freeze well (and are easier to crack when frozen), making them easy to accumulate over time. Like the kernels of other stone fruits, plum kernels contain amygdalin, a compound that can convert into hydrogen cyanide if the kernels are consumed whole and in large quantity. However, infusing them into cream or milk draws out only their aromatic qualities, not their toxicity, making this a safe technique.

Set a plum pit on a cutting board and smack it with a hammer. Extract the kernel (the inner seed) and discard the pit. Continue until you have about 60 grams of kernels.

Peel the thin skin from the kernels. Place the peeled plum kernels in a container, add the milk and sugar, and blend with an immersion blender until smooth. Pour into a vacuum bag and add the cream. Seal on 100% vacuum and refrigerate overnight to infuse. Strain the cream through a fine-mesh nylon sieve. You can reserve the kernels and do a second infusion, but know that the second infusion won't be as potent as the first. Reserve the cream in an airtight container in the refrigerator for up to 2 days. Use it in any dessert that calls for heavy cream, or whip it to Chantilly texture and use it as sweetened whipped cream.

Crack open the plum pits with a hammer and retrieve the inner kernels.

Peel off the outer skins. Combine the peeled plum kernels, milk, and sugar in a container and blend with an immersion blender until smooth.

Transfer to a vacuum bag and add the cream. Seal and refrigerate overnight to infuse.

Strain the plum kernel cream through a fine-mesh nylon sieve. Refrigerate in an airtight container for up to 2 days. Use in desserts in place of heavy cream or whip and use as sweetened whipped cream.

Pralines and Sweet Sauces

In this section, you'll find recipes for sweets that we call pralines. They don't have much in common with classic French *pralinés* (nuts cooked with sugar and then ground to a paste), and the individual recipes don't have much in common with each other, either. One of our Noma pralines is more savory than sweet, one is nutty and fruity, another is almost like a flavoured sugar, and the last is a luscious salty-caramelly whipped confection. So what's Noma's definition of a praline? We don't have one, and we don't really care. What we do care about is how we think about the definition, how we explore and experiment and ask the question, "What is essential about a praline?" Our answers are varied, and they are all delicious.

A wet mill is an essential tool at Noma.

The final recipes in this section stand on their own merits—hot chocolate sauce, to which we say, "Yes, please," and a version of Japanese mochi made from chestnuts, to which we say, "Why not?"

Pumpkin Seed Praline

Makes about 725 grams

250 grams pumpkin seed pulp (reserved from making Pumpkin Seed Oil*)
75 grams dried ceps
20 grams Noma Umami Salt (page 113)
200 grams muscovado sugar
65 grams Larch Wood Oil (page 190)
165 grams Parsley Oil (page 178)

We created this praline because we wanted to use the oil-less pulp that is extruded from the hot nut press when we make our pressed oils (see page 149). We had tried to use it in fermentation—hazelnut and walnut misos, for example—with some success. Noma creative director Thomas Frebel had the idea to run pumpkin seed pulp through a wet mill with various additives. The result was this complex praline, with strong savory flavours, caramel notes from the muscovado sugar, and a freshness from the herb and wood oils . . . plus plenty of umami from the salt. We first used it for the Ocean season in 2022 in a petit four called Mushroom Tart, which featured candied chanterelle mushrooms on a pie shell made of frozen cream with a bit of this praline for seasoning. The pumpkin seed oil was used earlier in the menu, so this dish allowed us to upcycle a by-product and create a delicious finishing bite for guests.

Place the pumpkin seed pulp, ceps, and umami salt on a dehydrator tray. Dry in a dehydrator set to 60°C (140°F) overnight to ensure everything is very dry. Transfer the ingredients to a Thermomix, add the sugar, and blend on high for 30 to 60 seconds, then transfer to a wet mill. Run the mill for 1 minute, then slowly pour in the larch wood oil, followed by the parsley oil. Run the mill until a smooth paste is formed, about 30 minutes. Strain through a fine-mesh nylon sieve, if needed. Use right away, keep refrigerated in an airtight container for up to 2 weeks, or freeze for longer-term storage.

Berry Praline

Makes about 500 grams

300 grams hazelnuts
45 grams muscovado sugar
2 grams raw licorice powder
0.5 gram saffron
100 grams Dried Rose Oil*
30 grams freeze-dried black currants
20 grams freeze-dried raspberries
10 grams freeze-dried blueberries

In our catalog of pralines, berry praline is a relative outlier, relying on natural sweetness from the hazelnuts and freeze-dried berries, with just a touch of added sugar. Make sure the freeze-dried fruit is bone-dry and has not absorbed any moisture from the air; if it has, dry it in a dehydrator before using. This praline is highly versatile and has found its way into both savory dishes (a golden beet and trout roe serving) and sweet ones (a woodruff mousse with phacelia flower honey and Ant Honey, page 425).

Spread the hazelnuts over a sheet pan and toast in a 160°C (320°F; 100% fan) oven until they are a rich, even brown, 5 to 8 minutes. Remove from the oven and let cool.

Meanwhile, place the sugar, licorice powder, and saffron in a spice grinder and grind them as finely as possible.

Transfer the cooled hazelnuts to a blender, add the rose oil, and blend until smooth and semi-liquid, then transfer the hazelnut mixture to a wet mill. Grind the hazelnut mixture through the mill, then add the sugar mixture and grind to incorporate. Add the freeze-dried black currants, raspberries, and blueberries and grind until smooth, about 1 hour. The praline should be used the same day it's made but can be reserved in an airtight container in the refrigerator for up to 1 day.

Toast the hazelnuts until they are an even golden brown.

Grind the sugar, licorice, and saffron in a spice grinder.

Grind the hazelnuts and rose oil in a blender first, then transfer them to a wet mill and grind. Add the sugar mixture and grind to combine.

Add the freeze-dried berries to the wet mill and grind for about 1 hour.

The finished praline should be homogeneous but not completely smooth. Use immediately or refrigerate in an airtight container for up to 1 day.

Pine Praline

Makes 345 grams

300 grams sugar
40 grams Douglas fir needles
5 grams frozen ants
Liquid nitrogen

This recipe was developed by former Noma sous chef Riccardo Canella, and it's perhaps the closest thing we've got to a traditional praline, in which you cook sugar to a dark caramel, add nuts, let it harden, and then grind the hardened mixture to use in pastries and desserts. Here we use pine needles, which contribute a grapefruit flavour, and ants, which are lemony. The resulting praline powder has an intriguing citrus flavour that's beautiful on fresh raspberries, great on ice cream, and fantastic as a topping for Chantilly cream.

Heat the sugar in a dry skillet over medium heat until melted and amber colored (about 160°C/320°F). Add the Douglas fir needles and ants and cook, stirring, for about 1 minute, then pour the mixture onto a Silpat-lined sheet pan and let cool to room temperature. Transfer the mixture to a stainless-steel bowl and freeze with liquid nitrogen. Once frozen, transfer to a mortar and use the pestle to grind it into a powder. Reserve in an airtight container at room temperature for up to 1 week.

Heat the sugar in a dry skillet over medium heat.

Cook until the sugar has melted and is mostly caramelized. Add the Douglas fir needles and the ants. Cook, stirring, until the needles are evenly coated, about 1 minute.

Transfer the mixture to a Silpat-lined sheet pan and let cool. Transfer to a stainless-steel bowl and freeze with liquid nitrogen.

Transfer the frozen mixture to a mortar and grind into a coarse powder with the pestle. Reserve in an airtight container at room temperature for up to 1 week.

Poppy Seed Praline

Makes about 190 grams

Poppy Seed Paste
120 grams black poppy seeds
70 grams neutral oil

Poppy Seed Praline
1 vanilla bean
150 grams Poppy Seed Paste
20 grams neutral oil
20 grams sweet licorice syrup

Denmark has a long tradition of pastries garnished with poppy seeds, most of them based on the baking traditions of Central and Eastern Europe. Our poppy seed praline, developed by Test Kitchen head Mette Søberg, is something altogether different. The flavour of poppy seed is subtle, but when ground into a paste, its earthy nuttiness becomes more apparent, as do light hints of licorice and vanilla, which heighten the perceived natural sweetness of the poppy seeds. You'll need a wet mill (see page 481) and at least 3 hours to grind the tiny seeds into a paste, but the resulting glossy black sauce is worth the effort. We featured this praline on a simple dessert of yogurt mousse, as well as in Saffron Ice Cream and Poppy Seed, a dessert served in a beeswax bowl during the Forest season in 2022.

Make the poppy seed paste: Combine the poppy seeds and oil in a Thermomix and blend on high speed for 5 minutes. Transfer the mixture to a wet mill and grind it for 3 hours. Remove the paste from the mill and set aside.

Make the poppy seed praline: Halve the vanilla bean lengthwise and scrape the seeds into a medium bowl. Add the poppy seed paste, oil, and licorice syrup and stir until well mixed. Pass the mixture through a conical sieve, pressing on the solids. Reserve in an airtight container in the refrigerator for up to 5 days. Warm the glaze to 65°C (150°F) before using.

Chestnut Praline

Makes 245 grams

Chestnut Praline Base
150 grams chestnuts
150 grams heavy cream
25 grams muscovado sugar

Chestnut Praline
⅓ vanilla bean
75 grams heavy cream
15 grams muscovado sugar
5 grams Noma Roasted Umami Salt (page 115)
150 grams Chestnut Praline Base

Noma roasted umami salt gives this creamy praline a sweet-salty edge—think salted caramel ice cream, but more addictive. It is excellent as a base for berry tarts or a frosting for cake or cookies.

Make the chestnut praline base: Combine the chestnuts, cream, and sugar in a medium saucepan and bring to a simmer. Cook for 1 hour, then transfer to a blender and blend until smooth. Strain the praline base through a tamis lined with a fine-mesh nylon sieve. Let cool, then reserve in an airtight container in the refrigerator until needed.

Make the chestnut praline: Halve the vanilla bean and scrape the seeds into a saucepan. Pour in a small amount of the cream, then add the sugar and roasted umami salt and cook over low heat, stirring, until the sugar and salt have dissolved. Stir in a small amount of the chestnut praline base, then stir in the remaining cream. Add the remaining chestnut praline base and simmer, stirring, until well combined. Transfer the mixture to a wide, shallow container, lay a piece of plastic wrap directly against the surface, and refrigerate for at least 2 hours before using. The chilled praline will develop a thicker, silky texture, like crème pâtissière. Reserve in an airtight container in the refrigerator for up to 3 days.

Place the chestnuts in a medium saucepan with the cream and muscovado sugar and bring to a simmer.

Simmer the chestnut mixture for 1 hour.

Scrape the vanilla seeds into a saucepan and add a small amount of the cream. Stir in the sugar and roasted umami salt and cook, stirring, until the sugar and salt have dissolved.

Stir a small portion of the praline base into the cream mixture, then whisk in the remaining cream.

Blend the mixture until completely smooth.

Pass the praline base through a tamis lined with a fine-mesh nylon sieve; reserve in the refrigerator.

Add the remaining chestnut praline base and mix well. Simmer, stirring, until well combined.

Transfer the praline to a shallow container, cover, and refrigerate for at least 2 hours before using. Refrigerate in an airtight container for up to 3 days.

Hot Chocolate Sauce

Makes 440 grams

26 grams Elderflower Syrup (page 417)
10 grams confectioners' sugar
5 grams Noma Roasted Umami Salt (page 115)
200 grams good-quality dark chocolate, chopped (we use 180 grams La Rifa chocolate and 20 grams Valrhona 75% dark chocolate)
200 grams Dried Rose Oil*
Salt

During the research and development phase for Noma Mexico, we discovered La Rifa, a small *chocolatería* in Mexico City who source cacao from sustainable producers in Chiapas and Tabasco. We were especially taken by their Blanco Jaguar chocolate—a dark chocolate with remarkable fruitiness and layered depth. After working with La Rifa for Noma Mexico, we knew we couldn't live without their chocolate back in Copenhagen and have been importing it ever since.

Inspired by this incredibly delicious Mexican chocolate, the Test Kitchen began developing ways to use it in savory-sweet applications. While a hot chocolate drink was the initial goal, it didn't quite land after multiple rounds of testing. But the idea evolved into something more versatile: a warm sauce that could be used in surprising ways. It became the dressing for a dessert salad of herbs, flowers, and berries—and a dipping sauce for intensely tart Danish sumac brought to us by our forager Zenia Samlersen. The sauce is rich, floral, and aromatic, thanks to rose oil and elderflower syrup, and provides a beautiful balance to sharp or acidic ingredients.

Place the elderflower syrup, confectioners' sugar, and roasted umami salt in a saucepan and warm them gently over low heat, swirling the pan until the sugar and salt dissolve into the syrup. Melt the chocolate over a double boiler. Whisk the rose oil into the melted chocolate until emulsified, then slowly whisk in the elderflower syrup mixture; the syrup can crystallize, so do this carefully. Season the sauce with salt. Use the sauce the same day you make it; reserve at room temperature until needed, then rewarm gently before serving.

Chestnut Mochi

Makes about 200 grams

750 grams frozen chestnuts
750 grams filtered water
Cep Oil (page 164) or other flavoured oil, for shaping (optional)

Noma has a long-standing love affair with Japanese cuisine. When we discover local items that remind us of Japanese products, we get excited, which is how Test Kitchen head Mette Søberg developed chestnut mochi.

Japanese mochi—a confection made from pounded glutinous rice—is often used in sweets, most notably as a wrapper for super-popular ice cream balls. The starch from the rice gives mochi a distinctive chewy texture. Mette had been experimenting with slowly reducing nut milks, including chestnuts, a favorite ingredient at Noma. In addition to containing a lot of natural sugar, chestnuts have a high starch content—something that we often struggled with when we wanted to serve them raw; the starch made them too crumbly to thinly slice. That troublesome feature, however, became a benefit for Mette. Through the slow reducing process, she noticed that chestnut milk became noticeably sweeter, but also began to bind to itself and pull away from the sides of the double boiler. Further cooking in a nonstick pan removed more of the chestnuts' water content and yielded something that resembled a pure chestnut dough.

Mette took the next logical step (for a Japanophile chef, anyway)—she began to pound the chestnut "dough" in a mortar and pestle, yielding a result similar to actual mochi. The chestnut dough became more structured and cohesive, and the starch molecules aligned to become more chewy and enhanced the perceived sweetness of the dough. "Nordic mochi" became a reality.

As with actual rice mochi, we've used this chestnut mochi in dishes both savory, as little dumplings wrapped around walnuts and truffle, and sweet, for an ice cream sandwich with milk ice cream, Blueberry (Bilberry) Reduction (page 262), and Chestnut Praline (page 467).

Place the chestnuts and water in a Thermomix and blend on high speed for 3 minutes. Transfer the mixture to a superbag, hold it over a clean container, and wring out all the liquid. Strain the chestnut liquid through a fine-mesh nylon sieve to remove any remaining solids. Pour the chestnut liquid into a heatproof bowl set over a saucepan of simmering water and cook over low heat, stirring every now and again and scraping down the sides to prevent dried flakes from forming, for at least 24 hours or up to 48 hours, until the liquid has reduced to a paste so thick that it can just barely be passed through a tamis lined with a fine-mesh nylon sieve.

Transfer the chestnut paste to a Thermomix and blend for 1 minute to break up any lumps, then pass the mixture through a tamis lined with a fine-mesh nylon sieve; work quickly, because the paste will stiffen as it cools. Transfer the paste to a nonstick pan and cook over low heat, working it with a flexible spatula by spreading the paste over the surface of the pan and scraping it back onto itself, until it begins to caramelize and enough moisture steams off that the paste no longer sticks to the pan. While still warm, transfer the paste to a large mortar and beat it with the pestle for 5 to 10 minutes to cool it and incorporate some air, and also to pound out any lumps that may have formed. Transfer the mochi to an airtight container; use right away or refrigerate for up to 5 days. When ready to use, knead the mochi again to make it pliable.

To shape the mochi into a wrapper, if desired, coat your hands with a bit of cep oil. Tear off a small portion of the mochi and work it in your hands until warm and pliable, like a pasta dough, stretching and flattening it to an even thickness. To make the mochi even thinner, sandwich it between two pieces of parchment paper coated with a thin layer of cep oil and run it through a pasta roller to create a thin, even sheet.

Place the chestnuts and water in a Thermomix (as Mette Søberg does here) and blend on high speed for 3 minutes.

Strain the blended chestnuts through a superbag, wringing out as much liquid as possible, then strain again through a fine-mesh nylon sieve.

Continue cooking, stirring and scraping with the spatula, until the paste no longer sticks to the pan.

Transfer the chestnut paste to a mortar and pound with the pestle to cool and slightly aerate it and to pound out any remaining lumps.

Cook the chestnut liquid in a double boiler over low heat for 1 to 2 days, until very thick, occasionally scraping the bowl with a flexible spatula to prevent dried flakes from forming.

Transfer the thickened chestnut liquid to a nonstick skillet. Cook over low heat to steam off more liquid and slightly caramelize the chestnut paste.

Use the mochi right away or refrigerate in an airtight container for up to 5 days. Knead until pliable before use. To use the mochi as a wrapper, coat your hands lightly with cep oil and stretch the mochi to refine the texture further.

To flatten further, sandwich the mochi between lightly oiled parchment sheets and pass it through a pasta roller.

Suggested Uses

Ice Cream and Praline

Make a classic dessert by drizzling warm Poppy Seed Praline (page 465) over a scoop of vanilla ice cream; coffee ice cream would be delicious as well. Berry Praline (page 459) also makes a sweet-savory topping for ice cream or thick yogurt.

Pound Cake with Lemon Thyme Syrup

Bake a lemon-cornmeal pound cake. While the cake is still warm, brush it generously with Lemon Thyme Syrup (page 419).

Strawberry-Elderflower Pavlova

Make a Pavlova filled with fresh strawberries and whipped cream, and drizzle it with Elderflower Syrup (page 417).

Strawberry-Tomato Sauce

Use strawberry leather (see page 329) to add fruitiness to a savory dish: Make a quick fresh tomato sauce and drop a few torn pieces of the fruit leather into the sauce to finish. Cook just until melted and incorporated.

Profiteroles with Chestnut Praline and Hot Chocolate Sauce

Bake small cream puffs or éclair shells and fill them with Chestnut Praline (page 467). Serve plain, or dusted with confectioners' sugar, or drizzled with Hot Chocolate Sauce (page 470).

Chocolate Mousse with Crumbly Topping

Make a simple chocolate mousse and top it with crumbled Milk Crumb (page 447).

Pine Praline–Dusted Berries

Using a tea strainer, sift a light dusting of Pine Praline (page 462) over fresh raspberries to add a touch of sweetness and an intriguing "foresty" note.

Opposite, top to bottom:
Ice Cream and Praline;
Strawberry-Tomato Sauce
Right: Pine Praline–Dusted Berries

Chestnut Mochi Ice Cream Balls

Roll portions of Chestnut Mochi (page 472) until very thin, punch out rounds using a pastry cutter, and brush lightly with Cep Oil (page 164). Fold the wrappers around small balls of ice cream; rose ice cream is an excellent flavour pairing with the chestnut.

Japanese Quince Crostata

Make a jam tart along the lines of an Italian *crostata di marmellata*, using a sweet tart dough and Japanese Quince Compote (page 445) for the filling. Top the tart with a lattice crust.

Sweet-and-Sour Candy

Cut a sheet of White Currant Leather (page 429) into long strips. Dust the strips with sugar or Pine Praline (page 462). Roll up the strips and serve as a sweet-and-sour candy.

Chocolate-Coated Aronia Kelp

Cut Aronia Kelp (page 436) into portions. Pat the surface dry and dip the aronia kelp in tempered good-quality dark chocolate. Gently press freeze-dried berries, such as blueberry or black currant, onto the chocolate as it is setting.

Plum Kernel Risalamande

Make the traditional Danish Christmas dessert, but use plum kernel cream instead of normal whipped cream: Make sweet rice porridge by cooking short-grain rice in whole milk with vanilla and a bit of sugar. Cool the porridge and fold in whipped Plum Kernel Cream (page 454) and toasted slivered almonds, leaving one almond whole.

A New PB and J

Use Pumpkin Seed Praline (page 458) instead of peanut butter in a peanut butter and jelly sandwich.

Brownies with a Surprise

Cut a handful of Candied Pine Cones (page 450) in half and add them to a dark chocolate brownie recipe for a fudgy and "piney" surprise.

Panna Cotta with Rhubarb Compote

Make a yogurt panna cotta, ideally using sheep's-milk yogurt and infusing the cream with pine shoots. Serve a scoop of the panna cotta with Rhubarb Compote (page 442); garnish the panna cotta with a few tender pine shoot needles.

Opposite: Chestnut Mochi Ice Cream Balls
Right: Panna Cotta with Rhubarb Compote

Key Equipment

While it's no secret that we have some pretty neat toys at Noma, none of the equipment listed here can replace the fundamental skills in which we expect our chefs to be proficient. These tools enhance and extend our skill set, taking the impossible and making it merely difficult.

Centrifuge: A centrifuge spins so quickly and with so much force that it is capable of separating substances by density. We've embraced the centrifuge (originally used in blood analysis) as a versatile addition to our arsenal of tools. It can clarify opaque liquids, producing crystalline consommés without the need for egg whites or heat, and it drastically increases the yield of all of our oils by spinning the last drops of aromatic liquid out of the pulp. Most important, it can instantly drain yogurt, for those moments when you have an insatiable craving for tzatziki and no time to drain off the whey.

Dehydrator: Dehydrators afford us time and control over our reductions. Many of our reduced preparations would burn if they were heated in a pan on the stove, but with a dehydrator, we can slowly reduce the water content of a liquid without it acquiring any burnt or overcaramelized flavours.

Pacojet: A Pacojet is a countertop appliance with a super-high-speed blade that shaves frozen ingredients, creating ultra-smooth purees. We use ours to make ice creams and sorbets, which is a typical use for this fairly expensive piece of equipment. On the savory side, it ensures that our Parsley Puree (page 311) is smooth and vibrant. By shaving frozen ingredients to order, the machine preserves volatile aromas.

Refractometer: A refractometer measures the level of dissolved solids in a liquid, expressed in degrees Brix (°Bx). Taking this measurement lets us know when a reduction has reached the desired concentration. Using a refractometer eliminates the guesswork, meaning the reduction will taste the same no matter which chef makes it.

Thermomix: A Thermomix is a powerful multitasker that goes far beyond a traditional high-speed blender. Common in both home and professional kitchens, particularly in Europe and Australia (but not so much in the United States), this mega-blender blends, cooks, stirs, and holds temperature with remarkable accuracy. As one of our former Italian sous chefs once said, "It's not just for grandmas making quick risotto!" It's excellent for emulsions and general blending, but especially effective when blending raw materials into neutral oil—a process that sometimes benefits from a little heat.

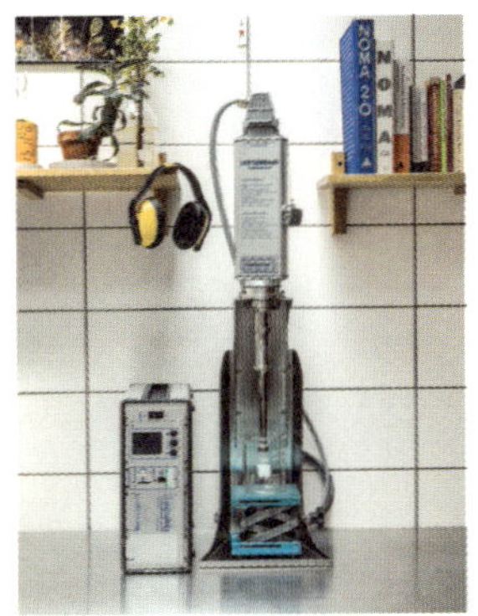

Ultrasonic homogenizer (sonicator): The ultrasonic homogenizer, commonly called a sonicator, is designed for industrial use, where its ultrasonic vibrations can clean the most minuscule particles of dirt from delicate tools and equipment, but we have repurposed it for use in the Fermentation Lab. The varying degrees of vibration promote emulsification between liquids that otherwise don't want to mix. The sonicator also allows us to make "hyper infusions," such as sonicating vinegar and oak barrel chips to create a "barrel-aged" flavour in minutes instead of years, or infusing the delicate flavour of beeswax into a liquid.

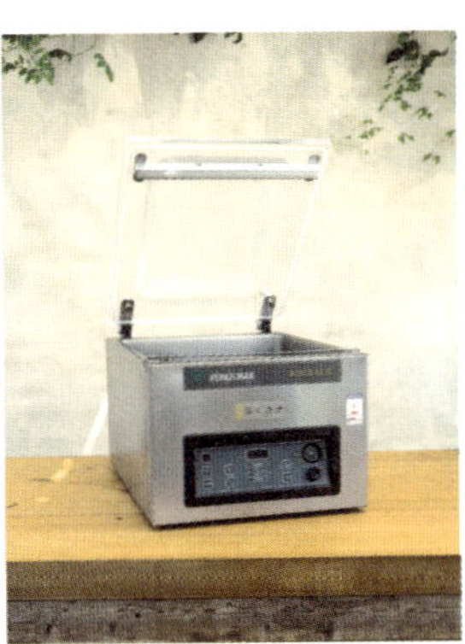

Vacuum sealer: At Noma, we use our vacuum sealer constantly for preservation, fermentation, inflation, compression, clarification, and infusion. Essentially a large box with a clear lid, a professional chamber vacuum sealer lowers the pressure inside the entire chamber, which also lowers the boiling point of any liquid inside. This is why liquids can start to boil at room temperature—or lower—if you're not careful, and why it's common to see bags overflow during sealing. But that same effect helps degas liquids and infuse flavours more efficiently. It also creates an airtight seal that protects ingredients from oxidation or contamination.

Wet mill: A wet mill, sometimes referred to as a melanger, allows us to refine the particle size of some of our pastes and sauces. While a blender can be used to puree an ingredient, running it through a wet mill creates an even finer texture without the risk of blade friction heating up the ingredient and affecting delicate flavours.

Noma's Basic Pantry

Every kitchen relies on ingredients that don't call attention to themselves but that are essential for getting the job done. Here are some of our most-used staples.

Butter

Danes love butter—it's on the table at almost every meal—and Danish butter is renowned for its rich flavour and luxurious mouthfeel. It's made from the milk of grass-fed cows, which gives it a golden color and enhances its flavour and nutritional benefits. It also has a high butterfat content—between 82% and 85%.

Eggs

We use free-range organic eggs, generally graded "large," which weigh about 60 grams in the shell.

Oil

Neutral oil is effective at capturing aroma, and therefore flavour, making it essential in our kitchen. We use an organic cold-pressed grapeseed oil for its clean taste and reliable consistency. It serves as the base for many of our flavoured oils, as well as a cooking medium.

Salt

We use noniodized fine salt for our brines, to ensure that there is no metallic or bitter aftertaste. For everything else, including seasoning, we use a flake salt from Iceland, which we often grind into more consistently sized grains for ease of use. The crystal structure of our Icelandic salt is similar to that of Maldon salt, a widely available flake salt from England.

Sugar

Our Noma palate isn't sugar-heavy, but we do use a variety of sugars in dishes both sweet and savory. We choose the sugar we use depending on our goal. Our most commonly used sugar, granulated white cane sugar, brings pure sweetness without many other flavour notes; it stays out of the way. Confectioners' sugar (icing sugar) is great for a simple hit of sweet; it dissolves quickly because of its fine texture. We use dark brown muscovado sugar, as well as *brun farin* (a Danish-style brown sugar), when we want deeper caramel flavours. And we can't forget about birch syrup, a very Scandinavian sweetener made by reducing the sap of birch trees, which has a deep, savory molasses flavour.

Vinegar

In addition to the vinegars we make, we use two commercially available vinegars. The first is an aged apple balsamic vinegar made in Denmark using a traditional artisanal process. With its rounded, almost sweet, fruity flavour and containing 5% acetic acid, this vinegar works well with delicate ingredients. We also use a white wine vinegar, which, at 6% acetic acid, has a sharper flavour but is still versatile.

Water

At Noma, we use filtered water for anything where the flavour of the water used will be noticeable. Denmark's groundwater comes primarily from limestone aquifers, especially in eastern regions like Zealand (home to Copenhagen). As rainwater filters through the limestone, it dissolves calcium carbonate, enriching the water with calcium and magnesium ions—the key components of hard water. Our local water is perfectly lovely to drink, but it does have a slight mineral flavour, which we don't want in our dishes. If you like the flavour of your local tap water, feel free to use that instead of filtered water.

Gastronomique

Powders and Dried Goods

Corn Bushi Powder

1 ear corn bushi

With gloved hands, remove the kernels from the ear of corn bushi. Use a spice grinder or blender to grind the kernels into a powder. Reserve in an airtight container at room temperature.

Dried Bergamot Skin

Fresh bergamot

Using a sharp knife, pare the skin from the bergamot, taking care to minimize the amount of white pith. Place the skin in a perforated gastro container and dry in a combi oven set to 60°C (140°F) for 12 hours, or until well dried. Transfer to a vacuum bag, seal at 80% vacuum, and reserve at room temperature.

Dried Ginger and Dried Ginger Powder

1 kilogram fresh ginger

For dried ginger: Peel the ginger and thinly slice on a mandoline. Lay the sliced ginger on dehydrator trays in a single layer and dry in a dehydrator set to 60°C (140°F) until completely devoid of moisture.

For dried ginger powder: Blitz in a Thermomix to yield a fine powder. Pass the powder through a fine-mesh nylon sieve and reserve in an airtight container at room temperature.

Dried Horseradish and Dried Horseradish Powder

1 kilogram fresh horseradish

For dried horseradish: Peel the horseradish and thinly slice with a mandoline. Lay the sliced horseradish on dehydrator trays in a single layer and dry in a dehydrator set to 60°C (140°F) until completely devoid of moisture.

For dried horseradish powder: Blitz in a Thermomix to yield a fine powder. Pass the powder through a fine-mesh nylon sieve and reserve in an airtight container at room temperature.

Dried Norwegian Spruce

1 kilogram fresh Norwegian spruce branches with needles

Break down the spruce into smaller branches, place them in a gastro container, and dry in an oven set to 60°C (140°F) for 12 hours. Strip the needles from the branches and discard the bare branches. Transfer the dried needles to vacuum bags, seal on 80% vacuum, and reserve at room temperature.

Kanzuri Oil and Kanzuri Sediment

1 kilogram kanzuri paste
Neutral oil

Set up a barbecue grill for smoking. Seal the kanzuri paste in a vacuum bag and spin in a centrifuge to separate the solids from the liquid. Pour off the liquid and reserve for another use. Transfer the kanzuri pulp to a tamis and smoke it lightly over the grill for 3 weeks. Once sufficiently smoked and dried, weigh the pulp, then transfer to a Thermomix and add three times its weight in oil. Blend on high for 10 minutes. Pour the blended oil into a nonstick pan and slowly bring it up to 160°C (320°F), stirring continuously, then cook, still stirring continuously, for 5 minutes more. Reduce the heat to lower the temperature of the mixture to 80°C (175°F), stirring as it cools, then cook at 80°C (175°F) for the entire day, stirring every 5 to 10 minutes. Remove from the heat, cover, and let stand at room temperature overnight to infuse.

The following day, stir the kanzuri mixture to combine, then transfer to a Thermomix and blend on high speed for 5 minutes. Set the Thermomix to 100°C (212°F), turn the speed down to 6, and blend for 5 minutes more. Strain the oil through a fine-mesh nylon sieve, reserving the sediment. Transfer the kanzuri oil to a vacuum bag, seal, and freeze. Transfer the kanzuri sediment to an airtight container and reserve in the refrigerator.

Powdered Dried Japanese Quince

10 Japanese quince

Cut the quince into eighths. Dry them in a dehydrator set to 60°C (140°F) until completely devoid of moisture. Blitz in a Thermomix to yield a fine powder. Pass the powder through a fine-mesh nylon sieve and reserve in an airtight container at room temperature.

Roasted Kelp, Kelp Powder, and Kelp Flour

250 grams fresh kelp

For roasted kelp: Spread the kelp over sheet pans and roast in an oven set to 160°C (320°F; 100% fan), dry heat, for 45 minutes, until aromatically toasted and deeply browned. Remove from the oven and let cool. Break up the roasted kelp and reserve in an airtight container at room temperature, or use to make roasted kelp powder.

For kelp powder and kelp flour: Blitz the roasted kelp in a Thermomix to yield a fine powder. Reserve the kelp powder in an airtight container at room temperature, or pass the powder through a fine-mesh nylon sieve and reserve the kelp flour in an airtight container at room temperature.

Roasted Yeast

1 kilogram fresh biodynamic baker's yeast
Neutral oil

Crumble the yeast onto sheet pans and roast in a combi oven set to 160°C (320°F), dry heat, for 45 to 60 minutes, until the yeast is no longer moist inside. Transfer to vacuum bags, seal, and reserve at room temperature until needed.

Oils and Butters

Chamomile Oil

300 grams pineappleweed (wild chamomile, *Matricaria discoidea*) buds and leaves (a few tender stems are okay)
600 grams neutral oil

Blend the pineappleweed and oil in a Thermomix on high speed for 7 minutes. Transfer to a container set over an ice bath and refrigerate overnight to infuse. Strain the oil through a fine-mesh nylon sieve and set aside. Vacuum seal the pulp and spin in a centrifuge to maximize yield. Strain off the resulting oil and mix it with the rest of the flavoured oil to homogenize. Vacuum seal and freeze to prevent oxidation.

Dried Rose Oil

500 grams dried rose petals
1 kilogram grapeseed oil

Blend the dried rose petals in a Thermomix on high speed for 30 seconds to yield a fine powder. Add the oil and blend on high speed for 6 minutes. Transfer the blended oil to an airtight container and refrigerate overnight to infuse. Pour the infused oil into a container lined with a fine-mesh nylon sieve, cover, and let stand in the fridge for 24 hours. Compost the pulp. Vacuum seal the oil and freeze to prevent oxidation.

Koji Oil

500 grams dried koji (any variety)
1 kilogram neutral oil

Blend the dried koji and oil in a Thermomix on high speed for 7 minutes. Transfer the blended oil to an airtight container and refrigerate overnight to infuse. Transfer the oil to a fine-mesh nylon sieve set over a container, cover, and let stand in the fridge for 24 hours. Compost the pulp. Vacuum seal the oil and freeze to prevent oxidation.

Note: Any variety of koji (see page 492) can be used for this oil. The koji should be crumbled and dried in an oven at 40°C (105°F) overnight.

Morita Chile Oil

100 grams morita chiles, stemmed
1 kilogram neutral oil

Blend the chiles and oil in a Thermomix on high speed for 1 minute, then turn the speed down to 6, set the temperature to 80°C (175°F), and blend for 9 minutes. Transfer the oil to a container and refrigerate overnight to infuse. Transfer the oil to a fine-mesh nylon sieve set over a container, cover, and let stand in the fridge for 24 hours. Compost the pulp. Vacuum seal the oil and freeze to prevent oxidation.

Pumpkin Seed Oil

1 kilogram pumpkin seeds

Preheat a nut press. Spread the pumpkin seeds over a sheet pan and toast in an oven set to 160°C (320°F; 100% fan) for 8 to 10 minutes, stirring them once. Transfer the seeds to the nut press and run them through to extract their oil. Compost the solids. Vacuum seal the oil and freeze to prevent oxidation.

Walnut Butter

1 kilogram shelled walnuts
Filtered water

Blanch the walnuts in boiling water five times, using a fresh pot of boiling water each time and shocking them in ice water after each blanching. Drain the nuts and weigh them. Transfer to a Thermomix and add an equal weight of filtered water. Blend on high speed for 2 minutes (be sure not to overfill the blender). Transfer the walnut milk to an airtight container and refrigerate overnight to infuse.

The following day, pour the walnut milk in a superbag and squeeze to extract the liquid until the pulp is dry. Bring the walnut milk to a boil in a medium saucepan, then transfer it to a heatproof bowl set over a saucepan of simmering water.

Cook over low heat all day, scraping down the sides and stirring every hour or so and blending with an immersion blender a couple of times to bring it together. Transfer the mixture to an airtight container and refrigerate overnight. The following day, return the mixture to a heatproof bowl set over a saucepan of simmering water and repeat. It should take the mixture 2 days to reduce on the stove in this manner. The final texture should be thick, butter-like, dark, and caramelized. The walnut butter may be split by this point. Set the bowl over an ice bath and whisk to reemulsify it. Refrigerate for up to 4 days.

Broths, Waters, Teas, and Juices

Carrot Juice

1 kilogram carrots

Rinse and peel the carrots. Trim the tops and juice the carrots using a centrifugal juicer. Strain the liquid through a fine-mesh nylon sieve. Use immediately or seal in vacuum bags and freeze for up to 3 months.

Celery Reduction

5 heads celery, leaves removed

Juice the celery and strain the juice through a conical strainer, then through a fine-mesh nylon sieve. Bring to a boil in a large pot, then skim off the chlorophyll and reduce the juice slowly by 75%. Transfer the reduction to a 1-liter container and place it in a dehydrator set to 60°C (140°F). Reduce until syrupy (60°Bx as measured by a refractometer). Let cool, then vacuum seal and freeze to prevent oxidation.

Japanese Quince Juice

100 grams Japanese quince, frozen

Defrost the quince. Using a wine press lined with cheesecloth, squeeze and press the quince to yield as much juice as possible. Reserve the juice in an airtight container in the refrigerator for up to 2 days or vacuum seal and freeze.

Peaso Water

4 kilograms filtered water
600 grams Peaso (page 490)

Blend the water and peaso with an immersion blender to combine. Transfer to 1-liter airtight containers and freeze. Remove the frozen bricks of peaso water from the containers and hang them in a cheesecloth-lined perforated gastro pan set over a deep gastro pan to catch the liquid as it thaws. Cover and let stand in the fridge for 2 to 3 days, until completed thawed. Do not press on the residual solids or you will cloud the liquid. Reserve the peaso water in an airtight container in the fridge.

Reduced White Wine

100 grams white wine

Bring the wine to a boil and cook until reduced to 30 grams. Let cool. Reserve in an airtight container in the refrigerator for up to 2 days.

Sea Buckthorn Juice

1 kilogram ripe sea buckthorn berries

Blend the sea buckthorn berries in a Thermomix using the paddle attachment, using a slow enough speed to break apart the berry flesh but not damage the stones of the fruit. Once all the flesh is broken down, pass the fruit though a conical sieve to harvest the juice. Reserve in an airtight container in the refrigerator for up to 2 days.

Tomato Water

1 kilogram vine-ripe tomatoes

Quarter the tomatoes and blitz them in a Thermomix for 45 seconds, until broken up and liquefied. Pour the tomato puree into 1-liter airtight containers and freeze.

Remove the frozen bricks of tomato puree from the containers and hang them in a cheesecloth-lined perforated gastro pan set over a deep gastro pan to catch the liquid as it thaws. Cover and let stand in the fridge for 2 to 3 days, until completely thawed and devoid of any further easily extractable liquid. Do not press on the residual solids or you will cloud the liquid. Vacuum seal and freeze to prevent oxidation.

White Currant Juice

1 kilogram white currants, frozen

Defrost the currants. Using a wine press lined with cheesecloth, squeeze and press the currants to yield as much juice as possible. Strain the juice through a fine-mesh nylon sieve, then vacuum seal and freeze.

Miso and Shoyus

Elderflower Peaso

800 grams dried yellow split peas
Cold filtered water
1 kilogram Barley Koji (page 492)
Centrifuged elderflower pulp (reserved from making Elderflower Oil, page 179)
100 grams salt, plus more if needed

Place the dried peas in a large container and add double their volume in cold water. Soak at room temperature for at least 4 hours to rehydrate them. Drain the peas, place them in a large pot, and add double their volume in fresh cold water. Bring to a boil, then reduce the heat to maintain a simmer and cook, stirring every 10 minutes and skimming off any foam that rises to the surface, until the peas are soft enough to crush between your thumb and forefinger without applying much pressure, 45 to 60 minutes. Drain the peas and spread them out on a sheet pan. Let cool to room temperature.

Weigh the peas. You should have close to 1.5 kilograms, but this may vary. Add enough of the koji to equal 66.6% of the weight of the cooked peas. Grind the peas and koji, weigh the mixture, then add enough of the elderflower pulp to equal 5% of that weight and mix well with gloved hands. Check the texture and moisture content by squeezing a small handful of the mixture in your hand; it should easily form a compact ball. If the mixture crumbles, it's too dry, and you'll need to hydrate it; to do so, make a quick 4% brine by blending 4 grams salt into 100 milliliters water with an immersion blender or a whisk until the salt has completely dissolved, then add a bit of the brine at a time to the mixture until you've achieved the proper texture. Weigh the mixture, add enough salt to equal 4% of that weight, and mix thoroughly once more.

One handful at a time, transfer the peaso to a sanitized fermentation vessel, packing it in as tightly as possible. Start at the edges of the bucket, forcing any air out, then work your way toward the center. Punch the mixture down with your fists after each addition to ensure it's well packed. Smooth and flatten the top of the peaso, wipe down the sides of the vessel with a paper towel, and lightly sprinkle the surface with salt to help prevent mold growth. Press a sheet of plastic wrap directly against the surface of the peaso, making sure it reaches all the way to the edges. Wipe down the walls of the vessel again with a clean paper towel.

Find a flat dinner plate that fits snugly inside your fermentation vessel. Place the plate right-side up on top of the peaso and press it down with your hand. Place a heavy rock in a plastic bag to keep things sanitary and set it on top of the plate to weight it down. Cover the vessel with a clean kitchen towel or cheesecloth and secure it with a couple of large rubber bands. Ferment the peaso in a chamber held at 28°C (82°F) for about 3 months.

The peaso is finished when the texture has softened significantly, the taste of salt has subsided slightly, and sweet, nutty tones have emerged through the perfumed floral notes of the elderflower pulp. It should have a mild acidity without being overly sour. Vacuum seal and freeze to prevent further fermentation.

Fava Rice Shoyu

600 grams dried fava beans
600 grams sushi rice
1 (20-gram) pack koji tane (*Aspergillus oryzae* spores)
1.9 kilograms filtered water
365 grams salt

Soak the dried fava beans in double their volume of cold water for 4 hours at room temperature.

Meanwhile, spread the rice over a large sheet pan and toast in the oven set to 170°C (340°) for 1 hour, stirring every 15 minutes. The grains should be very dark. Remove the rice from the oven and let cool to room temperature. Crack the rice using a tabletop grain mill on its coarsest setting and set aside.

Drain the soaked beans and put them in a pot with double their volume in fresh cold water. Bring the water to a boil, then reduce the heat to maintain a bare simmer and cook, skimming off any foam that accumulates on the surface, for 45 to 60 minutes, until the beans are soft enough to crush between your thumb and forefinger with light pressure. Take care not to let the beans overcook to the point of mushiness, but even more important is not undercooking them; if the beans aren't soft enough, the koji's mycelium won't be able to penetrate their flesh and take hold. Drain the beans and let cool to body temperature.

Weigh out 1.125 kilograms of the cooked fava beans and place in a large bowl. Add 600 grams of the cracked rice and mix thoroughly. Line an inoculation tray with a clean, lightly dampened towel. Spread the fava bean mixture over the towel. Using a fine tea strainer with a handle, sift the koji spores over the mixture. Place the tray on a speed rack in a chamber held at 25°C (77°F) for 24 hours, making sure it doesn't sit on the bottom of the chamber or too close to the heat source. Leave the chamber open slightly to allow fresh air in and heat out.

After 24 hours have passed, you should see the first inklings of mold growth. Wearing gloves, break up and turn the koji, then furrow it into three rows. Increase the heat in the chamber to 29°C (84°F) and let the koji sit for another 24 hours, after which you'll see a fairly drastic color change.

Just before the koji is finished, bring 950 milliliters of the filtered water to a boil, add the salt, and whisk to dissolve. Remove from the heat and add the remaining filtered water to cool down the brine. Set aside until the temperature of the brine falls below 35°C (95°F).

489

Crumble the koji into a sanitized fermentation vessel. Pour the cooled brine over the koji and give it a good stir with a whisk; this is your moromi. Weigh the vessel with its contents and note that number on the side of the vessel. Press a sheet of plastic wrap directly against the surface of the moromi, then cover with either a loosely fitting lid left slightly ajar or with a breathable towel secured with a rubber band (either way, just ensure the mixture can vent). Place the vessel in a spot held at slightly cooler than normal room temperature, with normal humidity, and ferment for 4 months. Once a day for the first 2 weeks, stir the moromi well with a whisk. After that, stir once a week.

After 4 months, calculate how much water was lost to evaporation and add that amount of fresh cold water. Transfer the moromi to a mesh bag and use a small cider press to extract the liquid (as you would press fruits for their juice). Once you've extracted all the shoyu, strain it through a fine-mesh nylon sieve. Vacuum seal and freeze to prevent oxidation.

Nordic Shoyu

600 grams dried yellow peas
600 grams whole-grain wheat
1 (20-gram) pack koji tane
(*Aspergillus oryzae* spores)
1.9 kilograms filtered water
365 grams salt

Place the dried peas in a large container and add double their volume in cold water. Soak at room temperature for 4 hours to rehydrate.

While the peas are soaking, spread the wheat over a large sheet pan and roast it in an oven set to 170°C (340°F; 100% fan) for 1 hour, stirring every 15 minutes. The grains should be very dark. Remove from the oven and let cool to room temperature, then crack the wheat using a tabletop grain mill on its coarsest setting. Set the cracked wheat aside. Drain the soaked the peas and put them in a large pot. Cover again with double their volume in fresh cold water. Bring to a boil, then reduce the heat to maintain a bare simmer and cook, skimming any foam that accumulates on the surface, for 45 to 60 minutes, until the peas are soft enough to crush between your thumb and forefinger with light pressure. Take care not to let the peas overcook to the point of mushiness, but even more important is not undercooking them; if the peas aren't soft enough, the koji's mycelium won't be able to penetrate their flesh and take hold. Drain the peas and let cool to body temperature.

Weigh out 1.125 kilograms of cooked peas, place in a large bowl, and mix thoroughly with 600 grams of the cracked wheat. Line an inoculation tray with a clean, lightly dampened kitchen towel. Spread the pea mixture over the towel. Using a fine tea strainer, sift the koji spores over the mixture. Place the tray in a chamber held at 25°C (77°F) for 24 hours, making sure it doesn't sit on the bottom of the chamber or too close to the heat source. Leave the chamber open slightly to allow fresh air in and heat out.

After 24 hours have passed, you should see the first inklings of mold grown. Wearing gloves, use your hands to break up and turn the koji, then furrow it into three rows. Increase the heat in the chamber to 29°C (84°F) and let the koji sit for another 24 hours, after which you'll see a fairly drastic color change.

Just before the koji is finished, bring 950 milliliters of the filtered water to a boil, add the salt, and whisk to dissolve. Remove from the heat and add the remaining filtered water to cool down the brine. Set aside until the temperature of the brine falls below 35°C (95°F).

Crumble the koji into a sanitized fermentation vessel. Pour the cooled brine over the koji and give it a good stir with a whisk; this is your moromi. Weigh the vessel with its contents and note that number on the side of the vessel. Press a sheet of plastic wrap directly against the surface of the mixture, then cover the vessel with a breathable towel and secure it with a rubber band. Place the vessel in a spot held at slightly cooler than normal room temperature, with normal humidity, and ferment for 4 months. Once a day for the first 2 weeks, stir the moromi well with a whisk. After that, stir once a week.

After 4 months, calculate how much water was lost to evaporation and add that amount of fresh cold water. Transfer the moromi to a mesh bag and use a small cider press to extract the liquid (as you would press fruits for their juice). Once you've extracted all the shoyu, strain it through a fine-mesh nylon sieve. Vacuum seal and freeze to prevent oxidation.

Peaso

800 grams dried yellow split peas
Cold filtered water
Fresh kelp
1 kilogram Barley Koji (page 492)
100 grams salt, plus more if needed

Place the dried peas in a large container and add double their volume in water. Soak the peas at room temperature for at least 4 hours to rehydrate them. Drain the peas, place them in a large pot, and add double their volume in fresh cold water, measuring how much water you add. For every liter of water, add 23 grams of kelp. Bring to a boil, then reduce the heat to maintain a simmer and cook, stirring every 10 minutes and skimming away any foam that rises to the surface, for 45 to 60 minutes, until the peas are soft enough to crush between your thumb and forefinger without applying much pressure. Drain the peas and spread them out on a sheet pan. Let cool to room temperature.

Remove the kelp, then weigh the peas. You should have close to 1.5 kilograms, but the weight can vary. Add enough of the koji to equal 66.6% of the weight of the cooked peas. Grind the peas and koji and mix well with gloved hands. Check the texture and moisture content by squeezing a small handful of the mixture in your hand; it should easily form a compact ball. If the mixture crumbles, it's too dry, and you'll need to hydrate it; to do so, make a quick 4% brine by blending 4 grams salt into 100 milliliters water with an immersion blender or a whisk until the salt has completely dissolved, then add a bit of the brine at a time to the mixture until you've achieved the proper texture. Weigh the mixture, add enough salt to equal 6.6% of that weight, and mix thoroughly once more.

One handful at a time, transfer the peaso to a sanitized fermentation vessel, packing it in as tightly as possible. Start at the edges of the bucket, forcing any air out, then work your way toward the center. Punch the mixture down with your fists after each addition to ensure it's well packed. Smooth and flatten the top of the peaso, wipe down the sides of the vessel with a paper towel, and lightly sprinkle the surface with salt to help prevent mold growth. Press a sheet of plastic wrap directly against the surface of the peaso, making sure it reaches all the way to the edges. Wipe down the walls of the vessel again with a clean paper towel.

Find a flat dinner plate that fits snugly inside your fermentation vessel. Place the plate right-side up on top of the peaso and press it down with your hand. Place a heavy rock in a plastic bag to keep things sanitary and set it on top of the plate to weight it down. Cover the vessel with a clean kitchen towel or cheesecloth and secure it with a couple of large rubber bands. Ferment the peaso in a chamber held at 28°C (82°F) for about 3 months.

The peaso is finished when the texture has softened significantly, the taste of salt has subsided slightly, and sweet, nutty tones have emerged. It should have a mild acidity without being overly sour. Vacuum seal and freeze to prevent further fermentation.

Note: Peaso can be made with any variety of koji (see page 492) depending on the desired result.

Black Pepper Tamari

1 kilogram Peaso (page 490)
10 grams black peppercorns, toasted
2 liters filtered water

Place the peaso in a large container. Grind the peppercorns into a powder and add it to the peaso. Add the water and use a large immersion blender to blend until homogeneous. Transfer the mixture to 1-liter airtight containers and freeze.

Remove the frozen bricks of peaso mixture from the containers and hang them in a cheesecloth-lined perforated gastro pan set over a deep gastro pan to catch the liquid as it thaws. Cover and let stand in the fridge for 2 to 3 days, until completely thawed and devoid of any further easily extractable liquid. Do not press on the residual solids or you will cloud the tamari.

Transfer the tamari to clean containers, place in a dehydrator set to 60°C (140°F), and reduce until the liquid reaches 67°Bx (as measured by a refractometer). Vacuum seal and freeze.

Red Pepper Tamari

500 grams red bell peppers, seeded
Peaso (page 490)
Filtered water
Fresh red bell pepper juice

Weigh the seeded peppers, chop them into pieces small enough to fit into the jug of a Thermomix, and blend until finely chopped. Add an equal weight of peaso and blend again to homogenize. Transfer the mixture to a sanitized fermentation vessel. Press a sheet of plastic wrap directly against the surface of the mixture, then top with a plate and cover with a lid. Ferment in a chamber held at 60°C (140°F) for 7 days. Weigh the pepper-peaso mixture, add twice its weight in water, and blend with an immersion blender. Transfer the mixture to 1-liter airtight containers and freeze.

Remove the frozen bricks of pepper-peaso mixture from the containers and hang them in a cheesecloth-lined perforated gastro pan set over a deep gastro pan to catch the liquid as it thaws. Cover and let stand in the fridge for 2 to 3 days, until completely thawed and devoid of any further easily extractable liquid. Do not press on the residual solids or you will cloud the tamari.

Transfer the tamari to clean containers, place in a dehydrator set to 60°C (140°F), and reduce until the liquid reaches 70°Bx (as measured by a refractometer). Season the tamari to taste with fresh red bell pepper juice and let cool. Vacuum seal and freeze.

Truffle Tamari

1 kilogram Peaso (page 490)
500 grams black winter truffles
4.5 kilograms filtered water

Working in batches, blend the peaso, truffles, and water in a blender. Transfer to a container and mix until homogeneous. Transfer to 1-liter airtight containers and freeze. Remove the frozen bricks from the containers and hang them in a cheesecloth-lined perforated gastro pan set over a deep gastro pan to catch the liquid as it thaws. Cover and let stand in the fridge for 2 to 3 days, until completely thawed and devoid of any further easily extractable liquid. Press on the residual solids well to extract as much liquid as possible. Transfer the liquid to a pot and bring to a boil, then pour the liquid into shallow containers and place in a dehydrator set to 60°C (140°F). Reduce until the sugar content reaches 63°Bx (as measured by a refractometer). Vacuum seal and freeze.

Garums

Beef Garum

225 grams Barley Koji (page 492)
1 kilogram lean ground beef
300 grams filtered water
240 grams salt

Using gloved hands, break the koji into small pieces and transfer to a sanitized nonreactive fermentation vessel. Add the ground beef, water, and salt and blend with an immersion blender to combine, then press a sheet of plastic wrap directly against the surface of the mixture. Cover the vessel with a lid and ferment in a chamber held at 60°C (140°F) for 10 weeks. Every day for the first week, skim off any fat that rises to the surface and stir the garum, then skim and stir once a week after that. Cover again with the plastic wrap and lid after each skimming. The mixture will separate and the solids will remain on the bottom of the vessel.

Strain the finished garum through a fine-mesh nylon sieve. Skim off any residual fat from the garum, vacuum seal, and freeze to prevent its flavour from changing.

Umami Salt Shrimp Garum

6 grams Tarry Lapsang souchong tea leaves
1 kilogram cold filtered water
140 grams Noma Umami Salt (page 113)
17 grams plus 60 grams salt, plus more if needed
1 kilogram peeled Norwegian shrimp
200 grams Øland Wheat Koji (page 492), broken into small pieces

Combine the tea leaves and water in a 1-liter airtight container. Refrigerate overnight (8 to 12 hours) to infuse. Strain the tea and reserve in an airtight container in the fridge.

Place 700 grams of the tea in a medium pot (reserve the rest for another use). Add the umami salt and stir to dissolve it into the tea. Use a salt content refractometer (not a sugar one) to measure the salt content of the liquid. It should read 3.5% salinity. If it does, add 17 grams of the salt to bring the salinity up to 5% (if it is under or over 3.5% to start, adjust the added salt slightly). We are going to add the shrimp and koji to this liquid, which will dilute the salinity of the liquid. To ensure it maintains 5%

salinity, add the remaining 60 grams salt.

Heat the liquid over medium heat to 70°C (160°F). Place the shrimp in a sanitized fermentation vessel, then pour the liquid over them. Stir, then add the koji. Press a sheet of plastic wrap directly against the surface of the mixture. Ferment in a chamber held at 60°C (140°F) for 24 hours. Stir the mixture with a sanitized utensil, then return it to the 60°C (140°F) chamber to ferment for 5 days more.

Transfer the vessel to the fridge to cool and rest for 2 weeks. Strain the finished garum through a fine-mesh nylon sieve, vacuum seal, and freeze to prevent further fermentation.

Mushroom Garum

2.5 kilograms cremini mushrooms
1.06 liters filtered water
202 grams salt
363 grams Rice Koji (page 492)

Rinse the mushrooms of any dirt and remove the very bottoms of their stems. Transfer to a sanitized nonreactive fermentation vessel. Combine the water and salt in a pot and bring to a boil to dissolve the salt. Pour the salted water over the mushrooms and use a large immersion blender to blend them into a paste, adding some of the koji bit by bit to evenly spread it throughout the paste. Once totally blended, press a sheet of plastic wrap directly against the surface of the mixture and cover the vessel with a lid. Ferment in a chamber held at 60°C (140°F) for 5 weeks. Strain the finished garum through a fine-mesh nylon sieve, pressing the pulp lightly to maximize yield. Vacuum seal and freeze to prevent oxidation

Ferments

Barley Koji

1 kilogram pearl barley
Salt
Filtered water
1 (20-gram) pack koji tane (*Aspergillus oryzae* spores)

Soak the barley in an ample amount of lightly salted filtered water in the fridge overnight. Rinse the barley in a conical strainer under running water until any excess starch has washed off and the water runs clear. Transfer the barley to a perforated gastro tray and steam in a combi oven set to 90°C (195°F; 90% humidity, 80% fan) for 45 minutes. Remove the tray from the oven and place on a wire rack on a clean counter.

Line a clean perforated gastro tray with a damp, clean towel. Wearing gloves, break up the barley into individual grains, transferring it to the lined gastro tray as you work. Let cool to 25°C (77°F).

Using a fine tea strainer with a handle, take a small amount of the koji tane and gently knock it over the barley as if you were dusting a cake with sugar. Once you have completed one pass, use gloved hands to turn the barley to mix it, then sprinkle another round of koji tane over the top. Still wearing gloves, mix the barley one more time and cover it with a lightly dampened cloth. Place the tray on a speed rack in a chamber held at 30°C (86°F) and 80% relative humidity for 24 hours.

After 24 hours have passed, you should see the first inklings of mold growth. Wearing gloves, mix the barley and furrow it into two rows. Cover with a freshly dampened cloth and let sit in the same conditions for another 24 hours. At this point, the barley should be fuzzy and set into a cake. The koji is now ready. Let it mature in the fridge for 2 days before use; for storage beyond that, transfer it to an airtight container and freeze.

Note: This recipe can be adapted to make other varieties of koji, including, but not limited to awamori koji (using *Aspergillus awamori* spores) and citric koji (using *Aspergillus luchuensis* spores). These can be used in other recipes calling for koji.

Øland Wheat Koji

1 kilogram polished Øland wheat
Filtered water
1 (20-gram) pack koji tane (*Aspergillus oryzae* spores)

Soak the wheat in an ample amount of filtered water in the refrigerator overnight. Rinse the wheat in a conical strainer under running water until any excess starch has washed off and the water runs clear. Transfer the wheat to a perforated gastro tray and steam in a combi oven set to 100°C (212°F; 90% humidity, 80% fan) for 45 minutes. Remove the tray from the oven and place it on a wire rack on a clean counter.

Line a clean perforated gastro tray with a damp, clean towel. Wearing gloves, break up the wheat into individual grains, transferring it to the lined gastro tray as you work. Let cool to 25°C (77°F).

Using a fine tea strainer with a handle, take a small amount of the koji tane and gently knock it over the wheat as if you were dusting a cake with sugar. Once you have completed one pass, use gloved hands to turn the wheat to mix it, then sprinkle another round of koji tane over the top. Still wearing gloves, mix the wheat one more time and cover it with a lightly dampened cloth. Place the tray on a speed rack in a chamber held at 30°C (86°F) and 80% relative humidity for 24 hours.

After 24 hours have passed, you should see the first inklings of mold growth. Wearing gloves, mix the wheat and furrow it into two rows. Cover with a freshly dampened cloth and let sit in the same conditions for another 24 hours. At this point, the wheat should be fuzzy and set into a cake. The koji is now ready. Let it mature in the fridge for 2 days before use; for storage beyond that, transfer it to an airtight container and freeze.

Rice Koji

5 kilograms polished sushi rice
Salt
Filtered water
1 (20-gram) pack koji tane (*Aspergillus oryzae* spores)

Soak the rice in an ample amount of lightly salted filtered water in the fridge overnight. Rinse the rice in a conical strainer under running water until any excess starch has washed off and the water runs clear. Transfer the rice to a perforated gastro tray and steam in a combi oven set to 87°C (189°F; 90% fan, 100% steam) for 45 minutes. Remove the tray from the oven and place on a wire rack on a clean counter.

Line a clean perforated gastro tray with a damp, clean towel. Wearing gloves, use your hands to break up the rice into individual grains, transferring it to the lined gastro tray as you work. Let cool to 25°C (77°F). Using a fine tea strainer with a handle, take a small amount of the koji tane and gently dust it over the rice as if you were dusting a cake with sugar. Once you have completed one pass, use gloved hands to turn the rice to mix it, then sprinkle another round of koji tane over the top. Still wearing gloves, mix the rice one more time and bring it in from the sides of the tray so the rice is only sitting over the perforations in the tray to maximize airflow. Cover the rice with a clean, lightly dampened cloth and place the tray on a speed rack in a chamber held at 38°C (100°F) and 80% relative humidity for 24 hours. After 24 hours have passed, you should see the first inklings of mold growth. Wearing gloves, mix the rice and furrow it into two rows. Cover with a freshly dampened cloth and let sit in the same conditions for another 24 hours. At this point, the rice should be fuzzy and set into a cake. The koji is now ready. Let it mature in the fridge for 2 days before use; for storage beyond that, transfer to an airtight container and freeze.

Lacto Fermentations

Lacto Koji Water

1 kilogram koji (any type—see page 492)
2 liters filtered water
60 grams fine salt

In two batches, blend the koji and water in a Thermomix on high speed for 1 minute. Mix the batches of blended koji water together to ensure a homogeneous finished product. Add the salt and whisk briefly to incorporate. Transfer the salted koji water to a vacuum bag and seal on 100% vacuum. Ferment in a chamber held at 28°C (82°F) for 2 to 3 days, until the pH drops to 4.5 or below. The finished mixture should be sweet, sour, and fruity—if it tastes vinegary or alcoholic, it has fermented too far. Pour the fermented koji water into 1-liter airtight containers and freeze.

Remove the frozen bricks of koji water from the containers and hang them in a cheesecloth-lined perforated shallow gastro pan set over a deep gastro pan to catch the liquid as it thaws. Cover and let stand in the fridge for 2 to 3 days, until completely thawed and devoid of any further easily extractable liquid. Do not press on the residual solids or you will cloud the liquid. Vacuum seal the koji water and freeze to prevent further fermentation.

Lacto Cep Water

2 kilograms frozen ceps
30 grams salt

Place the mushrooms and salt in a sous vide bag and mix the contents around thoroughly before sealing the bag on 100% vacuum. Place the bag in a chamber held at 28°C (82°F) for 5 days, or until the mushrooms have let out much of their liquid, yellowed, and soured. Strain the contents of the bag through a fine-mesh sieve and reserve the liquid. Transfer the mushrooms to a new vacuum bag, seal, and freeze for use in applications calling for lacto ceps. Transfer the liquid to a 1-liter container and freeze.

Remove the frozen brick of mushroom liquid from the container and hang it in a cheesecloth-lined perforated gastro pan set over a deep gastro pan to catch the liquid as it thaws. Cover and let stand in the fridge for 2 to 3 days until completely thawed. Vacuum seal the lacto cep water and freeze to prevent oxidation or further fermentation.

Vinegars and Pickled Goods

Pumpkin Vinegar

4 kilograms pumpkin, halved and seeded
Apple balsamic vinegar (see page 483)
Ethanol (96% ABV)

Cut the pumpkin into manageable pieces, leaving the skin on. Wearing gloves, pass the pumpkin through a juicer. Strain the juice through a fine-mesh sieve and weigh it. Pour the juice into a sanitized fermentation vessel and add 20% of its weight in vinegar. Weigh the mixture and add 8% of the total weight in ethanol. Place an air stone in the vessel so that it rests on the bottom and run the hose out of the top to an air pump. Cover the vessel with cheesecloth and secure it with a rubber band. Transfer to a chamber held at 28°C (82°F) and turn on the pump. Ferment for 10 to 14 days. Strain the pumpkin vinegar through cheesecloth, vacuum seal, and freeze to prevent further fermentation.

Sake Vinegar

Dry sake
Pear vinegar

Mix the sake with 20% by volume of vinegar and transfer the mixture to a clean fermentation bucket. Place an air stone in the vessel so that it rests on the bottom and run the hose out the top to an air pump. Cover the vessel with cheesecloth and secure it with a rubber band. Transfer to a chamber held at 28°C (82°F) and turn on the pump. Ferment for 10 to 14 days. Strain the sake vinegar through cheesecloth, vacuum seal, and freeze to prevent further fermentation.

Whisky Vinegar

1.5 liters plus 350 milliliters 80-proof whisky
Filtered water
400 milliliters unpasteurized apple cider vinegar

Heat a tall, deep pot till very hot but not smoking. Add 500 milliliters of the whisky to flash-boil it. Exercising extreme caution, use a grill lighter to ignite the boiling whisky and let the alcohol burn off. When the flames have subsided, add 500 milliliters more whisky and repeat the process; repeat again with another 500 milliliters of the whisky. When the initial 1.5 liters of whisky has burned off, add enough filtered water to the pot to bring the total volume of liquid up to 1.25 liters. Add the remaining 350 milliliters whisky and the vinegar.

Transfer the mixture to a sanitized fermentation vessel, place an air stone in the vessel so that it rests on the bottom, and run the hose out of the top to an air pump. Cover the vessel with cheesecloth and secure it with a rubber band. Transfer the vessel to a chamber held at 28°C (82°F) and turn on the pump. Ferment for 14 days, tasting frequently toward the end of this time frame, until the desired flavour is achieved. Strain the whisky vinegar (if necessary), vacuum seal, and reserve in the fridge or freezer.

Acknowledgments

Thank you to all the people who contributed to the making of this book:

Lia Ronnen, Martha Holmberg, Kevin Jeung, Nate French, Mette Søberg, Evan Sung, Ditte Isager, Sonya Dyakova, Archie Anderson, Paula Troxler, Jane Treuhaft, Ivy McFadden, Arielle Johnson, Thomas Frebel, Junichi Takahashi, Nadine Levy Redzepi, and Matthew McGuigan.

And finally, to the countless friends, collaborators, foragers, farmers, scientists, cooks, and curious souls who have shaped the world of Noma over the years: Your fingerprints are on every flavour in these pages. This book is a shared creation. Thank you for walking this path with us.

Index

NOTE: Page references in *italics* refer to photos.

C

D

E

F

G

H

I

J

P

R

S

T

U

V

W

Y

Z

Copyright © 2026 by René Redzepi
Photographs copyright © 2026 by Evan Sung, except on pages 9, 14, 15, 29, 30, 46, 47, 87, 88, 110, 111, 130, 131, 145, 146, 166, 167, 211, 212, 224, 225, 248, 251, 294, 295, 306, 309, 316, 317, 336, 339, 378, 379, 392, 393, 397, 411, 412, 440, 441

Hachette Book Group supports the right to free expression and the value of copyright. The purpose of copyright is to encourage writers and artists to produce the creative works that enrich our culture.

The scanning, uploading, and distribution of this book without permission is a theft of the author's intellectual property. If you would like permission to use material from the book (other than for review purposes), please contact permissions@hbgusa.com. Thank you for your support of the author's rights.

Library of Congress Cataloging-in-Publication Data is on file.

ISBN 978-1-57965-719-2 (hardcover)
ISBN 978-1-64829-566-9 (signed edition)
ISBN 978-1-64829-564-5 (ebook)

Design and art direction by Atelier Dyakova

Artisan books may be purchased in bulk for business, educational, or promotional use. For information, please contact your local bookseller or the Hachette Book Group Special Markets Department at special.markets@hbgusa.com.

The publisher is not responsible for websites (or their content) that are not owned by the publisher.

The Hachette Speakers Bureau provides a wide range of authors for speaking events. To find out more, go to hachettespeakersbureau.com or email HachetteSpeakers@hbgusa.com.

Published by Artisan
an imprint of Workman Publishing,
a division of Hachette Book Group, Inc.
1290 Avenue of the Americas
New York, NY 10104
artisanbooks.com

The Artisan name and logo are registered trademarks of Hachette Book Group, Inc.

Printed in China (APO) on responsibly sourced paper

First printing, February 2026

Cover © 2026 Hachette Book Group, Inc.

10 9 8 7 6 5 4 3 2 1